P9-AOD-660

1915 Fir Avenue West
Fergus Falls, MN 56537

WITHDRAWN

PAUSE AND REFLECT

by

Ofelia Aguinaldo Dayrit-Woodring

DORRANCE
PUBLISHING CO
EST. 1920
PITTSBURGH, PENNSYLVANIA 15238

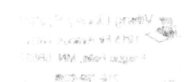

The contents of this work, including, but not limited to, the accuracy of events, people, and places depicted; opinions expressed; permission to use previously published materials included; and any advice given or actions advocated are solely the responsibility of the author, who assumes all liability for said work and indemnifies the publisher against any claims stemming from publication of the work.

All Rights Reserved
Copyright © 2017 by Ofelia Aguinaldo Dayrit-Woodring

No part of this book may be reproduced or transmitted, downloaded, distributed, reverse engineered, or stored in or introduced into any information storage and retrieval system, in any form or by any means, including photocopying and recording, whether electronic or mechanical, now known or hereinafter invented without permission in writing from the publisher.

Dorrance Publishing Co
585 Alpha Drive
Suite 103
Pittsburgh, PA 15238
Visit our website at www.dorrancebookstore.com

ISBN: 978-1-4809-3835-9
eISBN: 978-1-4809-3858-8

From the deepest core of my heart, this book is lovingly, warmly, and sincerely dedicated to my cherished loved ones.

Tom, William, Susana, Logan, Kaleb, Librada, Nestor, Felicisma, Manny, Missy, and Ori.

AD IESUM PER MARIAM (TO JESUS THROUGH MARY)

PART I

Guides for Daily Life

Ways and Means to Enhance Daily Life

Pieces of Advice for Christian and Better Living - Parts I to XI

Guides for Daily Life

Praise
Always praise, bless, thank, and glorify God. Above all, never cease loving and serving God and your neighbors all the days of your life.

Integrity
Integrity is doing the right things even when nobody is looking. Be a person of high integrity and be trustworthy. Preserve your integrity! Never, or do not, lose your integrity.

Talent
Share your God-given talents with the world for the benefit of humanity.

Charity
Have a generous heart and give to charity. Choose a charitable organization and support it benevolently with your hard-earned money, effort, and precious time.

Service
Your life is not your own. As Christians, you live for others as well. You are called to serve. Live in fervent service of God and neighbor. Serve the flock of the Lord with your utmost best for the praise and greater glory of God!

Kindness
Be kinder to yourself, neighbors, family, friends, relatives, co-workers, et al more than necessary.

Cool
Maintain your cool at all times no matter how bad the situation is. Keeping cool in a dire situation is classy. Do not go down to the level of the person who provokes you.

Enthusiasm
Show enthusiasm and caring about the success and happiness of others, even if you are somewhat envious. If you can't congratulate them, just smile. Don't rain

on their parades. Let them have the center stage for one swift, glorious, and triumphant moment! Be not jealous of their success!

The Best
Give the best of yourself in everything you do that your supervisors, co-workers, family members, relatives, friends, et al can say proudly, "YOU ARE SIMPLY THE BEST!"

Loyalty
Be loyal. Do not betray anyone's trust.

Family
Love your family. Always show them how much you love and care for them, even if it is as simple as saying the words, "I love you." These are magical words and have a strong, positive effect in the life of family members, especially children. Kids want so much to be loved.

Ways and Means to Enhance Everyday Life

Time for God

Set aside time for the Lord. Say your prayers daily. Make God a high priority in your life. Do not put God on the back burner.

The Representative of God

Love your priest. He is the representative of God on Earth. Think of Jesus Christ, our Lord God, when you see a priest. No one can celebrate Holy Mass, the memorial of the Lord God, Jesus Christ's, Passion, Death, and Resurrection, the most sacrosanct and Divine Liturgy without a priest. God has given each of us a unique individual talent. Serve God by using that talent in the service of the Lord and His flock. Help your priest in shepherding the Lord's flock and volunteer to be an extraordinary minister of Holy Communion, a lector, an usher, a cantor, a choir member, a member of the parish council (president, vice president, secretary, etc.), Sunday school teacher, wedding coordinator, ministry scheduler, hospitality host, etc. Sign up your young children to serve as altar servers. At an early age, they will develop a love for God and neighbors.

Angel

Be an angel in someone's life.

Smile

Begin your day with smile, and thank God you are alive. Make your day a smiley day. In the evening when you retire to sleep, smile. You made it through the day.

Friends

Friends are relatives we create for ourselves. Be good and helpful to your friends. Lift your friends. Appreciate and compliment them.

Time

Tempus fugit (Latin phrase for "time flies"). Yes, indeed, time flies. Use your precious time wisely. Time lost can never be retrieved. Do not waste time.

Grateful

Always remember to thank the Lord God above before each meal.

Living Plant

Have a living thing, like a plant, in your home, or something nice to behold like a rose, lily, violet, peony, or a magnolia from your garden. When you see the plant and flower as you wake up in the morning, thank God for every moment you live and every breath of life He gives you. A live plant is a reminder of the gift of life God continuously gives you. Your gift of life is a wonderful blessing from the loving and everlasting God!

A Knight

Be a knight in shining armor and rescue a maiden or someone in distress.

Words

Words spoken can never be retrieved. Choose words wisely before you speak. People may forget a good deed, but they will not forget hurtful words you uttered to them.

A Promise

Be wary in making promises. When you make a promise, it becomes a commitment and a responsibility. Keep your promises. Having word of honor makes you a reliable and respectable person. In addition, it makes you a person of class.

Pieces of Advice for Christian and Better Living
Part One

Relax
Take time to sit down and watch the world go by. Smell the orchids, roses, hyacinths, dahlias, magnolias, or the peonies, etc. They are the most fragrant flowers. Relax, take a deep breath, meditate, and spend time in prayer. Feel God's presence. It is ethereal and spellbinding. The Lord is near!

Honor
The good persons carry out their affairs with honor. Be righteous and lead a clean-living life.

Tact
Exercise tact. Be diplomatic. Try your best not to alienate anyone.

Envy
Envy is very bad. It is a monster! It causes troubles. Try your very best to avoid envy. You can prevent hurts - ill feelings and heartaches, and make this world a better place to live if you refrain from envy. Be happy for others if they have more than you. Say a prayer if you have the urge to be envious of others. Ask God to grant you wisdom and grace to refrain from envy.

Compliment
Compliment your spouse, children, parents, grandparents, neighbors, et al. It will make them feel very good, brighten their lives, and lift their spirits.

Positive
Be the most positive, hopeful, and exuberant person in the world. It makes your personality pleasing.

Punctuality
Make it a habit to be punctual in everything you do.

Students: Don't be late for your classes. Always arrive on time and be ready. Don't be late for Holy Mass on Sunday, any other important appointments, or social engagements, etc.

Manners
Have flawless and refined manners. It gives you a touch of class.

Be a Blessing
Be a blessing to someone who is sick and bring him/her some beautiful flowers or a delicious home-cooked meal.

Prime Importance
It is absolutely of prime importance to tell your wife you love her. It is vital as well to tell your husband you love him. Make it a high-priority to tell your children you love them. It is essential to appreciate your children and show your love for them. It is crucial to tell your parents you love them, for you may not know when it is too late. You may not know how long they will still be here with you.

Exercise
The body is meant to be mobile. Keep moving the body and exercising. It is indispensable for your health. Go for a brisk walk for thirty minutes every day. Increase the brisk walking from thirty to forty-five to sixty minutes, if you can. If you can't do it every day, at least every other day. The benefits of brisk walking are enormous for your whole body especially for cardiovascular health.

Make Someone's Day
Brighten, or make someone's day, let someone go in front of you in traffic, give your change to any charity collector on the street or the homeless.

Pieces of Advice for Christian and Better Living
Part Two

Optimism

Positive attitude truly conquers the enormous obstacles. Be the most optimistic person in the world. An optimistic person is always looking for the best in any given situation. Optimistic people are known to be healthier in body, mind, heart, and soul. They are a lot happier, and they enjoy daily life much more. Be with enthusiastic and supportive people. They can be a magnitude influence in your everyday life. Positive people can handle adversities, tribulations, and storms in life calmly and better than the people with negative attitudes.

Yesterday, Tomorrow, and Today

Yesterday is gone. It is the past and can never be retrieved. Whatever regrets you have, leave them in the mercy of God. Tomorrow is God's secret. The future is unknown and unpredictable. Entrust it in the divine providence of God. Now, today, the present is a wondrous gift. Put it in the protective care and love of God and you will go on well.

True Christian

A true Christian resolves to be a reflection of God's love.

Righteous

The righteous person resolves to conduct every aspect of his/her life with honesty.

Stipend

Holy men and women of God, give stipend/tithing to help your local church. Your parish needs financial assistance for the on-going programs and projects they undertake.

Blessed

It is blessed to give, but it is much more blessed to give to those who can't repay you!

Bless

Bless someone. Be a person who uplifts and inspires. It is magical.

The Best Gift

Giving someone a material thing for a gift is very good, but the best gift you can give to someone is a part of yourself.

Awesome

Be awesome to someone. It is a wonderful feeling.

Be True

Be true to yourself! Pretending to be someone else may cause you heartache, stress, and anxiety. I don't think you must measure up with the Gates, the Buffets, the Ellisons, the Waltons, the Vanderbilts, the Hearsts, the Rockefellers, the Kennedys, et al.

Don't you think it is better not to bite more than you can chew? Most of all, do not go into debt trying to measure up with your rich relatives and friends. True relatives and friends will like you for who you are, whether you are affluent or not. If they don't like you for who you are, then they are not your true friends and relatives.

Brighten, or Make Someone's Day

Brighten someone's day. Make your co-workers day, bake your best goodies/cookies, and bring them to work for your co-workers.

For Filipinos – Better yet, bring some lumpias (spring rolls) to your co-workers. Everybody loves lumpias. I have not met anybody who did not like lumpias. Everyone raves for lumpias. Men and women always say nice and lavish things about lumpias. Brighten someone's day, smile, and say hello nicely to a total stranger. Brighten someone's day and be the first to say good morning, good afternoon, or good evening.

Treasure the Family

The family is the foundation of our society. Treasure your family. Love the members of your family. Keep the family strong.

The Good God

God is good. Today, and every day, God is there. He is giving you his light, peace, joy, hope, care, and love. He is lending you his enduring strength, and sending abundant blessings your way. He is giving you the gift of a brand-new day. Be happy. Cheers!

Pieces of Advice for Christian and Better Living
Part Three

The Loving Heart
The heart God has given us is meant to love. It is meant for compassion; it is not meant to hate. Harbor no hate, hard feelings, or grudges on anyone. Help this vital organ stay healthy by letting go of hate, hard feelings, or grudges. The heart may suffer stress, anxiety, and possibly trigger a heart attack if you hold on to hate, hard feeling, or grudges. Forgive and let go of the ill feelings.

The Sweet Tongue
God has given us a tongue meant to speak the law of kindness. It is not meant to speak ill of anyone. Speak only uplifting, encouraging, kind, and inspiring words. The good Christian resolves never to speak ill of someone. Remember, words spoken can never be retrieved.

The Incredible Mind
One of the amazing and fascinating gifts God has given us in our body is the mind (brain). It is meant to think only of righteous things! It is not meant to plot evil! The true Christian thinks only of good, virtuous, upright, ethical, honorable, and angelic things that are very pleasing to the Lord God. Think no bad things, or plot no evil against your neighbors.

The Devout Christians
The devout Christians resolve to serve one another in love and follow gladly the exemplary works of Jesus Christ who came into the world, not to be served, but to serve.

The Pious
The pious person resolves to be kind and considerate with the young, sensitive, and compassionate with the old, understanding with the struggling, and un-biased with the frail. You may never know soon you may be one of these. One thing I know for sure is you will get old someday!

The Good Christians

The good Christians resolve never to judge anyone. The Lord Jesus Christ did not judge anybody. Why should you? Peter denied him, not only once, but thrice, yet He did not judge him. Instead, He trusted him with the keys of the Kingdom of Heaven.

The Perfect Gentleman

I went to the base chapel to attend daily Holy Mass.

The priest saw me and said, "I will open the door for you." I let him.

He opened the door for me, and I said, "Oh, Father, you are a perfect gentleman."

He said, "Yes."

Holy men of the Lord God, make someone's day and hold the door open for somebody. Be perfect gentlemen like the priest. Chivalry is not dead.

Note: Men: With offense towards none.

Face the Music

Life will not go on smoothly at all times. Sometimes there are bumps and curves, and we are thrust into an overwhelming situation we do not like, but we face the music even if we do not like the unpleasant and sour melody. We try our best to handle the formidable problem or ominous situation with inner courage and intense strength. We pray to God earnestly to help us, guide us, and get us through triumphantly. We should not give up! God will carry us lovingly on his shoulder. He loves us and will not let us down. We must entrust everything in the open arms of the Lord God. The new dawn will come! There will be a beautiful rainbow after the violent storm. A bright light will loom in the horizon! You will see!

The Joyful Heart

A cheerful heart does great like a tonic. It rejuvenates and stimulates.

The Friends

Treasure your friends like they are valuable gems – diamonds, emeralds, pearls, rubies, amethysts – Your cherished friends are absolutely precious!

The Small Stuff
Don't sweat the small stuff – the trivial things, let go!

Dwell Not
Dwell not on anything unpleasant or bad experience in the past. Use it as an avenue for growth or a valuable lesson, then block it out of your mind. What really matters is now, today. Live your day filled with joy, love, understanding, caring, kindness, and uplifting thoughts. Then, spread the joy, love, understanding, caring to others as well.

The Treasures
Blessed are they who are compassionate and feed the poor, homeless, impoverished, hungry, and less fortunate people for they are gathering treasures in Heaven where no thieves can break in and steal.

Lean On
Lean on the Lord God, and everything is possible. In a reading from the holy Gospel according to John (John, Chapter 21), Simon Peter, Thomas, Nathanael, James, John, et al went out fishing and caught nothing. Jesus told them to cast the net over the right side of the boat and they will find something. So, they did. They caught so many fish and were not able to pull the net in because of the number of fish. The impossible is possible with the Lord God. Rely upon the Lord! Put your confidence in the hands of God.

The Appreciation
Appreciate your priest/pastor, members of your family, relatives, friends, coworkers, doctor, nurse, pharmacist, et al. Always look for ways and means to make them feel needed and important. You will uplift their heart and mind. They will feel very good, and it makes you a remarkably caring and charismatic person.

Pieces of Advice for Christian and Better Living – Part Four

Your Church

Quit grumbling about your church. It is not a community of saints. It is a community of people, and people are not perfect. If it is perfect, I think, perhaps, you couldn't become a member.

The Apple

Remember, you are the "apple of God's eye" (Psalm 71-8). As such, you are precious, and you are treasured by God! Always have faith, hope, and love and fill your heart with ardor for the Lord God.

Accept What Cannot Be Changed

Life is not perfect. Really, not all things in life are perfect. Practical, sensible, and happy people accept bravely problems, challenges, disappointments, misfortunes, complications, and difficulties in their life in which they don't have any control, or they cannot change. Instead, they put their best effort on changing what they can control to improve the situation they are thrust into. Easier said than done, but they try their very best!

After the Storm

Stay calm in the midst of a storm. Be a rainbow stretching across a violent and stormy sea giving great hope and a quiet assurance of peace that must come. Tomorrow is a new and bright day. Dawn will come. It is inevitable. The sun will shine marvelously. New light, strength, and courage will loom in the horizon.

A Cell Phone Call Away

Whenever your heart and mind are in pain or you are hurting, say a prayer. Call God. He is only a cell-phone call away. He does not have a busy number. He has a special line you can call twenty-four hours every day, any time of the day. Prayer opens the closed door to inner comfort, healing, and peace. You'll see. God will not let you down.

True Disciple

The good Christian is a true disciple of Jesus Christ who bears much fruit.

Best Remedy

Sometimes in life, the best remedy is a friend's call over the cell/smartphone. A friend's sweet and calming voice is the best cure. It can give one an invigorating effect. Give your friend a call.

Poisons of Life

Hatred, bitterness, grudges, ill feelings, intense anger, envy, jealousy, and bad-talk poison the good life.

Hope

The loving Christian is a beacon of hope for someone.

Win

Win and influence people/friends by your own nice words and actions, and don't lose or drive them away by your very own words and actions.

The Splendor

Splendor, majesty, and sublime are attributed to the Lord God. Endless joy and praise are in His holy abode. Let us all rejoice! Exult in the Lord, and be happy. We are His people! Alleluia! Alleluia!

Never-Ending Glory

Cease not in giving never-ending glory and earnest praise to the Lord God who gives life and light to our existence. Those who dwell under the haven of His magnificent roof are devout Christian men and women who live in accordance with the Gospel; holy men and women who keep the word of God. Great and many are their blessings.

What to Pray For

Pray not for wealth, but pray for wisdom and grace. God will provide the wealth like He provided to Solomon after you seek Him first.

Happiness

Bear in mind true happiness is not based on wealth, influence, or prominence, but on how well you treat your family, relatives, and friends, et al - the persons you care for, cherish, and regard in high esteem.

Little Notes

Leave "I love you" notes for your husband to find in his pocket, his briefcase, or on the dashboard of his car.

Leave "I love you" notes for your wife to find in her purse, her pocket, or on the dashboard of her car.

Smile and Laughter

On a daily basis, you must smile and laugh. It is rejuvenating. It restores your youthful vigor!

Your Children

If you feel like you're being impatient with your children, pause and think momentarily. Take a deep breath! They can be very difficult sometimes, but count your blessings. They are well and alive. They are breathing. You can see, feel, and touch them. You can hug and talk to them. They are there with you. Rejoice gloriously! They are not dead. What an amazing miracle. Thank God for the blessing!

Let your children (adults or kids) catch you (on purpose) saying nice comments about them to other people. My brother Nestor always did that. When he talked on the phone to his friends or relatives and said nice things about me, he spoke loudly, letting me catch him complimenting me.

Pieces of Advice for Christian and Better Living - Part Five

Jesus Christ

Christ is our light and salvation; venite adoremus (come, let us adore). Pray the Lord God grant us a calm and peaceful day and night.

Glory to God

Sublime and glorious is the work of God. Give our God and Father sincere glory and thanks! Alleluia!

Captivating

Give everyone you meet a winning and captivating smile that knocks their socks off, melts their hearts, and takes their breaths away.

The Potentials

The gracious God has given each of us marvelous potentials. Be not afraid to use them for God's service. They are not meant to be hidden, but they are meant to be utilized in building God's Kingdom on Earth.

The Very Best

Give the very best of yourself to your spouse and children. They are your immediate family. Worry not if you cannot give them the most beautiful of material things. Give them love!

Obedience

Be loyal and obedient to Jesus Christ, and your life will go on well.

The Loving God

Spend time with the awesome, loving, and merciful God in prayer and meditation. He loves to talk to you. He is always there waiting for you all the time.

The Joy of Giving

Absolutely, share what you have with the poor. It is a true joy, an indescribable feeling of euphoria as if you can see God smiling at you and telling you, "Well done, you did it for me."

Spread Good Things

Spread cheers, goodwill, joy, love, kindness, compassion, friendliness, and charity. Make them contagious!

Walk

Let us walk in the presence of the Lord God in the company of Momma Mary, the angels, and the saints, and remain righteous all the days of our life.

Your Precious Gifts

Your kids did not ask to be born. They are your precious gifts of life from the good Lord God. Give them your very best. Bring them up loving God and their fellowmen/women. Instill in them righteousness, honesty, ethical values, integrity, compassion, and honor.

Teach them affable social skills as well. It is, likewise, indispensable. They need to learn to be friendly, charming, gracious, kind, good-natured, jolly, and courteous. Getting along with their schoolmates, siblings, friends, parents, et al and being interactive are factors of success. At home, teach them cooperation and teamwork to help in preparing them to succeed in this world, currently that is so highly competitive.

Attend your children's school activities like ballgames, math, spelling, or literary contests, theater plays, or violin, dance, and piano recitals.

Positive Thinking

You can even climb the summit of Mount Everest in the Himalayas, the highest mountain in the world, or Mont Blanc (White Mountain), one of the highest mountains, or one of the highest peaks in Europe, or El Capitan, the mountain in Yosemite National Park in California, if you have positive thinking.

The Best Gift

Give the best gift that anyone can give - the gift of prayer. It is the best gift anyone can receive.

The Gift of Faith

The gift of faith is another precious gift to give to someone. Invite someone who has not gone to church for a while. We are called to be disciples of

Jesus Christ and bear much fruit. Modern day discipleship does not necessarily mean you should go to the boondocks to preach. Your friend, an acquaintance, or next-door neighbors who have not gone to church for a few, or several, years may just be waiting for you to invite them and give them the gift of faith.

The Life

Sometimes daily life is not easy. You may encounter a friend or relative who may say to you: "You're looking swell baby!" You are not feeling swell, and there is something bothering you. There are bumps on the road; there are storms, and life is not always swell. Trust in the Lord when that happens. He will get you through no matter how difficult the situation may be. There is always hope. Tomorrow is a new day. The sun will shine.

The Destination

Walk confidently hand in hand with God, and you will reach your destination.

Jealousy

Blessed are they who are not jealous of others, but who have learned to appreciate and admire and not be jealous.

Tonic

Prayer is tonic. No side effects! Pray often. Spend time with the Lord God. Worry not about anything. God will take care of you. Leave it in the palm of His hands.

God's Blessings

God loves you. God will bless you mightily today. Count your blessings. See what God has done for you.

Wear Your Faith

Wear your faith on your sleeve - Deuteronomy 6:4-9 - My reflection on the Holy Scripture reading: Don't be afraid to "wear your faith on your sleeve" and let everyone know you are a Roman Catholic, or any other Christian religion – Anglican, Episcopalian, Baptist, Protestant, etc. In the deepest core of your heart, know the One and only One in whom you believe.

Note: I am a fan of Tim Russert (Timothy J. Russert), an American journalist and lawyer who was the moderator of NBC's *Meet the Press* for more than sixteen years. I watched *Meet the Press* every Sunday when he was alive. He died of a sudden heart attack on June 13, 2008. Watching him on TV for several years, and having the same faith, a common bond, I felt he was a part of my family. He wore his faith on his sleeve. I am so proud he always wore his Roman Catholic faith. I was sad when he died, as if a family member of mine died.

Pieces of Advice for Christian and Better Living
Part Six

The Eyes

Use the eyes to see the beautiful things in people. Not only physical beauty, but beauty within the heart and soul. Use not the eyes for finding, or looking for faults and wrong in people. Delight not in other people's mistakes, sins, and shortcomings. Remember, every human being is a creation of God. Every human person is worthy of honor and respect.

Note: God has given us an astonishing body. He has given us two eyes, two ears, two nostrils, two hands, two feet, two kidneys, two breasts, two ovaries (for women), two testicles (for men), and two lungs. Isn't that something? If something goes wrong with one of the two parts, there is a spare. He has also given us an amazing immune system. We would get sick easily if it were not for this immune system that fights germs, viruses, and bacterium. Because of our immune system, we only get sick when the germs, viruses, or bacterium are too strong for the immune system to fight. Thanks be to God for these blessings!

Respect

Respect each individual person and anyone God puts in your path.

The Invitation

Show your love for your priest, the representative of Jesus Christ, and invite him to dinner. Spoil him and prepare his favorite food! Use your fine china, beautiful silverware, nice Waterford or Mikasa crystal glasses, exquisite table cloth, and decorative napkins.

We invited our priest friend, Father R.R., one day to have dinner at home. After dinner, he said to me, "Fely, thank you for the dinner fit for a king!"

I was so overwhelmed by his kind words. I said, "Thank you." I thought I would choke. He was too kind!

The Lord God

Let us praise the name of the mighty Lord! Praise Him for the Lord is good! Come, let us rejoice, worship, and give Him homage. Alleluia!

The Right Path

Ensure that our path is not vile. We should follow the right path that leads to eternal glory! Pray God will guide us that we will never trek the wrong path!

At Work

In the workplace, always be at your best! Stay calm. Never lose your cool. Maintain your composure!

The Resplendent Day

Enjoy the resplendent day. In the movie, *Dead Poets Society*, Robin Williams, who played the role of John Keating, an English teacher, often told his students to, "Carpe diem!" I love this movie. See it if you have not yet. ("Carpe diem" is a Latin phrase for "Seize the Day" by Horace, a Roman poet).

The Savior

Jesus Christ is the ultimate sacrifice that redeemed us. Come you all, let us praise, adore, bless, and give profound thanks to the kind God who laid down His life for us! This is what profound and true love is.

Who would lay down their lives for their brothers and sisters? Saint Maximilian Kolbe did!

In February 1941, Maximilian Kolbe was arrested by the German Gestapo and sent to Auschwitz. Franciszek Gajowniczek was one of the men chosen and sentenced to die in the starvation bunker. Kolbe volunteered to take his place so Franciszek could live to take care of his wife and children. He traded places with Franciszek Gajowniczek. He died as a "martyr of charity" on August 14, 1941. This is an exemplary manifestation of Christian love, laying down one's life for a brother!

Stupendous

When someone asks, "How are you?" say, something like, "Stupendous, awesome, marvelous, never been better." Try your best not to grumble about the world.

Morale Booster

Make it a good habit to lift someone – your spouse, relatives, friends, children, co-workers, et al. Say something uplifting that will boost their morale. Be a morale booster.

The Virtue of Patience

Patience is a virtue. It is the ability to accept or tolerate delay, or suffering without getting mad, or upset. Be patient.

You can shop and find a good price if you have the patience to wait in a long queue for bargains before the stores open especially on the Friday after Thanksgiving Day.

The Virtue of Our Baptism

By virtue of our baptism, let us be salt of the earth and be light of Christ for the world as we are called upon to do. Let us be kind, courteous, compassionate, and patient with one another. Let us concentrate on being holy.

The Guests

Invite and feed the poor on your birthday and make them the guests of honor during the birthday celebration, for you are echoing God's deep love and concern for the poor.

Enjoy Life

Enjoy your one and only life while there is time, and while you can. If possible, visit places you would like to see.

Treat yourself, if you could. If you could afford it, spend money on yourself.

See your old friends, current friends, and classmates – you are not getting any younger. Eat the best food you can afford, and your health allows. Grasp the moment! Smile often!

Pieces of Advice for Christian and Better Living
Part Seven

God Knows

"God has called you by your name" - Isaiah 43:1. He knows you by heart, and he loves you. Sing a new song unto the Lord and give Him endless praise.

The Footprints

How wonderful it is to leave footprints in people's hearts that when they think of you, they have a lovely smile on their faces because they remember you very fondly as you have left your footprints in their hearts.

Guard Them

Guard your name and honor as much as you value your one and only precious life. Your name and honor once compromised may not be restored!

The Fine Manner - Common Courtesy

Practice common courtesy. Make it a serious duty to acknowledge a gift. Write thank you notes immediately. Do not wait for the giver of the gift to have to ask you if you have received the present.

Cease Not

Cease not in giving glory to God now and always. Glory and praise to our God! He alone gives a bright light to our everyday life. Many are the blessings He gives to those who put their trust in His hands 100%, with no reservations.

The Fine Manner – Respond to R.S.V.P. Invitations

When you are invited to a wedding, a birthday celebration, a graduation party, a Baptism, or a First Holy Communion you are thought of very highly. It is an honor and a privilege to be invited to a momentous occasion. Take time to respond promptly to R.S.V.P. invitations, especially when a stamp has already been affixed in the return envelope. If a phone number is provided, call as soon as possible. If you could not attend the event after responding, let the host know immediately. Be considerate to the host who goes to great length planning the important event, especially the reception. Remember, a notification that you can't come will save the host money. The host will cancel your reservation and does not have to pay for your reserved meal. It is classy to have fine manner, or courtesy!

Wrong
Wrong is wrong! Make no excuses for what is wrong. Do what is right. Correct the wrong!

The Lord God of the Earth and the Universe
In Jesus Christ's dying and rising lies our salvation. Let us give thanks and praise! He is ever faithful and true. Venite adoremus! Come, let us worship! How great our Lord God is through all the Earth and the Universe. Give Him our never-ending glory!

The Ears
Although the gift of gab is important, being a good listener provides an advantage as well. God gave you two ears, so you can be a good listener. Lend your ears to your family, relatives, and friends, et al when they need you. Do not ignore them, but hear them. Use not your ears for listening to gossips, vile, and innuendos.

Credit Card
A credit card is meant for convenience. Use it only for this purpose. When the bank has paid for the purchase, pay the bill as soon as possible. It will save you a good amount of money so you do not have to pay for interest charges.

Love and Care
Today, God is there giving you His enduring love and tender care. He is giving you strength and sending abundant blessings your way, and giving you the wonderful gift of a beautiful brand new day. Let us bow and kneel before the Lord.

PIECES OF ADVICE FOR CHRISTIAN AND BETTER LIVING
PART EIGHT

Share
As a Christian, remember to do good. Share what you have with those people in need. Such sacrifices are very commendable and pleasing to the Lord.

Bless the Lord
Let us bless the Lord God at all times; God's glory and grandeur on our lips. Jesus Christ dwells in our midst, let us give Him praise.

Your Precious Health
Take good care of yourself especially your precious health. Good health is affluence! It is everybody's main source of wealth. It is priceless. Good health is happiness beyond compare.

Sing a New Song
God is our courage and strength. Let us give Him our profound praise and sing a new song unto the Lord for He is gracious. His mercy endures forever. Live today in appreciation of His love. Alleluia!

The First Time
Do everything right the first time. Rework is costly. You can save quite a bit of money if you do not have to redo.

The Only Life
You only have one life to live. Keep calm. Keep cool. The astounding mystery to enjoying a wonderful and tranquil life is to be very thankful and appreciative for what each day and moment bring.

Real Success
To have become wise, loving, generous, and kind is the true and real success.

The Magnificent Lord God
The Lord is magnificent as ever in His angels, saints, prophets, apostles, and martyrs. Come, let us praise and glorify Him now and forever.

Reach Out

We, the Christian people, are called upon to reach out with one another in love and generosity. Everything we have is a blessing from God. All our material things, affluence, and whatever we possess are gifts from our God. We are stewards of God's gifts. We are called upon to share our blessings with the poor. When you provide assistance to the poor, or the homeless, they say "God bless you." You are the answer to their prayers. That is genuine and heart-felt love!

Real and Loyal Friends

Real and sincere friends warm you with their visits, trust you deeply with their innermost thoughts, and think of you in their prayers.

The Lord God

Let us praise the name of the mighty Lord! Praise Him for the Lord is good! Come, let us rejoice, worship, and give Him homage. Alleluia. Sing praises and psalms to the Lord God. Give earnest thanks to His holy name. You who love Him dearly. Alleluia!

Marvels

What marvelous works the Lord has done for us! His words are faithful and true. Let us put our trust in the Lord, and give Him thanks upon the lyre, piano, organ, guitar, violin, trumpet, ten-stringed harp, flute, etc., and sing Him lovely songs. O sing Him some songs, play them loudly, make the music blast out at full volume with all your might.

Upward Mobility

Climb up the corporate ladder. Look for opportunities for upward mobility. Look for promotion announcements. Put in application for all the promotion announcements for which you are qualified. Take a refresher course on how to excel in an interview for a promotion. Dazzle the panel of interviewers. Make it an outstanding, impressive, and a phenomenal interview that will knock their socks off. Show them you are a stellar, remarkable, and hard-working employee; you do a super, fantastic, and A+ job. Shine dramatically that will make you stand apart from the rest of the candidates, and convince the panel of interviewers to select you as the best candidate to fill the higher graded position.

Keep in Touch

Keep in touch with your friends and relatives and send a "Thinking of You" card. In the complimentary closing, just above your signature, write either one of the following below:

> From someone who thinks you are marvelous,
> From someone who thinks you are a gem,
> From someone who thinks you are an angel in my life,
> From someone who thinks you are an absolute delight,
> From someone who thinks you are terrific,
> From someone who thinks you are sweet,
> From someone who thinks you are wonderful,
> From someone who thinks you are amazing,
> From someone who thinks you are awesome,

Then sign your name.

Say something nice.

Don't tell anyone, "You look weary and unhappy." Say something better than that. Say something nice and uplifting like any of the following below:

For a lady: Wow, you look fabulous. You look gorgeous. You look beautiful. Wow, you had your hair cut in a becoming new style. That dress is very becoming on you. Wow, you look like a million-dollar lady.

For a gentleman: Wow, you look handsome. You look distinguished. That jacket or suit is very becoming on you. Wow, you had your hair cut in a becoming new style. Wow, you look like a million-dollar gentleman. You look marvelous.

Fine Things

Use the fine and beautiful things you have and reserve for parties like your delicate china dishes, elegant silverware, exquisite Waterford crystal glasses, lovely silver plate servers, regal cloth napkins, deluxe table cloth cover, grand candelabra, etc. even if you don't have guests. It feels good to treat yourself with fine and beautiful things every now and then. You are just as important and as precious as your distinguished or honored guests.

Pieces of Advice for Christian and Better Living
Part Nine

The Obstacles
Use obstacles you encounter along the way as stepping stones to lead the way to triumph, accomplishment, or success.

Living
Living is a tremendous adventure! Life is easy and happy sometimes, difficult at one time or another, all is well most of the time, unbearable when you are facing uncertainties, or when you lost a loved one, as if the world would end, but there is hope. Keep moving. You should savor and enjoy every aspect of life. It is a journey, and live by the grace of God.

The Belief
Your faith in God brings an ardent and deep strength, spiritual illumination, and overwhelming joy and peace. Have faith and believe in God.

Breath of Fresh Air
Tell your new friend, "You are a breath of fresh air! You are refreshing!" When you see a relative, or a friend you have not seen for a few years, say the same words to him/her, "You are a breath of fresh air! You are refreshing!"

These wonderful words have the power to make a difference in anybody's life! These words made a difference in my life when they were said to me.

"You are a breath of fresh air."

My supervisor said these words to me during appraisal time in 1999 when we first moved to another state. The following year during appraisal time in 2000, he said, "You are refreshing."

When my grandson Logan was born in 2001, he said these words to me again, "Oh, Fely, you are so refreshing with all of your excitement in becoming a grandma."

Today
Cherish today! Relish each second, minute, and hour of the brand-new day, or brand new year!

The Door

If the door closes on you, go through the window. Remember, there are several other avenues or paths to get through a closed door.

The Prayer

A day without prayer is a meaningless, lonely, and an aimless, empty day.

"La Vita E Bella"

See the movie "La Vita E Bella" (Life Is Beautiful) starring Roberto Benigni, Giorgio Cantarini, Nicoletta Braschi, et al. This movie won an Academy Award for Best Picture, Best Foreign Language Film. The film was a financial success. It won Roberto Benigni, the leading actor, the Academy Award for Best Actor at the 71st Academy Awards. This film, directed by Benigni, also won the Academy Award for Best Original Dramatic Score.

Life is worth living, and indeed it is beautiful.

Improvement

Constantly make room for improving yourself. Accumulate wisdom. Learn a foreign language. Stimulate your brain. Solve crossword puzzles. Read a book. Explore reading some of the plays of William Shakespeare, or read bestselling books, etc. Do some complicated tasks. Memorize your favorite poems, or songs. Memorize psalms from Holy Scriptures such as Psalm 23 – The Lord Is My Shepherd, Psalm 130, Psalm 51 - Miserere (Have Mercy), etc. The following prayers: Te Deum Laudamus (Thee, God, We Praise), Canticle of Zechariah, and Canticle of Mary, etc. are wonderful prayers to know by heart. Accept a challenging task.

The Holy Bible

The Bible is the number one most read book in the world. Read the Holy Bible. There are so many amazing and fascinating stories. To mention a few – the creation, Abraham's test of faith, Noah and the Ark, the exodus, Moses and the Ten Commandments, the story of David and Solomon, the birth of Jesus and the salvation of mankind, the apostles - Saint Peter, Saint Andrew, Saint Matthew, Saint James, the Great, son of Zebedee, Saint Bartholomew, Saint Thomas, Saint James, the Less, Saint Matthias, Saint Philip, Saint Judas Thaddaeus, Saint John, and Saint Simon Cananeus, the Zealot . Read about

Saint Paul as well. Tons of wisdom you can accumulate by reading the Bible, wisdom you can apply in your daily life.

Pieces of Advice for Christian and Better Living
Part Ten

Christ-like
Become more and more Christ-like in everything you do in words and actions.

Sing
Sing whenever you can, even if you can't carry a tune. Singing is very therapeutic. It is absolutely divine.

Radiating
Be a delightful Christian person who radiates joy and cheer. It is infectious.

The Conversation
A conversation is an art; an exchange of ideas. In a conversation, listen! Do not monopolize the conversation; ensure you let other people talk too.

The Love
Love is one thing that money can't buy, although you have all the millions, trillions, and billions in this world! Love sincerely.

True Light
Christ is our true light. Come all, let us find His way now and forever!

Jesus, the Lord
The Lord is our shepherd, light, hope, and guard. In the shelter of His love, let us gather together and give Him our endless thanks and praise!

Excellent Deeds
Do good! Laugh! Love! Pray, Forgive!

The Movie *Hook*
Watch the movie *Hook* with your kids. If you have seen it already, watch it again. It is an exemplary family movie that can bring tears to your eyes and possibly melt your heart. It is also a good time to bond with your kids.

The Caring
If you are a supervisor, include love, caring, and compassion in taking care of your employees. You can't go wrong!

Be Pleasant
Be pleasant, and smile a lot when you are at work even if the job is challenging, complex, and difficult, and even if your co-workers or supervisors are difficult sometimes.

Brighten the Day
Brighten, or make someone's day, and let someone go in front of you to pay for their purchase at a convenient store. Everyone seems to be in a hurry most of the time. You will make them feel better, if you let them go ahead of you.

PIECES OF ADVICE FOR CHRISTIAN AND BETTER LIVING - PART ELEVEN

Do It Now

Do whatever you want to do now. Do not wait until tomorrow. Time flies very fast. It does not wait for you. There are only so much tomorrows. Tomorrow may be too late. Live now, seize every moment of the day, so one day when you look back at your life, you don't have any regrets that you did not get to do this and that!

Spend Precious Time for Yourself

- Feel the cool zephyr brush on your cheeks.
- Call a cherished friend.
- Fix the broken fences.
- Smell the roses, the queen of all flowers.
- Slow down, relax.
- Forgive. Heal the wound.
- Appreciate your liberty. You are lucky. You live in a county where you are free.
- Commemorate diversity. Many of us are immigrants.
- Scatter good deeds; the harvest is amazing.
- Be yourself. No need to measure up with others.
- Do it right always.
- Live and love by the grace of God.

The Importance

With a heart that is gentle and kind, humbly, consider others as more important than yourselves.

God Bless You!

If someone is unpleasant to you, say "God bless you." Hopefully, this person will realize the unpleasant attitude and may change for the better when you have asked God to bless this individual.

The Day

Make the best of each day God has given you. Make it bright, cheerful, and blissful. Make it not chilly, gloomy, and joyless.

Growing in Holiness

Be nearer to God always. Give the magnificent God precious time in prayer. Keep growing in holiness, and hopefully achieve the sanctity and dedication of a saint. We are called upon to be saints!

Lemons

If life gives you lemons, make lemonade out of them and add some sugar.

The Words

Let the words of Christ dwell in you richly. Blessed is the only begotten Son of God who continuously feeds us the sublime and awe-inspiring words of life.

The Pets

If you can, have a pet – a dog, a cat, or a bird, etc. According to a survey, people (especially older people) with pets are calm, and they live longer. They are happier and more likely not to suffer from loneliness or depression.

The survey also said kids who have pets are well-adjusted. They are loving, nice, and kind, and they get along better with other kids.

Bury the Hatchet

Bury the hatchet with a friend or relative, et al whom you have been estranged. Make peace!

A Million Thanks

Let us always think of thanking our Lord God for the prolific and countless blessings He has bestowed upon us – for every breath of life He gives us and the members of our family, for our good health, home, shelter, our daily bread, etc., and for the numerous blessings He has lavishly showered on us.

THE PRAYER OF ST. FRANCIS BY SAINT FRANCIS OF ASSISI

If you feel like getting ballistic with someone who has provoked you, take a deep breath and say this prayer. It works and can calm your anger. It is one of the best-known prayers in the world. It is a very beautiful prayer. I pray it all the time.

> **The Prayer of St. Francis**
> Lord, make me an instrument of Your peace;
> Where there is hatred, let me sow love;
> Where there is injury, pardon;
> Where there is doubt, faith;
> Where there is despair, hope;
> Where there is darkness, light;
> And where there is sadness, joy.
> O Divine Master,
> Grant that I may not so much seek
> To be consoled as to console;
> To be understood, as to understand;
> To be loved, as to love;
> For it is in giving that we receive,
> It is in pardoning that we are pardoned,
> And it is in dying that we are born to Eternal Life.
> Amen.

Part II

Selected Holy Gospel Readings –
Commentaries or Reflections

Selected Holy Scripture Readings –
First and Second Readings, Commentaries or Reflections

The Spellbinding Journeys

THE GOOD SHEPHERD

We all need a shepherd. We need Jesus. Jesus Christ, the good Lord is our good Shepherd. He knows us by heart. He is there for us twenty-four hours a day watching and keeping us in His tender loving care. If we stumble and fall, He will pick us up, and put us affectionately on His shoulder. He is kind-hearted and merciful. If we get lost in the terrain, He will look us up, find us, and bring us home. He will never disown us, nor will He delete us from His living will.

It is only through Jesus we have received salvation. "I am the good shepherd; and I know My sheep, and am known by My own" (John 10:14). He gave us the ultimate sacrifice and laid down His life for us, so the Kingdom of Heaven was widely opened for us.

He came not to be served, but to serve. Let us therefore follow the exemplary deeds of Jesus. Let us warmly and fondly serve one another in love.

Oremus (Let us pray). O God, our loving and good Shepherd, may we always praise, glorify, thank, and serve you all the days of our life. May we serve one another in love as you have served us. My we exult in your everlasting love now and forever. O Lord God, hear our prayer. Amen.

Charity - A Genuine Love

A reading from the holy Gospel according to Luke 21:1-4:
Jesus saw the rich putting their gifts into the treasury. He saw a poor widow putting in two small copper coins. He said, "Truly I say to you, this poor widow put in more than all of them; for they all out of their surplus put into the offering; but she out of her poverty put in all that she had to live on."

Excerpts from a reading from the holy Gospel according to Luke 3:10-11:
The crowds asked John the Baptist, "What should we do?"

John replied, "Whoever has two coats must share it with anyone who has none; and whoever has food must do likewise."

My heart-felt reflections on these two Holy Scripture readings:
Have compassion for the poor and the homeless. Jesus Christ loved the poor. Benevolent goodwill toward humanity is a Christian duty. It feels good to be generous. Give your clothes, shoes, handbags, eyeglasses, and other things in your closet you have not used during the past two or three years to charitable organizations that assist the poor worldwide. Giving charity is gathering treasures that have merit in the Kingdom of Heaven. It will greatly benefit those who are needy and less fortunate than you are. Giving to the poor is a profound and genuine love for God and neighbor.

Support the charity drives at your local church. Donate your extra sweaters, clothes, shoes, canned goods, dry goods, toiletries, etc. to aid the needy and the suffering in your local community. If you don't have a charity drive in your local church, your church leaders can organize one.

Support the angel drive at your church. If you don't have this program in your parish, some of the parishioners can start this worthy cause. In our parish church, we have an angel drive every year during the Christmas season. Paper angels are placed on the Christmas tree. A written request is on each paper angel. If you take one angel, it will tell you what to give for a child in need – a dress for a two-year-old, shoes for a ten-year-old, a toy for a toddler, or pants for an eight-year-old boy, and so forth.

Participate in feeding the poor when your local church sponsors a "Food for the Poor Program" such as the Breakfast with Apung Kulas (San Nicolas de Tolentino Parish) in Capas, Tarlac (my hometown) in the Philippines, "Food for the Poor," "Feeding the Poor Programs," etc.

Have some dollar bills, or coins in your wallet? When you see beggars or homeless on the streets, give them a few coins or a couple of dollars. This kindhearted deed has merits in Heaven.

Oremus (Let us pray). O God, the world is hungry for food, love, and justice. May we make a difference in people's lives and show our love and compassion to you by giving our assistance in feeding the hungry people, we ask this in the name of Jesus Christ, Your Son, our Lord who lives and reigns with you in the unity of the Holy Spirit, one God for ever and ever. Amen.

THE TEN COMMANDMENTS

Excerpts from A Reading from the Book of Exodus 20:1-17:

In those days, God delivered all these commandments: "I, the Lord, am your God who brought you out of the land of Egypt, that place of slavery. You shall not have other gods besides me."

"You shall not take the name of the Lord, your God, in vain. For the Lord will not leave unpunished the one who takes His name in vain."

Commentary on the Scripture reading from the Book of Exodus:

The people of the United States, England, France, Ireland, Netherlands, etc. are free to worship God without fear or religious persecution all the days of their lives. We are lucky. We live in a democratic society. We have freedom. Although we are free, we live in a well-ordered society. It means we believe in the Rule of Law. We follow the laws, rules, and regulations. We can't just run-a-muck. The first reading from the Book of Exodus 20:1-17 speaks about the Ten Commandments of God. The Ten Commandments God has given to Moses in Mount Sinai.

Every faithful Christian (Catholic, Anglican, Protestant, Methodist, or Baptist, etc.) knows the Ten Commandments. These are the rules we follow as good and devout Christians. In these commandments, God beckons us to love Him earnestly, and to love our neighbors sincerely.

In this modern day and age, how do we love God? How do you love your neighbor? To love God is to love your neighbor, and to love your neighbor is to love God. How do we love God above all, and how do we love our neighbors in this modern time? We can truly love God above all by being righteous and following God's words - the Ten Commandments at all times. We can love our neighbors profoundly by caring for one another. You can show your love and caring by serving one another in love. Remember, Jesus came into the world, not to be served but to serve.

Love your wife, husband, children, parents, brothers, sisters, relatives, friends, etc. Take care of your family. Do not neglect them. Listen to your children and others who need it. Be kind to others. Be helpful to anyone who needs it. Give someone your beautiful smile, uplift someone, say a cheerful hello to anyone, be pleasant to everybody, etc.

Jesus said, "The spirit is willing, but the flesh is weak." – Matthew 26:41. The spirit is willing to do good, but the flesh is weak, and sometimes temptations prevail. What should you not do to love your neighbor? Do not steal from your neighbor. Do not cheat them. Do not talk bad, or gossip, and make up lies about your neighbor. Do not do any evil to them.

Have compassion for the poor. Jesus Christ loved the poor. His Holiness, Pope Francis loves the poor, as well, and asks us to have empathy for the poor. We are called upon to love the poor. There are so many references in the Holy Bible about the poor, poverty, and justice.

THE BIRDS

A reading from the Holy Gospel according to Matthew 6:24-34.

Jesus said to his disciples: "No one can serve two masters. He will either hate one and love the other, or be devoted to one and despise the other. You cannot serve God and mammon."

"Therefore, I tell you, do not worry about your life, what you will eat or drink, or about your body, what you will wear. Is not life more than food and the body more than clothing? Look at the birds in the sky; they do not sow or reap, they gather nothing into barns, yet your heavenly Father feeds them. Are not you more important than they? Can any of you by worrying add a single moment to your life-span? Why are you anxious about clothes? Learn from the way the wild flowers grow. They do not work or spin. But I tell you that not even Solomon in all his splendor was clothed like one of them. If God so clothes the grass of the field, which grows today and is thrown into the oven tomorrow, will He not much more provide for you, O you of little faith? So, do not worry and say, 'What are we to eat?' or 'What are we to drink?' or 'What are we to wear?' All these things the pagans seek. Your heavenly Father knows that you need them all. But seek first the Kingdom of God and His righteousness, and all these things will be given you besides. Do not worry about tomorrow; tomorrow will take care of itself. Sufficient for a day is its own evil."

Reflection on the Gospel of Matthew:

I love this Gospel reading. When I was contemplating retirement, I was praying to God to enlighten me and give me a sign when should I retire. Half of me wanted to retire and the other half did not want to retire. It was one of the most difficult decisions I had to make in my life. I was so afraid that if I retired, we may not have enough money for our material needs and not be able to support my lifestyle. In fact, I told my immediate supervisor I was not retiring. She told her supervisor who was my second-level supervisor I was not retiring. My second-level supervisor sent her an email and wrote, "Perfect. Glad to hear Fely is staying for a while; she is a stellar employee." My immediate supervisor forwarded the email to me. Oh, my second-level supervisor was very kind. Her kind words were touching, but I changed my mind after I witnessed a flock of birds. After Holy Mass one Sunday, I drove to the Antelope Plaza. When I got there, suddenly, I saw a flock of birds flying freely in the sky in Antelope Plaza. They came swarming around, then landed on the ground. I had crackers in my purse, and I gave them to the birds. I watched them happily as they vied eagerly for the crackers. A few of them got pieces of crackers and ate them. This Gospel reading about the birds in the sky suddenly dawned on me. God has finally showed me the sign that it was time to retire. The birds were the sign God will take care of us even if I would retire. God will provide for us just as he provides for the birds that do not sow or reap and gather nothing into barns, yet the loving God provides for them. This was the discernment I was waiting for. Then, I made my decision to retire and not worry. I placed my deepest trust in God, and submitted my papers for my retirement. I felt God must have sent me those birds, a sign it was time to give up working.

Indeed, God has provided for us very well, and He continues to provide for us through our retirement incomes. "For we walk by faith, not by sight" – 2 Corinthians 5:7, and entrust everything in the hands of God!

I probably would still be working now if it were not for this reading from Holy Scripture. My regret? I should have retired sooner! Oh, well, I can't return to the past. Not retiring sooner was not bad. Working longer means a better retirement pay.

I am enjoying retirement so much! We have travelled to Europe every year since I retired. It is glorious! Stress free life! It is wonderful! Thanks be to the gracious God for the blessing!

The Miracle

A reading from the Holy Gospel according to Matthew 14:13-21:
When Jesus heard of the death of John the Baptist, He withdrew in a boat to a deserted place by Himself. The crowds heard of this and followed Him on foot from their towns. When He disembarked and saw the vast crowd, His heart was moved with pity for them, and He cured their sick.

When it was evening, the disciples approached Him and said, "This is a deserted place and it is already late; dismiss the crowd so that they can go to the villages and buy food for themselves."

Jesus said to them, "There is no need for them to go away; give them some food yourselves."

But they said to Him, "Five loaves and two fish are all we have here."

Then, He said, "Bring them here to me," and He ordered the crowds to sit down on the grass. Taking the five loaves and the two fish, and looking up to heaven, He said the blessing, broke the loaves and gave them to the disciples, who in turn gave them to the crowds. They all ate and were satisfied, and they picked up the fragments left over – twelve wicker baskets full. Those who ate were about five thousand men, not counting women and children.

Reflection on the Gospel of Matthew:
Jesus asked the apostles to bring Him the five loaves and two fish. The apostles complied with the request. Jesus said the blessing, broke the loaves, and the five loaves and the two fish multiplied. Five thousand men, not counting women and children, were fed. Jesus performed a miracle, the miracle of the multiplication of bread. How do we apply this Gospel reading in this modern day and age? Jesus is calling each of us to give Him five loaves and two fish. If each of us will give Him five loaves and two fish, there will be plenty of loaves and fish to feed the hungry people in the whole world. There is so much hunger around the world. People are starving especially in third world countries and even in the United States of America (U.S.A.). Let each of us give Jesus five loaves and two fish and in combining these loaves and fish, we can multiply them and make a difference. We can feed the hungry people in the world. How do we do it? We can send our share in the form of checks or stipends to several charitable organizations that help in feeding hungry people world-wide.

Oremus (Let us pray). O God, there is abundant hunger in the world. May we show our special care to those who are hungry and make us instruments of your compassion. Keep us forever grateful, appreciative, and generous in your loving service. Help us to display our love to you by aiding the hungry people in the world. We ask this in the name of Jesus Christ, your Son, our Lord. Amen.

God and Solomon

A reading from the first Book of Kings 3:5, 7-12:

The Lord appeared to Solomon in a dream at night. God said, "Ask something of me and I will give it to you."

Solomon answered: "O Lord, my God, you have made me your servant, king to succeed my father David; but I am a mere youth, not knowing at all how to act. I serve you in the midst of the people so vast that it cannot be numbered or counted. Give your servant, therefore, an understanding heart to judge your people and to distinguish right from wrong. For who is able to govern this vast people of yours?"

The Lord was pleased that Solomon made this request. So, God said to him: "Because you have asked for this – not for long life for yourself, nor for riches, nor for the life of your enemies, but for understanding so that you may know what is right – I do as you requested. I give you a heart so wise and understanding that there has never been anyone like you up to now, and after you there will come no one to equal you."

Commentary on the Scripture reading from the first Book of Kings:

God has blessed Solomon with enormous wisdom! He prayed, and God gave him overwhelming prudence. He pleaded, and the spirit of wisdom was granted to him. The judgment he rendered to find out who is the real mother of the disputed child is indeed an awesome, super, and an exceptional wisdom.

Solomon said, "Divide the living child in two and give half to the one and half to the other."

One woman spoke to the king and said, "Oh, my Lord give her the living child and by no means kill him."

The other woman said, "He shall be neither mine nor yours; divide him." – 1 Kings, Chapter 3:25.

Who is the real mother of the child in this story? It is the most prudent decision anyone can ever imagine. Indeed, Solomon was renowned for his illustrious mind. If the Lord asks you for one thing you would want him to give you, what would be your answer? Would you ask for wisdom like Solomon?

May men and women in modern day not ask God for high power and distinction, affluence, beauty and fame, a large and splendid home, a beautiful and lavish car, nor precious gems – diamonds, pearls, and emeralds, but for wisdom, and the astute judgment of what is good and evil. Just like Solomon, may the Lord grant us wisdom to do what is right all the time. May He also give us an understanding heart, kindness, and compassion. May we not hurt anyone, but may we be a blessing to all. May we love and serve God always all the days of our life. May we help God in shepherding His people, the flock of the Lord.

The gracious God will provide for all the material things we need if we ask for wisdom like Solomon and seek Him first!

Oremus (Let us pray). O God, we ask you to guide us that in our everyday life we may always have the insight and astute ability to determine what is right from wrong. Give us wisdom to make wise judgment that everything we do is righteous, ethical, honorable, saintly, and pleasing to you. Hear our prayer, O God, in the name of Jesus Christ, Your Son, our Lord. Amen.

THE TEST

Abraham yearned for a child. God did not give him a child for a long time. In fact, his son Isaac was born in his old age and past the child bearing age of his wife, Sarah. There is nothing impossible with God. He finally gave the couple a son. Abraham and Sarah loved their son, Isaac, very much.

In a reading from the book of Genesis 22:1-2, 9a, 10-13, 15-18, God put Abraham to a test. He called to him and said, "Abraham!"

"Here I am!" he replied.

Then God said: "Take your son, Isaac, your only one, whom you love, and go to the land of Moriah. There you shall offer him up as a holocaust on a height that I will point out to you."

God asked Abraham to take his son, Isaac, his one and only son, whom he loved so much, to the land of Moriah, and there he shall offer him up as a holocaust. Abraham obeyed God without any question.

Can you imagine the horrified look on Abraham's face in placing his son on the altar, and then killing him to offer him up as a sacrifice? I am dazed just thinking about this!

How do we relate God's test in our world today? We do not have any exemption from trials and tribulations. We are not immune from sickness, suffering, trouble, misery, pain, anguish, tragedy, adversity, etc. We are susceptible to anything. We may have trials - a terrible sickness, loss of a loved one, loss of a job, marriage problem, problems with children, loss of a home, or business, etc.

When we are thrust into situations like these, we are called to have a profound faith and an extreme trust in God. Withhold not the trust! Do not let your hearts be troubled. After the trial comes the testimony. No matter how difficult the situation is, we are called to walk by faith. Do not give up! God will take care of us. He will not let us down. God is with us!

After passing the test, God blessed Abraham abundantly. God will bless us abundantly like He promised Abraham if we could pass the test! Be ready! Can you pass the test?

The Little Faith

A reading from the Holy Gospel according to Matthew 14:22-33:
When the apostles saw Jesus walking on the sea they were terrified. "It is a ghost," they said, and they cried out in fear.

At once Jesus spoke to them, "Take courage, it is I; do not be afraid."

Peter said to Him in reply, "Lord, if it is you, command me to come to you on the water."

He said, "Come."

Peter got out of the boat and began to walk on the water toward Jesus. But when he saw how strong the wind was he became frightened and, beginning to sink, he cried out, "Lord, save me!"

Immediately, Jesus stretched out his hand and caught Peter, and said to him, "O you of little faith, why did you doubt?" After they got into the boat, the wind died down.

Those who were in the boat did Him homage, saying, "Truly, you are the Son of God."

Meditation on the Gospel of Matthew:
"O you of little faith, why did you doubt?"

I was like Peter when we were traveling in Europe. We flew from the United States to Europe, and when we got there we had to fly constantly to several countries. Boarding an airplane rather than taking the train, or the Eurostar train from one country to another is easier. I love flying; it is really exciting, but I am also scared of the risk and the safety of the aircraft. I convinced myself I had to be brave, otherwise I would not be able to see the countries I would like to see. I told myself, "Fely, no guts, no glory." I had to take risks in order to achieve a goal or glory to see the historical and magnificent places I had studied in World History, as well as Church History. Like Peter, I had a little faith. I doubted about my safety.

When we crossed the English Channel from England to Calais in France and back to England we boarded a ferry. I was not afraid because the ferry boat is big. It is safe. When we were in Naples in Italy, we boarded a ferry to go to Capri. It is safe as well. In Capri, we boarded a little boat to see the Blue Madonna. The little boat carried around forty people. It was crowded. The boat floated on the sea while we were waiting for our turn to see the Blue

Madonna. The waves kept swaying the little boat. I was petrified! I thought it will sink. Again, like Peter, I doubted. I had a little faith.

After visiting several European countries successfully and enjoying the marvelous tours, we got home safe and sound. God had protected us, kept us alive, and freed us from all harm. Then, I told myself, "Fely, O you of little faith, why did you doubt like Peter? Did you think God would abandon you?" Indeed, God took care of us very well. I should have had more faith. I should have not doubted like Peter. I should have entrusted everything in the loving hands of the Lord God, instead of getting frightened unnecessarily.

When we seem to have a little faith, when we doubt, and when we have storms in our life, let God take over. Let Him be the captain of the boat. Allow Him to be in control to navigate and steer the boat. He will calm the strong wind and command the severe storms to vanish swiftly.

Oremus (Let us pray). O God when we have a little faith, when we doubt you, and when we have storms in our life, give us courage, and strengthen our faith. May we put our trust in you completely that you will stretch out your loving hands and catch us like you did to Peter. We trust you will not let us sink in the sea. Amen.

The Lost Sheep

A reading from the Holy Gospel according to Luke 15:4-7:
Jesus said, "What man among you having a hundred sheep and losing one of them would not leave the ninety-nine in the desert and go after the lost one until he finds it? And when he does find it, he sets it on his shoulders with great joy, and upon his arrival home, he calls together his friends and neighbors and says to them, 'Rejoice with me because I have found my lost sheep.' I tell you, in just the same way there will be more joy in heaven over one sinner who repents than over ninety-nine righteous people who have no need of repentance."

Commentary on the Gospel of Luke:
God's mercy is overwhelming. It is immeasurable. It is endless. God is good all the time. He is compassionate, loving, and kind. No matter how low you have gotten yourself, God will not write you off. He will not disown you. He will not remove you from His will. God did not disown King David after he committed sins. In the *Works of Saint Augustine*, he writes about how much he regrets having led a sinful life. God did not disown him. God will leave the ninety-nine sheep in the desert, and He will look for you until He finds you. When He finds you, He will carry you affectionately on His shoulder, and take you home.

Oremus (Let us pray). O God, help those who are lost to seek you; those who have gone astray to find you, and return to your fold. Guide and enlighten them that you are there waiting willingly and lovingly, that you would embrace them with sublime exultation when they return to you and come home. In their darkness and in the depths of their confusion and despair, illuminate their hearts and mind that you are a gracious and a compassionate God who is always ready to forgive and welcome them earnestly. Let them know you will stretch your arms and open the door for them with great joy. We ask you, O God, in the name of Jesus Christ, your Son, our Lord. Amen

THE FISHERS OF MEN

A reading from the Holy Gospel according to Mark 1:14-20:
As Jesus walked beside the Sea of Galilee, He saw Simon and his brother Andrew casting a net into the lake, for they were fishermen. "Come after me and I will make you fishers of men." At once they left their nets and followed Him. When He had gone a little farther, He saw James, son of Zebedee, and his brother John in a boat, preparing their nets. Without delay, He called them and they left their father Zebedee in the boat with the hired men and followed Him.

Reflection on the Gospel of Mark:
In this Gospel reading, Jesus said, "Come after me and I will make you fishers of men." He called Andrew, then Simon, followed by James, son of Zebedee, and his brother John. He called eight more people to be fishers of men. These are the twelve apostles who became fishers of men for God. Jesus beckons us to be fishers of people as well to proclaim the Gospel, the good news of God. The world is passing away. Time is running out. We can't run away from God. We have been called. The challenge is how do we respond to become apostles in this modern day and age?

I think today, being an apostle of Christ, is leading an exemplary Christian life. Be good, and be holy men and women who follow the commandments of the Lord God, and who are treating your neighbors with compassion, kindness, and dignity. You extend your helping hands to others in need. You listen to the cry of the poor and the less fortunate people. You reach out and touch someone. Be an angel in people's lives. Invite people to church. Do not hurt anybody. Forgive those who have hurt you, and more.

Oremus (Let us pray). O Lord God, we pray for the grace and the wisdom to let the light of your everlasting love shine brightly like the stars in the firmament through us all, so that everybody who sees us may praise and glorify your name. Work through us now and always that your greater glory may be known by all men and women. Help us to answer your call to discipleship and not hide, or run away from you like Jonah (Jonah 1:3-17). We pray to you O God in the name of Jesus, your Son, our Lord. Amen.

Through Jesus

A reading from the Holy Gospel according to John 14:6-14:
Jesus said to Thomas, "I am the way and the truth and the life. No one comes to the Father except through me. If you know me, then you will also know my Father. From now on, you do know Him and have seen Him."

Philip said to Him, "Master, show us the Father, and that will be enough for us."

Jesus said to him, "Have I been with you for so long a time and you still do not know me, Philip? Whoever has seen me has seen the Father. How can you say, 'Show us the Father'? Do you not believe that I am in the Father and the Father is in me? The words that I speak to you I do not speak on my own. The Father who dwells in me is doing His works. Believe me that I am in the Father and the Father is in me, or else, believe because of the works themselves. Amen, amen, I say to you, whoever believes in me will do the works that I do, and will do greater ones than these, because I am going to the Father. And whatever you ask in my name, I will do, so that the Father may be glorified in the Son. If you ask anything of me in my name, I will do it."

Brief contemplation on the Gospel of John:
We gain access to the Father through His beloved Son. We come to God through Jesus, His one and only begotten Son. As we have come to know Jesus is the way and the truth, and the life, may we make our life worthy of God's love. May we always remain upright members of the community – honest, virtuous, kind, and good Samaritan neighbors.

Oremus (Let us pray). O God, may we always praise, glorify, and adore you. Above all, may we continue to love and serve you with all our strength and do all things for your greater glory now and forever! Amen.

LOVE YOUR NEIGHBOR

A reading from the Book of Leviticus 19:1-2, 17-18:
The Lord said to Moses, "You shall not bear hatred for your brother or sister in your heart. Though you may have to reprove your fellow citizen, do not incur sin because of him. Take no revenge and cherish no grudge against any of your people. You shall love your neighbor as yourself. I am the Lord."

Reflection on the Book of Leviticus:
God calls us to truly love the members of our family, relatives, friends, neighbors, et al ceaselessly. We should not keep a grudge. Hold no hard feelings for no one. It is a heavy burden, and it is not healthy for the heart and mind. It causes undue stress! The joyful heart is meant to love unconditionally. That is what we are called upon as Christians.

Oremus (Let us pray). O Lord God, open our hearts that we may truly love one another as you love us. Hear our prayer in the name of Jesus, your Son, our Lord. Amen.

THE GREATEST COMMANDMENTS

A reading from the Holy Gospel according to Matthew 22:34-40:
When the Pharisees heard that Jesus had silenced the Sadducees, they gathered together, and one of them, a scholar of the law, tested Him by asking, "Teacher, which commandment in the law is the greatest?"

He said to him, "You shall love the Lord, your God, with all your heart, with all your soul, and with all your mind. This is the greatest and the first commandment. The second is like it: You shall love your neighbor as yourself. The whole law and the prophets depend on these two commandments."

Commentary on the Gospel of Matthew:
To love God is to love your neighbor, and to love your neighbor is to love God. How do we love God above all, and how do we love our neighbors in this modern time? We can truly love God above all by being righteous and following the Ten Commandments at all times. We can love our neighbors profoundly by caring for one another. You can show your love and caring for your neighbors by serving one another in love. The following examples below are suggestions on how you can love and serve your neighbors.

1. Visit your relatives and friends who are sick. Visit them if they are in the hospital and pray for them.
2. When they are discharged from the hospital, if they can eat, bring them homemade food.
3. Bring them flowers; if you cannot afford to buy flowers, pick some flowers in your garden.
4. Visit a new mother, bring her some flowers, a little something for the baby, or homemade food.
5. Give a few dollars to the homeless, or buy some hamburgers from fast food restaurants, such as Burger King or McDonalds, and give them to the homeless on the streets.
6. Visit old people in a nursing home, listen, and talk to them. They are happy to see someone.
7. Help your friends and relatives who need you. Be there for them. Sometimes, all they need is someone to listen.
8. Drive someone to church who can no longer drive.

9. Comfort families who lost a loved one. Be with them. Attend the funeral, give them a sympathy card, or a Holy Mass card, and some financial assistance, if you can.
10. Send donations to charitable organizations especially those who are helping the poor in the world, including third world countries.
11. Sponsor a child or an elderly person in need through the Unbound Organization, or send charity checks to Catholic Relief Services, etc.
12. Support the feeding of the poor program in the community. Render your service and assist in cooking the food. Extend your helping hand in serving the food for the poor, as well.
13. You may add what you wish to do for love of God and your neighbor.

THE PARABLE OF THE TALENTS

A reading from the Holy Gospel according to Matthew 25:14-30:
For it will be like a man going on a journey who called his servants and entrusted to them his property. To one he gave five talents, to another two, to a third one, each in proportion to his ability. Then he set out on his journey. The man who had received the five talents promptly went and traded with them and made five more. The man who had received two made two more in the same way. But the man who had received one went off and dug a hole in the ground and hid his master's money. Now a long time afterwards, the master of those servants came back and went through his accounts with them.

The man who had received the five talents came forward bringing five more. "Sir," he said, "you entrusted me with five talents; here are five more that I have made."

His master said to him, "Well done, good and trustworthy servant; you have shown you are trustworthy in small things; I will trust you with greater; come and join in your master's happiness."

Next the man with the two talents came forward. "Sir," he said, "you entrusted me with two talents; here are two more that I have made."

His master said to him, "Well done, good and trustworthy servant; you have shown you are trustworthy in small things; I will trust you with greater; come and join in your master's happiness."

Last came forward the man who had the single talent. "Sir," said he, "I had heard you were a hard man, reaping where you had not sown and gathering where you had not scattered; so I was afraid, and I went off and hid your talent in the ground. Here it is; it was yours, you have it back."

But his master answered him, "You wicked and lazy servant! So, you knew that I reap where I have not sown and gather where I have not scattered? Well then, you should have deposited my money with the bankers, and on my return, I would have got my money back with interest. So now, take the talent from him and give it to the man who has the ten talents. For to everyone who has will be given more, and he will have more than enough; but anyone who has not, will be deprived even of what he has. As for this good-for-nothing servant, throw him into the darkness outside, where there will be weeping and grinding of teeth."

Meditation on the Gospel of Matthew:

God beckons us to use our talents, our God-given gifts. The first person entrusted with five talents multiplied them to five - doubling them. The second person multiplied them twice as much. The third person did not do anything with the talent entrusted to him. Instead he buried it. God does not want us to bury our talents in the ground. He wants us to use, nurture, develop, and multiply them for the advancement of the Kingdom of Heaven. He does not want us to be lazy, and do nothing. Instead, He wants us to work for Him like the apostles and saints and bear much fruit.

Oremus (Let us pray). O God may we nourish and multiply our talents and unselfishly render service using the special and unique talents you have given each of us to serve you and humanity, and proclaim your greater glory! Hear our prayer O God in the name of Jesus Christ, your Son our Lord. Amen.

THE CALL TO DISCIPLESHIP

A reading from the Holy Gospel according to Matthew 16:13-19:
When Jesus went into the region of Caesarea Philippi He asked His disciples, "Who do people say that the Son of man is?"

They replied, "Some say John the Baptist, others Elijah, still others Jeremiah, or one of the prophets."

He said to them, "But who do you say that I am?"

Simon Peter said in reply, "You are the Son of the living God."

Jesus said to him in reply, "Blessed are you, Simon son of Jonah. For flesh and blood has not revealed this to you, but my heavenly Father. And so, I say to you, you are Peter, and upon this rock I will build my church, and the gates of the netherworld shall not prevail against it. I will give you the keys to the Kingdom of Heaven. Whatever you bind on earth shall be bound in heaven; and whatever you loose on earth shall be loosed in heaven."

Reflection on the Gospel of Matthew:
Jesus Christ built his church upon a rock and made Peter the head of the church, the first pope. We too are called upon to be disciples of Jesus Christ. We are called to have the zeal and the devotion of the blessed Apostles, Saint Peter and Saint Paul. Peter is the dynamic apostle, preacher, and martyr who established the early church, and spread the Christian faith. Paul is the indefatigable, outstanding, and tireless preacher. Let us pray our church may follow, uphold, and preserve the teachings of the apostles. May we continue to remain staunch followers of Jesus Christ. Like Saint Paul and Saint Peter, who had unselfishly and valiantly shed their blood proclaiming the Gospel (good news), may we remain stalwart in our faith and in God's love even in the midst of religious persecution that exists throughout the world, even today.

In Saint Peter's Square, just before the façade of Saint Peter's Basilica in Vatican City, are the statues of Saint Peter and Saint Paul. Saint Peter is holding two keys, and Saint Paul is holding a sword and a book. Jesus had given Peter and the disciples the authority to speak or act on His behalf as His representatives, to teach the teachings He taught them and to help everyone live the righteous way of the heavenly Kingdom of God.

Jesus said to Peter, "I will give you the keys to the Kingdom of Heaven. Whatever you bind on earth shall be bound in heaven; and whatever you loose on earth shall be loosed in heaven" - Matthew 16:19.

A book and a sword are the common attributes of Saint Paul. Saint Paul was beheaded. The sword is a reminder of the means of his martyrdom.

It was absolutely divine to behold such a holy place. I was spellbound looking at the statues of these two greatest apostles of Christ and the several statues of saints in the Colonnade of Saints at Saint Peter's Basilica when we went on a pilgrimage to Rome, the Eternal City, and Vatican City in 2015 and years earlier. It was very awe-inspiring. Wouldn't it be wonderful to be a saint? We can all try! We can encourage and inspire one another to be a saint. A saint to be, anyone?

Show No Partiality

A reading from the Letter of Saint James 2:1-5:
My brothers and sisters, show no partiality as you adhere to the faith in our glorious Lord Jesus Christ. For if a man with gold rings and fine clothes comes into your assembly, and a poor person in shabby clothes also comes in, and you pay attention to the one wearing the fine clothes and say, "Sit here, please," while you say to the poor one, "Stand there," or "Sit at my feet," have you not made distinctions among yourselves and become judges with evil designs? Listen, my beloved brothers and sisters. Did not God choose those who are poor in the world to be rich in faith and heirs of the kingdom that he promised to those who love him?

Commentary on the Letter of Saint James:
We are called upon to treat people fairly and should not allow partiality in living our Christian faith. We should not treat the rich differently because of their opulence. The affluent person should not be given a special seat, and a poor person should not be given an unobtrusive seat just because of lack of wealth. This letter shows the significance of our actions how we treat people. We should welcome everybody, rich or poor, well-dressed, or not. The poor people who have less material things have a very special place in Heaven. God gives special preferences to the poor. The Holy Scriptures contain many verses on the poor, God's overwhelming and profound love and social justice. We are called upon to reflect on these preferences.

Whatsoever You Do

A reading from the Holy Gospel according to Matthew 25:31-46:

"When the Son of Man comes in His glory, and all the angels with Him, He will sit upon his glorious throne, and all the nations will be assembled before Him. And He will separate them one from another, as a shepherd separates the sheep from the goats. He will place the sheep on His right and the goats on His left.

Then the king will say to those on His right, 'Come, you who are blessed by my Father. Inherit the kingdom prepared for you from the foundation of the world. For I was hungry and you gave me food, I was thirsty and you gave me drink, a stranger and you welcomed me, naked and you clothed me, ill and you cared for me, in prison and you visited me.'

Then the righteous will answer him and say, 'Lord, when did we see you hungry and feed you, or thirsty and give you drink? When did we see you, a stranger, and welcome you, or naked and clothe you? When did we see you ill or in prison, and visit you?'

And the king will say to them in reply, 'Amen, I say to you, whatever you did for one of these least brothers of mine, you did for me.' Then He will say to those on His left, 'Depart from me, you accursed, into the eternal fire prepared for the devil and his angels. For I was hungry and you gave me no food, I was thirsty and you gave me no drink, a stranger and you gave me no welcome, naked and you gave me no clothing, ill and in prison, and you did not care for me.'

Then they will answer and say, 'Lord, when did we see you hungry or thirsty or a stranger or naked or ill or in prison, and not minister to your needs?'

He will answer them. 'Amen, I say to you, what you did not do for one of these least ones, you did not do for me.' And these will go off to eternal punishment, but the righteous to eternal life."

Commentary on the Gospel of Matthew:

There is nothing wrong being ambitious. Everybody likes to have a good job, or to climb up to the top of the corporate ladder, etc. to have a better life. That is all right. I am ambitious as well. I am no exception, but no matter how lofty and prominent you have achieved, do not forget your duty to God and your fellowmen/women. Your life on Earth is ephemeral. It is transient. It is not permanent. We are all going on a pilgrimage, on a journey towards eternal life. When the time on Earth is up, and your journey has passed, I think the Lord is not going to ask you, if you became the President of the United States of America, Attorney General, the Chief Justice of the Supreme Court, the President of Italy, or the Philippines, or Austria, the Prime Minister of England, or Germany, a bank or a big corporation manager, an ambassador, a diplomat, a prominent neurosurgeon, an astronaut, the dean of a prestigious university like Harvard University, or Cambridge College, or a famous architect who designed an awesome building like the pyramid in the front of the Louvre Museum in Paris, or a lead technical editor and alternate chief in your organization, etc. No, God will not ask you any of these things. I think he will ask you the following questions:

- Did you feed the needy?
- Did you give food to the poor or the homeless?
- Did you give water to the thirsty?
- Did you clothe the naked?
- Did you visit the imprisoned?
- Did you visit the sick in the hospital or in their home?

If your answer is yes, I think God will tell you, "Awesome, super! You did an outstanding and exceptional performance! Well done my son/daughter. Welcome into my eternal Kingdom of Heaven." He may add, "Congratulations, bravo, or kudos to you. You've done so well."

If your answer is no, I think He will tell you, "I don't know you. I don't have any room for you. Find a place somewhere." Think about it. You know where that is.

THE LORD IS CALLING

A reading from the Holy Gospel according to John 1:35-42:

The next day John was there again with two of His disciples. When he saw Jesus passing by, he said, "Behold, the Lamb of God!" When the two disciples heard him say this, they followed Jesus.

Turning around, Jesus saw them following and asked, "What do you want?" They said, "Rabbi, where are you staying?"

"Come," He replied, "and you will see."

So, they went and saw where He was staying, and they spent that day with Him. It was about four in the afternoon. Andrew, Simon Peter's brother, was one of the two who heard what John had said and who had followed Jesus. The first thing Andrew did was to find his brother Simon and tell him, "We have found the Messiah," and he brought him to Jesus. Jesus looked at him and said, "You are Simon son of John. You will be called Cephas."

Commentary on the Gospel of John:

Jesus said, "Come, and you will see." Andrew was the first to respond to the call of Jesus and came. The second was his brother Simon whom Jesus called Peter. Peter means rock. Then, James, son of Zebedee. John came next. Then, came the rest of the apostles – Matthew, Thomas, Philip, Bartholomew, James, son of Alpheus, Thaddaeus, Simon the Zealot, and Judas. Then came Matthias after the betrayal of Judas. They are the apostles who responded to Jesus' loving call. They are the first witnesses to Jesus' ministry.

We are called the same way to be disciples of the Lord God. Are we ready to respond and accept the sublime invitation of the Lord Jesus Christ to come and follow Him like the apostles did? Time is near. Things on Earth are ephemeral. We are a pilgrim people on a journey every day of our life towards eternal life.

In the reading from the first Book of Samuel 3:1-10, 19-20, God called Samuel three times. Samuel replied, "Speak for your servant is listening." Like the apostles, Samuel likewise answered the call of God. If we respond to the call of God and become disciples, He will give us the grace of discernment, wisdom, strength, and courage. He will grant us His guidance, and help us do His work on Earth.

We are also invited to create a space for God, and take time in the company of the Lord like the apostles and Samuel to deepen our faith. We are called to invite one another as well. We are all in this journey together.

THE VINEYARD

A reading from the Holy Gospel according to Matthew 21:28-32:
Jesus said to the chief priests and elders of the people: "What is your opinion? A man had two sons. He came to the first and said, 'Son, go out and work in the vineyard today.' He said in reply, 'I will not,' but afterwards changed his mind and went. The man came to the other son and gave the same order. He said in reply, 'Yes, sir,' but did not go. Which of the two did his father's will?"

They answered, "The first."

Jesus said to them, "Amen, I say to you, tax collectors and prostitutes are entering the Kingdom of God before you. When John came to you in the way of righteousness, you did not believe him; but tax collectors and prostitutes did. Yet even when you saw that, you did not later change your minds and believe him."

Commentary on the Gospel of Matthew:
The man has two sons. He asked both sons to go out and work in the vineyard. The first son said that he will not, but went out and did the work anyway. The second son said yes he will go out and work in the vineyard, but did not do anything at all. In this parable, Jesus invites us to work in His vineyard. Others will say, yes they will accept the invitation, dedicate themselves to the cause, and work for Jesus' vineyard, while others will do nothing. Jesus presents us with many opportunities to join Him in His work and mission. Working for Jesus' vineyard may require a great deal of effort and endurance, huge responsibility, and absolute dedication. Contemplate how you can work for Jesus' vineyard.

Oremus (Let us pray). O God, may we respond to your loving call with zeal and work fervently in your vineyard. May we use our given talents to participate in your work and mission. May we enhance our spiritual growth as well, and be more cognizant of our devotion to you. We pray to you, O God, in the name of Jesus Christ, Your Son, our Lord. Amen.

THE GENEROUS GOD

A reading from the Holy Gospel according to Matthew 20:1-16a:
Jesus told his disciples this parable: "The Kingdom of Heaven is like a landowner who went out at dawn to hire laborers for his vineyard.

After agreeing with them for the usual daily wage, he sent them into his vineyard. Going out about nine o'clock, the landowner saw others standing idle in the marketplace, and he said to them, 'You too go into my vineyard, and I will give you what is just.' So, they went off. And he went out again around noon, and around three o'clock, and did likewise. Going out about five o'clock, the landowner found others standing around, and said to them, 'Why do you stand here idle all day?'

They answered, 'Because no one has hired us.'

He said to them, 'You too go into my vineyard.' When it was evening the owner of the vineyard said to his foreman, 'Summon the laborers and give them their pay, beginning with the last and ending with the first.' When those who had started about five o'clock came, each received the usual daily wage. So, when the first came, they thought that they would receive more, but each of them also got the usual wage.

And on receiving it they grumbled against the landowner, saying, 'These last ones worked only one hour, and you have made them equal to us, who bore the day's burden and the heat.'

He said to one of them in reply, 'My friend, I am not cheating you. Did you not agree with me for the usual daily wage? Take what is yours and go. What if I wish to give this last one the same as you? Or am I not free to do as I wish with my own money? Are you envious because I am generous?'

Thus, the last will be first, and the first will be last."

Commentary on the Gospel of Matthew:
The landowner in this parable is God, as revealed in Jesus Christ. Some of the laborers worked full day while the others only worked for a few hours, yet the pay was the same. It caused resentment and envy for the people who worked longer. Jesus preached the Kingdom to everyone, the holy people as well as the lost sheep. In fact, he dined with the tax collectors. If the holy and the lost will both accept Jesus Christ, they will be bestowed the same equal share in the Kingdom of God. The Gospel reading today strongly tells us

God unselfishly grants generosity and kindness to whomever - the righteous and the sinners. He forgives and forgets the transgressions. The merciful Lord God is near to everyone who calls upon Him. Just go into His vineyard, and He will give you what is just.

Oremus (Let us pray). O merciful God, may we conduct ourselves worthy of you, and call upon you when we seem to be lost, or when we seem to be envious like the other laborers. We know you are near and will rescue us from whatever situations we are in.

THE TOUCH

A reading from the Holy Gospel according to Mark 1:40-45:
A leper came to Him [and kneeling down] begged Him and said, "If you wish, you can make me clean."

Moved with pity, He stretched out His hand, touched him, and said to him, "I do will it. Be made clean." The leprosy left him immediately, and he was made clean. Then, warning him sternly, He dismissed him at once. Then He said to him, "See that you tell no one anything, but go, show yourself to the priest and offer for your cleansing what Moses prescribed; that will be proof for them."

The man went away and began to publicize the whole matter. He spread the report abroad so that it was impossible for Jesus to enter a town openly. He remained outside in deserted places, and people kept coming to Him from everywhere.

Meditation on the Gospel of Mark:
Jesus started performing His messianic work in Capernaum, the hometown of Simon and Andrew, His home base as well. He exorcised demons, performed miracles, and healed the sick. In this Gospel reading, a man afflicted with leprosy begged Jesus to cure him. Moved with pity, Jesus stretched out His hand, touched him, and said to him, "I will do it. Be made clean." The leper was healed. During that time when a person has leprosy, he is declared unclean. It is more or less like a death sentence. The person is ostracized. He is excluded from society.

How do we apply the Gospel reading today in our society today? I received a letter from a friend yesterday. She thanked me for the birthday card and calendar I sent her for her birthday.

In her letter, she mentioned, "Still not communicating with my son as well as my eight-year old grandson and five-year old granddaughter. I miss them very much and pray for reconciliation someday."

This is the kind of ostracism we have today. My friend was ostracized from his son and grandchildren. Isn't that painful she can't see her son and precious grandchildren? I hope her son realizes he is not only hurting his mom, but also himself and his own children in depriving them of the profound love of their grandmother. Today, we are called to cease estrangement from people -

family, relatives, friends, etc., and we should do our best effort to be reconciled with one another.

In this Gospel reading, we are also called upon to touch someone, just like Jesus. We are called upon to touch peoples' lives with our compassion, generosity, kindness, words, and actions. Encourage one another, build each other up, reach out to one another, and lift one another.

ABUNDANT HARVEST

A reading from the Holy Gospel according to Matthew 21:33-43:
Jesus said to the chief priests and the elders of the people: "Hear another parable. There was a landowner who planted a vineyard, put a hedge around it, dug a wine press in it, and built a tower. Then he leased it to tenants and went on a journey. When vintage time drew near, he sent his servants to the tenants to obtain his produce. But the tenants seized the servants and one they beat, another they killed, and a third they stoned. Again, he sent other servants, more numerous than the first ones, but they treated them in the same way.

Finally, he sent his son to them, thinking, 'They will respect my son.'

But when the tenants saw the son, they said to one another, 'This is the heir. Come, let us kill him and acquire his inheritance.' They seized him, threw him out of the vineyard, and killed him. What will the owner of the vineyard do to those tenants when he comes?"

They answered him, "He will put those wretched men to a wretched death and lease his vineyard to other tenants who will give him the produce at the proper times."

Jesus said to them, "Did you never read in the Scriptures: *The stone that the builders rejected has become the cornerstone; by the Lord has this been done, and it is wonderful in our eyes?* Therefore, I say to you, the Kingdom of God will be taken away from you and given to a people that will produce its fruit."

Commentary on the Gospel of Matthew:
The vineyard represents the Kingdom of God.

How do we apply this Gospel reading in this modern day and age? The vineyard is the Catholic Church led by Pope Francis. God is beckoning us to participate fully in the works of the church. We are summoned to become active members working in God's vineyard. We are called and encouraged to serve the church faithfully. How do we serve the church of God? Pray and meditate how you can serve. You may want to volunteer to be Extraordinary Ministers of Holy Communion (EMHC), lectors, choir members, lead singers (cantors), ushers, Catechism teachers, hospitality ministers, ministry scheduler, wedding coordinator, webmaster, community life, baptismal preparation teacher, wedding coordinator, leader of social activities, organizer of clothing/coats, toiletries, and food drives, Christmas angel drive, members of the Parish Council and become president, vice-president, secretary, etc. and help the priest in planning church activities that will benefit the people of God. The Church needs you to get fully involved so it can produce abundant harvest for the greater glory of God!

Encourage your kids to serve as altar servers. At a young age, they will be more cognizant of God. They will grow up to be upstanding young men and women who will love God, serve Him, and mankind. Isn't that what you want them to be?

The Salt of the Earth

A reading from the Holy Gospel according to Matthew 5:13-16:
Jesus said to His disciples, "You are the salt of the earth. But if salt loses its taste, with what can it be seasoned? It is no longer good for anything but to be thrown out and trampled underfoot. You are the light of the world. A city set on a mountain cannot be hidden. Nor do they light a lamp and then put it under a bushel basket; it is set on a lamp stand, where it gives light to all in the house. Just so, your light must shine before others, that they may see your good deeds and glorify your Heavenly Father."

Reflection on the Gospel of Matthew:
To my relatives, classmates, students, friends, and town mates, I can proudly say, "You are all the salt of the earth," and a reflection of God's love. In your daily life, you are following Christ's footsteps. You are serving as the light of Christ for the world. You are letting your light shine brightly like the stars in the vast firmament. Men and women see the many good deeds you do continuously. You exult, adore, and praise our heavenly Father in your everyday life. How truly blessed I am being surrounded by all of you – righteous, honest, fine, terrific, and God loving people.

THE BLIND MAN

A reading from the Holy Gospel according to Mark 10:46-52:
As Jesus was leaving Jericho with His disciples and a sizable crowd, Bartimaeus, a blind man, the son of Timaeus, sat by the roadside begging. On hearing that it was Jesus of Nazareth, he began to cry out and say, "Jesus, son of David, have pity on me." And many rebuked him, telling him to be silent. But he kept calling out all the more, "Son of David, have pity on me."

Jesus stopped and said, "Call him."

So, they called the blind man, saying to him, "Take courage; get up, Jesus is calling you." He threw aside his cloak, sprang up, and came to Jesus.

Jesus said to him in reply, "What do you want me to do for you?"

The blind man replied to him, "Master, I want to see."

Jesus told him, "Go your way; your faith has saved you."

Immediately, he received his sight and followed Him on the way.

Meditation on the Gospel of Mark:
Bartimaeus cried out loudly and called on Jesus, so he could see. Jesus heard him. And so it happened. Jesus performed a miracle, and opened the eyes of the blind man, and he could see! The Gospel reading calls us that we need to open our eyes and see God's works and His goodness. Look around you and see the splendid creation of God – the people around you, especially the ones in your life and the beauty of the earth you live in. Take a good look at the gorgeous flowers, the birds singing in the sky, the pristine brooks, the clear lakes, the flowing rivers, the resplendent meadows, the towering lush trees with luxuriant foliage, the evergreen grasses, the exuberant forests, the majestic mountains, and many, many more. Then, thank God you are not blind and can see His beautiful creations. Sometimes, we are blind to what we see! Let us open our eyes, and appreciate God's works and goodness. We need to follow Bartimaeus' example. Utter a joyous loud cry to the Lord God, and shout out loudly in constant prayer and in declaration of our faith.

The Gospel also calls us not to be blind, but to see the needy, the oppressed, the broken-hearted, the persecuted, the downtrodden, etc. Above all, let us not be blinded by power, prestige, and wealth!

BROTHERLY AND SISTERLY CARE

A reading from the Holy Gospel according to Matthew 18:15-20:
Jesus said to His disciples, "If your brother sins against you, go and tell him his fault between you and him alone. If he listens to you, you have won over your brother. If he does not listen, take one or two others along with you, so that 'every fact may be established on the testimony of two or three witnesses.' If he refuses to listen to them, tell the church. If he refuses to listen even to the church, then treat him as you would a Gentile or a tax collector. Amen, I say to you, whatever you bind on earth shall be bound in Heaven, and whatever you loose on earth shall be loosed in Heaven. Again, amen, I say to you, if two of you agree on earth about anything for which they are to pray, it shall be granted to them by my heavenly Father. For where two or three are gathered together in my name, there am I in the midst of them."

Reflection on the Gospel of Matthew:
The Catholic Church is a community of people with different educational, economic, social, cultural, and ethnic backgrounds. It is not a community of saints. Nobody is perfect. Human beings are not flawless. The Gospel reading tells us that, as Christians, we can correct and care for our brothers and sisters if they are not doing the right things. However, if we need to correct somebody, we should do it in the most gentle and loving way. We should not criticize or condemn. "We should not look at the speck of sawdust in our brother's eye without paying attention to the plank in our own eye." - Matthew's Gospel 7.3.

We are connected in Christ Jesus and share a common bond— belief in God. We are to encourage one another to follow the Lord. We can help reconcile to God our lost brothers and sisters by reminding them the sacrament of reconciliation. Help them remember God is waiting for them. He will be very happy when they return to Him, and turn away from evil, or sins. God's mercy is vast and limitless. No matter how bad the sin, God forgives and forgets. He does not hold the transgressions in His sacred and tender heart. God promised when we gather together in His name, there He is in our midst. He is in our midst seven days a week, twenty-four hours every day. This is a testimony God is very near and present in our lives.

Oremus (Let us pray). O God, as Christians, may we care for our brothers and sisters in Christ and urge one another to recognize you are a merciful God. You are in our midst all day long. May we pray always. May we honor and praise you at all times. Amen.

THE KINGDOM

A reading from the Holy Gospel according to Matthew 13:44, 52:
Jesus said to His disciples: "The Kingdom of Heaven is like a treasure buried in a field, which a person finds and hides again, and out of joy goes and sells all that he has and buys that field. Again, the Kingdom of Heaven is like a merchant searching for fine pearls. When he finds a pearl of great price, he goes and sells all that he has and buys it."

Meditation on the Gospel of Matthew:
The Earth is not our permanent home. Every day of our life, we are on a constant journey leading to eternal life. How do we spend this life's journey? Would you choose the way of the Lord? Would you sell your cherished possessions in exchange for the Kingdom of Heaven?

This parable emphasizes the Kingdom of Heaven as the sole and only thing worth owning. Seek Jesus then, and the Kingdom of Heaven. Relentlessly, gather treasures that have merits in the Kingdom of God, so when your pilgrimage on Earth has been completed, you will be with the Lord in His great and palatial abode in the heavens.

THE GOLDEN RULE

Excerpts from a reading from the Holy Gospel according to Matthew 7:7-12:
Jesus said, "Do unto others as you would have them do unto you. The is the law and the prophets."

Contemplation on the Golden Rule:
Living the Golden Rule is an excellent way to live our lives in perfect harmony with one another, a fundamental and an important principle that must be adhered to ensure smashing success in general, or in any certain activity.

Oremus (Let us pray). O heavenly Father and loving God, help us to live the Golden Rule always and treat others the same way as we ourselves would like to be treated. Amen.

CHRIST HAS NO BODY

By Saint Teresa of Avila (1515–1582)

"Christ has no body now on earth but yours;
 no hands, but yours; no feet, but yours.
Yours are the eyes through which the compassion of Christ
 must look out on the world.
Yours are the feet with which He is to go about doing good.
Yours are the hands with which He is to bless His people."

Reflection on the words of Saint Teresa of Avila:
We are called upon to serve as the body, the eyes, the feet, and the hands of
Jesus Christ in doing good for others. We are called to serve God, and our
neighbors, the flock of the Lord with the unique talent/s God has given us.
Let us use our God-given talent/s for the greater glory of God, for the ad-
vancement of His Kingdom, and bear much fruit.

BLESS THE CHILDREN

A reading from the Holy Gospel according to Mark 10:13-16:
People were bringing children to Jesus that He might touch them, but the disciples rebuked them. When Jesus saw this, He became indignant and said to them, "Let the children come to me; do not prevent them, for the Kingdom of God belongs to such as these. Amen, I say to you, whoever does not accept the Kingdom of God like a child will not enter it." Then He embraced the children and blessed them, placing His hands on them.

Meditation on the Gospel of Mark:
Following Jesus' exemplary deeds of love for the children, we all have an enormous responsibility in taking care of our children. They must be a top priority. Let us love our children. Take care of them in an outstanding manner. They will only be children once. They did not ask to be born. Bless the children! Let us give them our unparalleled support and attention. Let our focus shine on the children! The children are our greatest assets and the only hope for the future. From them will rise our future leaders - presidents of the country, prime ministers, priests, doctors, nurses, senators, ambassadors, educators, college professors, engineers, scientists, astronauts, bank managers, military officers, corporation managers, executives, etc.

In addition, also think of the poor children. Feed them! Help get them out of poverty, and provide assistance by sponsoring their education. It is a great and noble mission. Check Unbound on how to sponsor a child and provide for his/her education. Google them in the Internet.

A Letter of Saint Paul to the Corinthians 12:31-13:8:
"Love is always patient and kind. It is never jealous. Love is never boastful or conceited. It is never rude or selfish. It does not take offense and is not resentful. Love takes no pleasure in other people's sins, but delights in the truth. It is always ready to excuse, to trust, to hope, and to endure whatever comes. Love does not come to an end."

Commentary on the letter of Saint Paul:
I love this letter of Saint Paul to the Corinthians. It is great wisdom from Saint Paul. This is a good reminder for everybody especially married couples.

If your spouse is a little difficult at one time or another, read this letter. It may help you overcome the difficulty. For people who are anticipating to get married in the Catholic Church, this letter is a good choice for the reading during Holy Mass. Most Catholic Matrimonies are celebrated with a Holy Mass. I think this wisdom is an outstanding reminder for a solid and a strong foundation in starting a married life. I believe this reading is also good for anybody getting married in any Christian Church, or any non Christian Church as well. Don't you think?

The Couple

Husband, set aside time for you and your wife. The two of you - go to a romantic rendezvous like a candlelit dinner that provides soft, soothing, and splendid music while dining. Enjoy the evening, the food, and the time being together in each other's company. Relive the days when you were courting her – when everything was beautiful, full of sugar and spices, and everything nice. Tell her how much you love her. Wife, tell your husband how much you love him. Whisper sweet nothings into each other's ears. Then, when you get home, watch the movie "Fireproof." Later – at another time, watch the movie "Facing the Giants." These two movies may strengthen your marriage more. It is always best to keep on enhancing your marital bliss, and make it to the finishing line – "till death do us part."

I was inspired to write this advice because a week after I sang the song "That's Amore," a song popularized by Dean Martin at the Karaoke Club on a Friday, karaoke night, a young woman told Tom she was very happy I sang the song "That's Amore" because it reminded her of her wedding. The song was sung on her wedding day. Another person, a Hispanic guy, told Tom after hearing me sing "That's Amore," he was enlightened, and took his wife to a movie, and then to a romantic candlelit dinner. His wife was so happy. She enjoyed the movie, the dinner, and their time together. He too was very happy because he made his wife happy. I was very glad as well that somehow, in my own little way, I was able to make some people happy.

THE LIGHT

Excerpts from a Letter of Saint Paul to the Ephesians 5:8-14:
"Live as children of light for light produces every kind of goodness and right-eousness and truth. Try to learn what is pleasing to the Lord."

Brief commentary on the Letter of Saint Paul to the Ephesians:
May the unfruitful works of darkness caused by sins vanish in the world. May the great light of Christ shine forth to illuminate us that we may truly live as children of light. May the light of Christ, our Lord, grow in us stronger day by day that love, integrity, kindness, sanctity, and service may continue to dwell deeply rooted in our hearts always, now and forever.

"Prepare the Way of the Lord"

A reading from the Holy Gospel according to Luke 3:1-6:
In the fifteenth year of the reign of Tiberius Caesar, when Pontius Pilate was governor of Judea, and Herod was tetrarch of Galilee, and his brother Philip tetrarch of the region of Ituraea and Trachonitis, and Lysanias was tetrarch of Abilene, during the high priesthood of Annas and Caiaphas, the word of God came to John the son of Zechariah in the desert. John went throughout the whole region of the Jordan, proclaiming a baptism of repentance for the forgiveness of sins, as it is written in the book of the words of the prophet Isaiah:

A voice of one crying out in the desert: "Prepare the way of the Lord, make straight His paths. Every valley shall be filled and every mountain and hill shall be made low. The winding roads shall be made straight, and the rough ways made smooth, and all flesh shall see the salvation of God."

Reflection on the Gospel of Luke:
We are called upon to make straight the paths of the Lord as John the Baptist had announced. God is calling us to be blameless in His sight as we prepare to make straight His paths. It is embracing God with our whole body – heart and mind. It is being cognizant of God. It is spending time with God – time in prayer, meditation, and sorting things out. Whoever we are, whatever we do, we are called to do our very best – the best in the world. If you are a father, be a good father; if you are a mom, be a good mom; if you are a grandparent, be the best grandmother/grandfather; if you are a priest, be the best representative of Jesus Christ; if you are a technical editor, be the best technical editor in the whole organization; if you are a doctor/nurse, pharmacist, dentist, give it your best effort; if you are an educator, be the best teacher in town; if you are a diplomat, be the best in your line of work, etc. It is giving our best in the loving service of our Lord God.

Therefore, exult! Rejoice, be filled with exuberant joy! Continue to pray fervently. Have a grateful heart, and give thanks to the majestic God for all the blessings He has bestowed upon you. Count your blessings one by one. They are numerous. They are countless! Give glory and praise to the Lord God!

THE BAPTISM OF THE LORD

A reading from the Holy Gospel according to Luke 3:15-16, 21-22:
The people were filled with expectation, and all were asking in their hearts whether John might be the Christ.

John answered them all, saying, "I am baptizing you with water, but one mightier than I is coming. I am not worthy to loosen the thongs of his sandals. He will baptize you with the Holy Spirit and fire."

After all the people had been baptized and Jesus also had been baptized and was praying, heaven was opened and the Holy Spirit descended upon Him in bodily form like a dove.

And a voice came from Heaven, "You are my beloved Son; with you I am well pleased."

Meditation on the Gospel of Luke:
Jesus, the Lord God did not need to be baptized. He was sinless. He went through Baptism to identify with us. He was also a human being like us.

In this Gospel reading, God is calling us to renew our Baptismal promises - renounce Satan and sins, and the lure of evil and believe in God, the Father Almighty, Creator of heaven and earth and in Jesus Christ, His only Son, our Lord, who was born of the Virgin Mary, suffered death and was buried, . . . etc. (Baptismal promises from the Catholic Prayer Book). It is calling us to examine ourselves. We are called to repentance and turn from the wicked ways of this world, and to be righteous. Are we at peace with ourselves? Are we at peace with God? Are we at peace with our brothers, sisters, parents, neighbors, friends, et al? If we are not, we are summoned to make amends, and take the necessary steps to be at peace with God, our ourselves, and everybody. God is pleased with His beloved Son. Can our God truly and lovingly say He is pleased with us like He is pleased with His Son?

Oremus (Let us pray). O God, help us to be at peace with everybody. Forgive us our trespasses as we forgive those who trespass against us; and lead us not into temptation, but deliver us from evil. Amen. Kyrie eleison! Lord have mercy on us!

THE TEMPTATIONS

A reading from the Holy Gospel according to Luke 4:1-13:

Filled with the Holy Spirit, Jesus returned from the Jordan and was led by the Spirit into the desert for forty days, to be tempted by the devil. He ate nothing during those days, and when they were over He was hungry.

The devil said to Him, "If you are the Son of God, command this stone to become bread." Jesus answered him, "It is written, *One does not live on bread alone.*" Then he took Him up and showed Him all the kingdoms of the world in a single instant. The devil said to Him, "I shall give to you all this power and glory; for it has been handed over to me, and I may give it to whomever I wish. All this will be yours, if you worship me."

Jesus said to him in reply, "It is written: *You shall worship the Lord, your God, and Him alone shall you serve.*"

Then he led Him to Jerusalem, made Him stand on the parapet of the temple, and said to Him, "If you are the Son of God, throw yourself down from here, for it is written: *He will command His angels concerning you, to guard you,* and, *with their hands they will support you, lest you dash your foot against a stone.*"

Jesus said to him in reply, "It also says, *You shall not put the Lord, your God, to the test.*" When the devil had finished every temptation, he departed from Him for a time.

Reflection on the Gospel of Luke:

In this Gospel reading, Jesus was tempted by the cunning devil three times. The first temptation, the devil told Jesus to change the stone to become bread. The second temptation, the devil showed Jesus all the kingdoms of the world, and then offered Him all this power, and glory. The third temptation, the devil told Jesus to throw Himself from the parapet of the temple down below to prove He was the son of God. Jesus did not succumb to the three temptations of the devil. He resisted the temptations courageously and strongly.

Jesus is God, yet He did not have an exemption from temptations. Nobody is exempt to temptations. We are not spared from it. When temptations come, let us valiantly resist the devil. Refuse the temptations of the evil one. Let us not yield to the devil like what Jesus did. Respond to temptations with earnest prayers, and call on the Holy Spirit for help. Send the Holy Spirit a signal of extreme distress, an SOS (Save our Souls). Pray, the Lord's Prayer: "Lead us not into temptation; but deliver us from evil." If we have a fervent devotion to God, and we put our main focus on establishing a closer relationship with our Lord God, we will definitely succeed in overcoming evil, the temptations.

THE SALVATION

A reading from the Holy Gospel according to John 3:16-18:

"God so loved the world that He gave His only Son, so that everyone who believes in Him might not perish but might have eternal life. For God did not send His Son into the world to condemn the world, but that the world might be saved through Him. Whoever believes in Him will not be condemned, but whoever does not believe has already been condemned, because He has not believed in the name of the only Son of God."

Reflection on the Gospel of John:

God sent the angel Gabriel to a young woman named Mary who was betrothed to Joseph. The angel Gabriel announced to Mary, "Rejoice, O highly favored daughter! The Lord is with you. Blessed are you among women… Do not fear Mary. You have found favor with God. You shall conceive and bear a son and give Him the name Jesus." – Luke 1:18, 30-31.

God has chosen her to be the mother of God. In faith and confidence without hesitation, Mary willingly obeyed and said, "Behold, I am the handmaid of the Lord. May it be done to me according to your word." - Luke 1:38. Jesus was born a few months later. He grew up, and did his mission work on earth. In his early thirties (according to some scholars, He was about thirty-three), He gave the world the ultimate sacrifice. He died on the Cross for the salvation of mankind. The Paschal Mystery, Jesus dying and rising (Passover sacrifice of Jesus from death to life) opened the gate of Heaven for us all. We became heirs to the majestic Kingdom of Heaven. God gave us this precious inheritance.

We exult in the Cross of Jesus Christ! We firmly believe in the name of Jesus Christ, the only begotten Son of God who He sent into the world for our salvation. Jesus in Hebrew means, "God saves." We are saved! We give profound thanks to God for the precious gift of His only Son for our redemption.

Oremus (Let Us Pray). O gracious God, we thank you deeply for sending your only begotten Son, Jesus Christ, into the world to save us. It is your greatest and magnificent gift for us, and we are forever grateful. May we rejoice profoundly in the triumph of the Cross. When we wake up in the morning, may we begin each day with the Sign of the Cross and teach our children to do the same. Amen.

In God's Time

Many Christians often pray to God. We pray to give praise and glory to our Lord God, and thank Him for the many blessings He has bestowed upon us. We also pray for forgiveness for our sins. We pray, perhaps for God's prolific blessings, wisdom and grace, special favors, good health, healing of illness, etc. Possibly, we pray for a promotion to Major, Colonel, etc., or, if you are a federal government employee, you probably pray for a promotion to a higher General Schedule position and financial stability. Sometimes we pray to God for a comfortable home, a happy marriage, a nice car, a beautiful journey to see the world, and historical places, or a pilgrimage to Lourdes, Fatima, Vatican City, or the Holy Land, etc. Maybe we pray for reconciliation with loved ones, perhaps a brother, sister, mother, father, grandmother, grandfather, son, daughter, relative, friend, et al we have been alienated.

When our prayers are not answered, we may get impatient, and we could not wait for God to answer our prayers. We ask God, "Lord, when will you answer my prayers? I have been praying, and you have not answered me. Where are you Lord, God?" We feel God has abandoned us. Remember, it is always in God's time, not your time; not what you want, but God's will. Have a deep faith.

Oremus (Let us pray). O God, help us to be patient, and learn forbearance that we may stay calm. We trust you, O Lord God, and we put our earnest confidence in the palm of your hands.

THE OVERWHELMING FORGIVENESS

A reading from the Book of Genesis, Chapter 45:1-09:
The Truth Revealed. Joseph could no longer restrain himself in the presence of all his attendants, so he cried out, "Have everyone withdraw from me!" So, no one attended him when he made himself known to his brothers. But his sobs were so loud that the Egyptians heard him, and so the news reached Pharaoh's house. "I am Joseph," he said to his brothers. "Is my father still alive?" But his brothers could give him no answer, so dumbfounded were they at him.

"Come closer to me," Joseph told his brothers. When they had done so, he said: "I am your brother Joseph, whom you sold into Egypt. But now do not be distressed, and do not be angry with yourselves for having sold me here. It was for the sake of saving lives that God sent me here ahead of you. The famine has been in the land for two years now, and for five more years' cultivation will yield no harvest. God, therefore, sent me on ahead of you to ensure for you a remnant on earth and to save your lives in an extraordinary deliverance. So, it was not really you but God who had me come here; and he has made me a father to Pharaoh, lord of all his household, and ruler over the whole land of Egypt."

Reflection on the Book of Genesis:
I love the story of Joseph. It is one of my favorite stories in the Bible. In the book of Genesis Chapter 37:1-36, Jacob loved his son Joseph much more than his other sons. Jacob made a special robe for his son Joseph. The brothers were very jealous of Joseph because their father loved him more than them. They hated Joseph. They hated him more when he told them about his dream that his bundle of grains suddenly stood up, and it remained standing while their bundles gathered around his bundle and bowed down to it. Then, he told his father and brothers his other dream. The Sun, the Moon, and eleven stars bowed down to him. The brothers did not like the dream of Joseph that made them think he would take over as head of the family to rule them and bow to him. The brothers became more jealous of him and hated him much more.

One day, when his brothers tended sheep, they plotted to kill Joseph. Reuben, one of the brothers, convinced the other brothers not to kill Joseph, but instead, put him into an empty cistern with no water in it. So, they did.

A caravan of Ishmaelites were traveling from Gilead to Egypt. Judah came up with the idea to sell Joseph to the Ishmaelites instead of killing him. They all agreed. Joseph was sold to the Ishmaelites. The Ishmaelites took him to Egypt. In Egypt, Joseph was sold to Potiphar, one of Pharaoh's officials and captain of the guard. Joseph worked diligently. Potiphar made Joseph head of his household. Potiphar's wife seduced Joseph. Joseph refused her advances. She told her husband Potiphar Joseph attempted to rape her. Joseph was locked in prison.

While in prison, Joseph interpreted the dream of two fellow prisoners. The interpretation of the dreams proved to be accurate. Then, later, the Pharaoh had dreams he could not fathom. Since Joseph had an extraordinary gift in interpreting dreams, he was called upon by the Pharaoh. He told Joseph about his dreams. Joseph interpreted the dreams. He told the Pharaoh there would be seven years of abundant harvests, and after seven years there would be seven years of extreme famine in Egypt. Joseph advised the Pharaoh to start storing grain so when the famine struck in the land, there would be plenty of food for the people. Joseph was granted a royal pardon. The Pharaoh appointed him to be the economic planner and would lead this important job of storing grain. The Pharaoh made Joseph his right hand, second to him as the ruler of Egypt.

The severe famine occurred. There was no food in Canaan, as well. Jacob sent his sons to Egypt to procure grain. There, Joseph recognized his brothers. They bowed down to him, just like the Sun, the Moon, and the eleven stars bowing to him in his dream. Joseph revealed his identity to his brothers and told them he was Joseph, whom they had sold to the Ishmaelites. His brothers could not believe what they had just been told. They were stupefied.

Joseph forgave his brothers and told them, "Do not be distressed, and do not be angry with yourselves for having sold me here. It was really for the sake of saving lives that God sent me here ahead of you."

What a big, loving, and forgiving heart Joseph had. He never harbored any hard feelings, or intense anger at his brothers who intended to kill him, put him in a waterless cistern, and then sold him to the Ishmaelites. Instead, he gave them his overwhelming forgiveness and embraced them lovingly and joyfully in his arms. He asked them to move to Egypt to be with him and bring their father, Jacob. The story has a wonderful and happy ending. They all enjoyed living happily in Egypt. They did not starve or die of famine! The power of forgiveness!

Joseph and the Amazing Technicolor Dreamcoat: this London and Broadway musical is a glittering treasure of a show. I love it! I can see it again and again. Tom and I have seen it four times - first time in Reno, Nevada with our priest friend, Father R., second time in California, again with our priest friend, Father R., third and fourth times in my home state. The score was written by Andrew Lloyd Webber. The lyrics were written by Tim Rice. It is a spectacular and awe-inspiring family musical. It dramatizes the life of Joseph, son of Jacob. His trials and triumphs are moving and inspiring. It is brilliant, irresistible, warm-hearted, and moving. You come out of the show feeling very good, touched, and uplifted.

The melodies of the songs are gorgeous and ethereal. The lyrics are beautiful and marvelous with some fantastic sense of humor. The ardent forgiveness culminates this captivating and lovely musical.

If the touring Broadway show comes to your area, I recommend it. If it does not come to your area, you can buy the DVD movie. It is not expensive. It costs twenty dollars. It is available at Amazon.com. The touring company sells it, as well. If you attend the show if it tours in your area, you can buy the DVD from them.

Can you imagine the sons of Jacob calling their father on a cell phone during that time, centuries ago? Can you imagine the economic planners during that time carrying laptop computers? You will see much more. You will feel spellbound seeing the show.

Our priest friend, Father R., said to me during intermission, "Fely, I am enjoying the show so much. I am so happy you took me with you and Tom to see this awesome show."

The Solemnity of the Assumption of the Blessed Virgin Mary

Excerpt from a reading from the Book of Revelation 11:19a; 12:1-6a, 10ab:
A great sign appeared in the sky, a woman clothed with the Sun, with the Moon under her feet, and on her head a crown of twelve stars.

Every year on 15 August, we celebrate the Solemnity of the Assumption of the Blessed Virgin Mary.

On August 15, 2015, we were in Lourdes in the Pyrenees in southern France on a pilgrimage. We attended the liturgy of the Solemnity of the Assumption of the Blessed Virgin Mary held in the square in front of the Basilique de Notre-Dame de l'Immaculee Conception (Basilica of Our Lady of the Immaculate Conception). There were many pilgrims from several countries who attended the liturgy. There was a long procession. We bought our candles from the local store. A priest led the Rosary prayer. "The Lord's Prayer" (Our Father) (Pater Noster) was always prayed in Latin and the "Hail Mary" (Ave Maria) was prayed in Latin, French, Italian, and Spanish. The "Glory Be To The Father" was prayed in Latin. The song "Ave Maria" was sung after each decade of the Rosary. The Hail Holy Queen (Salve Regina) was said in Latin. The priest prayed all four mysteries of the Holy Rosary - Joyful, Luminous, Sorrowful, and Glorious.

Several infirm people on wheelchairs were brought to the front of the church during the liturgy. The members of the Legion of Mary, and many more associations devoted to the Blessed Virgin Mary, followed. I was so spellbound feeling God's presence when I was praying the Rosary in Lourdes. I whispered to the Lord, "My Lord, God, this is a life-long dream that I have just realized. I have always wanted to go to this holy place for a long time, and now, by your grace, I am here. Thank you."

The liturgy of the Solemnity of the Assumption of the Blessed Virgin Mary in Lourdes was one of the most beautiful liturgies I have ever attended. It was ethereal, awe-inspiring, and absolutely divine!

It was raining on that day, but I would have not missed it for the world.

Oremus (Let us pray). O Blessed Mother Mary, Mother of God, our mother as well, as we celebrate the feast day of your Assumption to Heaven, may we rejoice in the Lord, and our hearts may be filled with fire of love. May we follow your remarkable examples of faithful obedience and profound love for God. Watch over us, your children. Fill us with grace, and intercede for us. To you, we entrust our earthly journey and assist us that our path in life is not wicked, but guide us in the way everlasting. Holy Mary, Mother of God, ora pro nobis (pray for us). Amen.

Living Mercy in the Jubilee Year of Mercy

The Jubilee Year of Mercy commences on 8 December 2015.

Contemplation on Living Mercy during this significant Year of Mercy.

God's mercy is immeasurable. He forgives. Our sins wound the tender heart of God, but He forgives and forgets what we have been.

Then, Peter came and said to Jesus, "Lord, how often shall my brother sin against me and I forgive him? Up to seven times."

Jesus said to him, "I do not say to you, up to seven times, but up to seventy times seven." - Matthew 18:21-22.

God truly forgives no matter how many times we have stumbled and fell into sins. Peter denied Jesus three times, but he was forgiven.

I have met people who are alienated from their families. I know of a grandma who is not allowed to see her grandson because the wife of her son does not approve her. A friend of mine is estranged from her son. The son does not have anything to do with her. He did not invite her to his wedding. I do not understand how families get alienated, but they do. It happens in the best of families. I pray earnestly for these families. I could not bear the thought if I were alienated from my grandsons. That would be poignant and extremely painful. I don't think I could bear it. It is too excruciating.

During this Year of Mercy, we are called to forgive one another. We should replace the bitterness, hurt, and anger with deep love. I pray these families learn to forgive one another and be a family again.

We are also encouraged to go to confession in this "Year of Mercy." Confession is reinvigorating and soothing for the soul, mind, and heart. God blesses us through the priest when we go to confession.

In this Year of Mercy, we are called upon to be true disciples of Jesus and bear much fruit. We are inspired to find ways and means how we can strengthen charitable works and social justice, promoting equality for all people regardless of race, national origin, sex, or handicap, etc. in our faith community. We are urged to get involved lovingly. We should put our hands and feet in action to do good.

From the Catechism of the Catholic Church, 2447, below are the Corporal Works of Mercy and Spiritual Works of Mercy that can serve as fundamental guides in our efforts to genuinely participate in the Year of Mercy.

The Corporal Works of Mercy:

- Feed the hungry.
- Give drink to the thirsty.
- Clothe the naked.
- Shelter the homeless.
- Visit the sick.
- Visit the imprisoned.
- Bury the dead.

The Spiritual Works of Mercy:

- Admonish the sinner.
- Instruct the ignorant.
- Counsel the doubtful.
- Comfort the sorrowful.
- Bear wrongs patiently.
- Forgive all injuries.
- Pray for the living and the dead.

Check on the wonderful and indefatigable works of the Catholic Relief Services, Unbound, Food for the Poor Incorporated, Salesian Missions, Oblate Missions, Boys and Girls Town, etc. and find out how you can help, or perhaps give financial support for their worthy cause.

THE SPELLBINDING JOURNEYS

Visiting the sacrosanct and absolutely divine places in Europe was a spellbinding experience. I have listed several of the places we visited in Europe to inspire, move, uplift, and touch your life. In reading this section of the book, I encourage each one of you to travel in your imagination to these holy places. Visualize you are a pilgrim visiting these celestial and magnificent places conducive to a relaxed atmosphere that will enable you to pause and reflect. Then, I hope you will be spending quality time in prayer and in communion with the loving, gracious, and compassionate Lord God. I hope you will be spellbound and feel the presence of God.

Basilica Papale di San Pietro (Papal Basilica of Saint Peter) - Vatican City
This Basilica was designed by Donato Bramante, Michelangelo, Carlo Moderno and Gian Lorenzo Bernini. The style is Renaissance architecture. It is one of the two largest Roman Catholic Churches in the whole world. Many pilgrims flock to Saint Peter's Basilica. It is the greatest of all churches of Christendom.

I was spellbound touring Saint Peter's Basilica for the first time in the late 1990s, and for the second time in August 2015. It is one of the holiest Roman Catholic Churches. It is magnificent, breathtaking, and absolutely divine! I was overwhelmed. It was ineffable!

In this resplendent place of worship, we attended Holy Mass in Latin at Saint Peter's Basilica. I remember the Latin prayers, so I could pray in Latin comfortably. The Holy Mass was spellbinding, ethereal, and awesome. The solemn and enchanting organ music during Mass filled the whole church with heavenly atmosphere. It was blissful. I felt God's nearness like He was standing beside me, touching my shoulder.

The first and second time we visited Saint Peter's Basilica I prostrated in the Blessed Sacrament Chapel. I paused, reflected, and prayed earnestly. Looking at the magnificent Tabernacle, I was overwhelmed with happiness in communicating with the Lord. I cried tears of joy. I poured my heart out to God.

The interior of Saint Peter's Basilica is grand and magnificent. It is breathtaking! The sacredness of this extraordinary place took my breath away! I was totally breathless and full of awe! I was bewildered! It is an expansive space

The Papal Basilica of Saint Peter in Vatican City

The statue of Saint Peter at Saint Peter's Basilica in Vatican City

filled with many sculptures of saints, mosaics, and frescoes. Many of the amazing works by the greatest and finest artists, including Michelangelo, Bernini, Arnolfo di Cambio's etc. are found in this Basilica.

The high altar is magnificent – divine! There is an image of a Dove above the Chair of Saint Peter symbolizing the Holy Spirit. The image of the Dove representing the Holy Spirit with rays of light shines brightly.

Cathedra Petri (Chair of Saint Peter), also known as the "Throne of Saint Peter," is at the high altar. There is a Latin inscription: "O Pastor Ecclesiae, tu omnes Christi pascis agnos et oves" ("O Pastor of the Church, you feed all Christ's lambs and sheep"), above the Chair on the golden background of the frieze. The sculptures of Saint Augustine, Saint Ambrose, Saint Athanasius, and Saint Chrysostom, four doctors of the Roman Catholic Church are also at the high altar.

I prayed to Saint Peter for his intercession in front of his sculpture. Euphoria filled my heart when I touched the sculpture of Saint Peter, and wiped it with my white handkerchief. I felt the very presence of this great saint, an apostle, preacher, and martyr. He was one of the greatest and the most stalwart of the twelve apostles of Jesus Christ. According to Christian tradition, the tomb of Saint Peter is beneath the high altar of the Basilica. Christian tradition also believed he suffered martyrdom on this site.

Another captivating sculpture in Carrara marble inside the Basilica is the Pieta. It depicts the Lord Jesus on the lap of His mother, Mary, after the Crucifixion. It was curved by Michelangelo when he was twenty-four years old. Michelangelo signed his work on the marble sash of the sculpture of the Blessed Mother Mary. I marveled at this sculpture reminding myself of the intense pain and sufferings Jesus had endured for the salvation of mankind. It must have been heart-rending and poignant for Mother Mary holding her beloved son who died of an agonizing and violent death.

The Pieta is a world-renowned incredible work of art visited by tourists from around the world. It was enclosed in a glass case after a mad man damaged it with a hammer in May 1972.

The underground of Saint Peter's Basilica is a cemetery, a burial place for many popes. We took the elevator to get to the top of the Dome of Saint Peter's Basilica. The elevator does not go all the way to the top. We had to ascend several flights of stairs to get to the very top. Reaching the top, it was majestic and breathtaking. You can see the aerial view of the city of Rome, the

Eternal City. You can see the Colosseum, the gorgeous and lush Vatican Gardens, the Janiculum Hills, the Palatine Hills, the Castel Sant' Angelo, the Roman Forum, downtown Rome, etc.

Michelangelo designed the dome. The interior of the dome is filled with many awesome holy Christian paintings.

The Papal Audience ~ Vatican City

We woke up early to be the first in line for the Papal Audience. Seeing the Holy Father requires security check like you are boarding an aircraft. The queue was already very long when we arrived. During the whole month of August in 2015, anyone can attend the Papal Audience without a ticket. I was glad I did not have to go through the process of getting a ticket to see the Pope.

We attended the Audience with the Holy Father, Pope Francis. The Audience Hall was filled with hundreds of people from all over Europe and around the world. We were seated with the Portuguese people who kept shouting:

"Papa Francesco! Papa Francesco!"

I joined them and shouted, "Papa Francesco! Papa Francesco! Viva La Papa!"

When the Pope arrived, and was seated on stage, the ceremony began. It was full of pageantry and wonderful readings. One of the speakers, a bishop talked about divorced Catholics. He said divorced Catholics should ensure they bring up their children in the faith, that they are welcome in the church, that there are no easy answers about this matter, but we pray to God. Attending the Audience with the Holy Father was divine.

The Holy Father delivered his message to the public. He spoke softly and tenderly. He prayed in Latin - Pater Noster (Our Father), Ave Maria (Hail Mary) and Gloria Patri (Glory Be To The Father). Since I know these prayers in Latin, I was able to pray with the Holy Father in Latin. I recite some of the decades of the Rosary in Latin when I pray the Rosary every day. It was fascinating and wonderful to pray in Latin, the language of the Roman Catholic Church for many years. We also sang a heavenly song. We received the Pope's blessing imparted to all present and their families and friends. I was overwhelmed and filled with euphoria for being there. It was completely divine, marvelous, and awe-inspiring. The Holy Roman Catholic Church has many beautiful liturgies, pageantries, celebrations, etc. I love Catholicism very much! I would not know how to live without my faith.

I paused and reflected. I contemplated the many blessings of God. Being there in the Audience Hall with the Holy Father was a tremendous blessing.

Years earlier, we also attended the Audience with the Holy Father, Pope John Paul II, now Saint Pope John Paul II, the Great at the Audience Hall in

Ofelia attending the Papal Audience in Vatican City

The author in front of the Basilica of Saint Paul Outside the Walls in Rome, Italy

Vatican City. Many people from around the world and Europe attended the Audience with Pope John Paul II. It was totally divine as well.

A few days later, Tom, my husband, and I attended the Papal Blessing in Castel Gandolfo. Pope John Paul II held the Papal blessing on the balcony of the Apostolic Palace of Castel Gandolfo. He blessed the people below. We got blessed by Pope John Paul II for the second time.

Castel Gandolfo is the Pope's summer residence and vacation retreat.

Basilica Papale di San Paolo Fuori le Mura (Papal Basilica of Saint Paul Outside the Walls) - Rome, Italy

It is one of the four major Basilicas and the second largest in Rome. For all its grandeur, a tourist like me, I was breathless. It is magnificent, awe-inspiring, and celestial. Abundant and astounding frescoes and mosaics decorate the sublime church of worship.

We attended Holy Mass. It was beautiful, splendid, and heavenly. I paused and reflected. I prayed for me and my family. I also included in my prayers my relatives, classmates, students, friends, town mates, former co-workers, supervisors, and directors.

In front of this Basilica is the memorial statue of Saint Paul. According to the tour guide, Saint Paul was a Roman citizen. By Roman law, he could not be executed in Rome, hence, he was beheaded outside the walls. This is the site of his martyrdom. Saint Paul was a tireless apostle and a steadfast follower of Christ who remained committed in his profound faith, and died for it.

The Corinthian columns of this church are impressive. I marveled at this dazzling and majestic Basilica, feeling the nearness of God.

Basilica Papale di Santa Maria Maggiore (Papal Basilica of Saint Mary Major) - Rome, Italy

This is another major Basilica in Rome in addition to Saint Peter's Basilica. We toured the Papal Basilica of Saint Mary Major. The Basilica of Saint Mary Major is also known as the "Our Lady of Snows." It is the largest Roman Catholic Marian Church in Rome.

The most notable in this Basilica is the reliquary of the sacred relic of the Holy Crib of the infant Jesus in the lower level underneath the high canopied altar. Behind the Crucifix at the high altar is an exquisite painting of the Blessed Mother Mary and the child, Jesus.

At the Archbasilica of Saint John Lateran in Rome, Italy

Ofelia standing in front of the Saint Mark's Basilica in Venice, Italy

This Basilica is magnificent and awesome. The interior is filled with many sculptures of saints and fine, divine paintings. The church is filled with resplendent mosaic and fresco paintings. Side altars abound in the Basilica. It is an angelic place of worship to pause and reflect, to pray and to have a chat with the Lord God in one of the major Basilicas of Rome.

Arcibasilica Papale di San Giovanni in Laterano (Papal Archbasilica of St. John in the Lateran) - Rome, Italy

This is the cathedral of Rome, one of the four major Basilicas in Rome. The interior is filled with abundant and huge marble sculptures of saints, stunning and captivating holy Christian paintings, large and elegant chandeliers, awesome side altars, etc. Like the other three major basilicas, it is magnificent and astounding.

We attended Sunday Holy Mass in this Basilica twice. The music director of the choir led the singing. His powerful and crystal-clear tenor voice filled the entire church. He sang like the world-renowned tenor, Luciano Pavarotti. It was ethereal. The singing and the liturgy were completely enthralling. There were six priests, four of them concelebrated with the main celebrant. I was dazed and spellbound by it all. The beautiful liturgy took my breath away. My whole mind, heart, and spirit were entirely captivated by the presence of God! I paused and reflected. I prayed for me, my family, relatives, classmates, students, town mates, friends, former co-workers, supervisors, and directors. I prayed fervently and was in constant communion with the Lord God.

The Pantheon - Rome, Italy

Marcus Agrippa, a Roman statesman, general, and architect during the rule of Emperor Augustus authorized the construction of the Pantheon. You can still see clearly the engraving Agrippa on top of the building. It is a Roman temple dedicated to all the gods and deities of Rome when it was a pagan nation. It was completed by Emperor Hadrian.

Later, after Christianity became the official religion of the Roman Empire, the Pantheon was converted to a church dedicated to Saint Mary and the martyrs. Since the Renaissance, the Pantheon has also been used as a sepulcher. Among the people buried here are Raphael Sanzio, the artist, painter, two kings of Italy, Vittorio Emanuele II, Umberto I, his queen, Margherita, et al.

In front of the Castel Sant'Angelo in Rome

Today, the Pantheon is a Roman Catholic Church. Holy Masses are celebrated here on holy days of obligation, Sundays, etc. I sat on a chair in front of the altar and prayed earnestly.

Castel Sant'Angelo – Castle of the Holy Angel - Rome, Italy

Castel Sant'Angelo was formerly a Mausoleum of Emperor Hadrian. It is a mystical and towering edifice in Rome. It was commissioned by Emperor Hadrian to be his resting place. Later, the building was used by popes as a castle and a fortress. It also became the Pope's treasury. The bronze statue of the angel Michael, who is like the general of God, stands on the top of the enthralling Castel Sant'Angelo building. Inside the castle, there is also another statue of Saint Michael.

Today, it is a museum, the Museo Nazionale di Castel Sant'Angelo. Tom and I toured the museum. It is a fascinating, historical, enigmatic, and marvelous place to visit in Rome.

The Vatican Museums - Vatican City

The Vatican City is a favorite for millions of travelers from around the world. The Vatican Museums are some of the greatest museums in the whole wide world and significant tourist attractions. There are numerous collections of fascinating, magnificent, and awesome works of art - frescoes, exquisite Christian paintings, sculptures, and artifacts and collections of just about everything. Masterpieces by the greatest artists who ever lived are housed in the museum complexes.

Capella Sistina (Sistine Chapel) in Vatican City.

We toured the world-renowned Capella Sistina (Sistine Chapel) in Vatican City. It is the place where the college of cardinals gather to elect a new pope (known as the Papal Conclave). It was named after Pope Sixtus IV. The frescoes painted by Michelangelo (a genius of the Renaissance) are breathtaking! Some of the frescoes depict nine scenes from the book of Genesis - God separating light from darkness, the creation of the sun, moon, and the earth, the separation of water and land, the creation of Adam, the creation of Eve, Adam and Eve's fall and expulsion from Eden, the story of Noah, etc. There are also frescoes of prophets - Daniel, Joel, Jeremiah, Isaiah, Ezekiel, Zechariah, Jonah, etc. The fresco painting of "The Last Judgment" on the altar wall by Michelangelo is magnificent! It is awe-inspiring. Looking at this fresco, I prayed earnestly in front of it imagining Jesus talking to me. I prayed, paused, and reflected and spoke to God in my meditation. I was so spellbound feeling God's presence! It was ethereal; it was like Heaven on Earth!

I bought the painting (copy) of "The Last Judgment." I had it framed, and it is hung in the living room. It is a reminder for us that, yes, there is a God, and we should obey the Ten Commandments. You would like to wind up in the place where the righteous, not the wicked, are as shown in the painting.

The fresco of Jesus' "Sermon on the Mount" on the side wall is marvelous. Everything in the Sistine Chapel is awesome and amazing! It is indescribable – too ineffable! Absolutely divine to behold!

There is much, much more to the Sistine Chapel than Michelangelo. The chapel contains significant and resplendent works by great Renaissance artists (geniuses), such as Raphael, Bernini, and Botticelli, et al.

Basilica di San Pietro in Vincoli (Saint Peter's Basilica in Vincoli) - Rome, Italy
We toured this Saint Peter's Basilica in Vincoli. There are two chains on display in a box close to the entrance of the church.

The story goes, according to the tour guide - Saint Peter had double chains put on him when he was imprisoned. The chains fell off when the angel of the Lord appeared to Peter. What a miracle! The angel led Peter out of prison. They passed the first guard, then the second, and came to an iron gate that lead out to the city. He was freed by the angel of God! (The storytelling of the rescue of Peter by the angel of God is in the Acts of the Apostles, 12:1-11.)

What a holy experience seeing these chains and remembering the Lord's rescue of Saint Peter from Herod. Nothing is impossible with the Lord! Trust in the Lord, "for we walk by faith, not by sight" – 2 Corinthians 5:7.

Michelangelo is one of the geniuses of the Renaissance Period. He carved the statue of Moses displayed in the Church of Saint Peter in Vincoli in Rome. I stood, wondering how he created that magnificent marble sculpture. It is breathtaking! God had truly blessed Michelangelo di Lodovico Buonarroti Simoni with great talents – a sculptor, painter, architect, poet, and engineer of the High Renaissance.

Again, I paused and reflected on God's rescue of Peter with the assistance of an angel of the Lord. God will rescue us, like Peter, when we are in trouble.

The Imprisonment in Carcere Mamertino (Mamertine Prison) - Rome, Italy
This is the place where Saint Paul and Saint Peter were imprisoned. Saint Paul called Saint Peter "the pillar of the church."

Peter was imprisoned in Mamertine. He endured horrendous torture and was kept in complete darkness. Despite all the sufferings, Peter never gave up preaching. He converted some of his jailers. He needed water to baptize the new converts. The miracle of God happened. Out of nowhere, a small stream of water suddenly flowed from the ground by the miracle of God. Peter was able to have water to baptize the converts.

Christian tradition says Peter was crucified in Rome under Emperor Nero. He chose to be crucified upside down. He felt unworthy to be crucified in the same manner as Jesus.

Mamertine Prison is a good place to pause and reflect the Holy Scriptures and remember the poignant sufferings Saints Peter and Paul encountered to spread the Christian faith.

Scala Sancta (Holy Stairs) - Rome, Italy

There are twenty-eight white marble steps in the Chapel of Saint Lawrence. These steps are protected. They are encased in a frame structure of wooden steps. There is a written instruction in front of the steps that pilgrims should climb the steps on their knees to get to the chapel upstairs. You can't walk on these steps. They are delicate. This chapel was used as the personal chapel of the early popes. According to the tour guide, these are the very steps Jesus stepped on leading to the praetorium of Pontius Pilate in Jerusalem when he was tried. Helena, the mother of Emperor Constantine, brought the holy stairs to Rome in the fourth century. The Scala Sancta has captivated thousands of Christian pilgrims, including me and my spouse, who wish to give honor and glory to the Passion and Death of the Lord, Jesus.

In this mystifying and awe-inspiring Sancta Sanctorum (Holy of Holies) place of worship, I was very spellbound. I prayed, paused, and reflected on the Passion of Jesus Christ. I prayed fervently. Again, I prayed for me, my family, relatives, classmates, students, friends, town mates, and people who have touched my life.

The Chapel of Saint Lawrence is magnificent as well, like the other basilicas and churches in Rome.

Piazza di Spagna – Spanish Steps – Rome, the Eternal City

This is another piazza in Rome. Above the Spanish steps is the Triniti de Monti church, another resplendent church in Rome for pausing, reflecting, and wor-

At the Scala Santa (Holy Stairs) in Rome, Italy

At the Scala Santa (Holy Stairs) in Rome, Italy

shipping. The famous Barcaccia Fountain by Pietro Bernini and Gian Lorenzo is in this crowded, and much visited, place of interest in Rome. The leading attraction of the Piazza di Spagna square is the incredible staircase of Triniti dei Monti Church. This is another beautiful church in Rome.

Basilica di Santa Maria in Cosmedin (Basilica of Saint Mary in Cosmedin) - Rome, Italy

The Basilica of Saint Mary in Cosmedin housed the La Bocca della Verita (The Mouth of Truth). It is in the portico of the church. The mouth is world-renowned. Pilgrims and tourists around the world come to see the "Mouth of Truth." The story goes that the sculpture is believed to be a part of a first-century manhole cover or perhaps an old Roman fountain in ancient days.

The mouth is like a lie detector. The tour guide said if a person puts his/her hand in the mouth of the sculpture, the mouth will close, or will bite the hand, if the person lied. If the person did not lie, the mouth will stay open, and will not bite the hand of the person.

I put my right hand in the mouth of the sculpture. The mouth stayed open. It did not bite my hand. It meant I did not lie. We toured the resplendent church. I paused and reflected and prayed in this church for safety in all our travels.

The Basilica of Santa Maria in Trastevere - Rome, Italy

The Basilica of Santa Maria in Trastevere is a minor Basilica in Rome. It is one of the oldest churches in Rome. In the interior of the church is a mosaic of "The Annunciation, Life of the Virgin." One of the side chapels is the Avila Chapel. It was named after Saint Teresa of Avila.

This is another sublime church. According to the tour guide, there are close to 1,000 churches in Rome.

Piazza Navona - Rome, Italy

Piazza Navona is one of the most visited and spectacular squares in Rome. The fountain of the Four Rivers is one of the most important attractions of this square. The fountain displays four figures representing a river from four continents - the Ganges (Asia), the Danube (Europe), the Nile (Africa), and the Rio de la Plata (South America).

Another significant tourist attraction in Piazza Navona Square is the Church of Sant'Agnese in Agone. We toured this 17th century Baroque

Church. It is sublime. Frescoes and large-scale sculptures abound in the church. I sat down, paused and reflected. I prayed vehemently.

The Arch of Constantine, Historical Landmark, Rome

The Arch of Constantine is a triumphal arch in Rome honoring Emperor Constantine. Constantine believed his victory over Maxentius at the Battle of Milvian Bridge in the year 312 was the help of the Christian God who aided him in winning the battle. As a result of this belief, he proclaimed the Edict of Milan. The persecution of the Christians finally ended when Emperor Constantine signed the Edict of Milan allowing Christians to practice their faith, to worship God freely without fear all the days of their life. How wonderful and great it was when Christianity became the official religion of the Roman Empire. VIVA CHRISTUS! VIVA JESUS CHRIST! To Thee be honor and glory forever and ever! Thank God for Emperor Constantine.

The Catacombs - Appian Way - Rome, Italy

We hopped on a bus and took the tour to see the Catacombs. We toured the Catacombs of Saint Calixtus. They are among the most important in Rome. The tombs of several popes from the second to the fourth centuries are housed in here. Saint Cecilia's tomb and tombs of several saints are also in here.

There was a tour guide who explained the use of Catacombs. It was spooky and somewhat dark. It was really seeing a large cemetery many centuries old. The tour guide said Christians used the Catacombs to worship when they were hiding from the Roman authorities.

I was so spellbound touring Rome, the Eternal City, and seeing with my own eyes the unfolding of the history of Rome and the world. My favorite subjects are English and History. I am a history buff.

Our pilgrimage to Vatican City and Rome was entirely heavenly.

Thank God for the blessing that I had realized my lifelong dream of going to Rome and Vatican City on a pilgrimage! I was able to spend much time pausing and reflecting and communicating with the Lord God. God is good all the time.

Basilica di San Francesco d'Assisi – (Basilica of Saint Francis of Assisi) - Assisi, Italy

We toured Assisi and visited the Basilica di San Francesco d'Assisi. It is a majestic and an awe-inspiring Roman Catholic Basilica.

Saint Francis of Assisi founded the men's order of Friars Minor, the women's order of Saint Claire, and the third order of Saint Francis for men and women. He preached to the birds and animals. He told them to praise and love God, their Creator. He told the birds to fly freely, and not worry about their food as the Heavenly Father would provide for them.

In this day and age, he is a very popular saint. Saint Francis is an inspiration to our pope, His Holiness Pope Francis (Pope Jorge Mario Bergoglio). He chose Francis as his Papal name in honor of Saint Francis of Assisi. Saint Francis loved the poor; Pope Francis loved the poor as well.

The tomb of Saint Francis of Assisi is in this Basilica.

We attended Holy Mass in this Basilica and received Holy Communion. It is a great place to pause and reflect, and spend time in contemplation and prayer.

The Cattedrale di Santa Maria del Fiore (The Cathedral of Saint Mary of the Flower) - Florence in Italy

The Cattedrale di Santa Maria del Fiore is the main church of Florence in Italy. I marveled at the resplendent design of the Baptistery and Giotto's Campanile. The basilica is one of Italy's largest churches. The Gothic style of the church is splendid. Gothic design is elaborate, intricate, and stunning. It is magnificent! It is awesome and breathtaking. This cathedral is the mother church of the Archdiocese of Florence. Seeing various basilicas and cathedrals in the continent of Europe, Christianity unfolding before my eyes through the captivating and eye-catching masterpieces, works of art by great and world-renowned artists, attending Holy Mass at Saint Peter's Basilica, and several other basilicas and cathedrals in Europe make me ecstatic. I always feel God's presence in all of it. It is indescribable!

The Basilica di Santa Croce (Holy Cross) in Firenze (Florence), Italia

The Basilica di Santa Croce is the principal Franciscan Church in Florence in Italy. It is spectacular. It is the burial place of distinguished and prominent men in the Tuscany region such as: Michelangelo di Lodovico Buonarroti Simoni, Galileo Galilei, Niccolo Machiavelli, et al.

The architectural styles of the Basilica di Santa Croce are Gothic Revival, Renaissance, and Italian Neo-Gothic. It is a majestic church.

The interior is very sublime – It is fabulously and richly-decorated with stained glass and frescoes. Dante Alighieri, writer of the *Divine Comedy* has a sculpture standing in front of the church.

The Camposanto (Holy field) Vecchio in Pisa is a monumental cemetery. It was the burial place of the upper class and prominent people in Pisa. Roman and Etruscan sculptures, urns, etc. decorated the Camposanto. Many restored and amazing frescoes lined the walls. The most notable were The Triumph of Death, the Last Judgment, and Stories of the Anchorites. The frescoes about death served as pieces of advice for everyone to remember life on earth was transient. Death was inevitable, and living a good Christian life was essential.

In the beautiful Blessed Sacrament chapel, I sat down, paused and reflected. I prayed for me, my family, friends, relatives, classmates, students, and town mates, et al.

The Pisa Cathedral (Duomo di Pisa) in Pisa, Italy – As soon as I entered the Pisa Cathedral, I was spellbound. It is strikingly beautiful and absolutely divine. The massive granite Corinthian columns between the nave and the aps were stunning. I loved the fine marble façade of this magnificent cathedral in the Pisan Romanesque style. The Pisa Cathedral is located in the monumental Piazza dei Miracoli near the Leaning Tower of Pisa. The immense nave had a Cosmatesque marble pavement. The interior was mostly decorated with many, lovely Renaissance art. The interior of the cathedral was marvelous, beautifully decorated, and breathtaking. I was in awe marveling at all of the Christian sculptures, fine paintings, and life-size statues.

An extraordinary artwork was the pulpit by Giovanni Pisano. It was regarded as a masterpiece. How majestic and exquisite it was.

In the awesome Blessed Sacrament Chapel, I sat down and prayed. I prayed for me, my family, relatives, classmates, students, town mates, and friends.

The Battistero di San Giovanni (Baptistery of Saint John) in Pisa, dedicated to Saint John, the Baptist is resplendent. This is a Roman Catholic sacrosanct edifice in Pisa. It was constructed of marble. The architectural style was both Romanesque and Gothic. The interior of the Baptistery was enthralling and enigmatic. There is a column that portrayed several occurrences in the life of Saint John the Baptist.

Piazza San Marco (Saint Mark's Square) in Venezia (Venice) – Italia (Italy)
The Saint Mark's Square in Venice, the Floating City, is the main public square. In this square is the Patriarchal Cathedral Basilica of San Marco (Saint Mark). It is the cathedral church of the Roman Catholic Archdiocese of Venice in Italy. It is the most well-known Basilica in Venice. At the top of the church

is the sculpture of Saint Mark holding a book. He is surrounded by angels. Below his statue is a winged lion, the symbol of Saint Mark and Venice. The Italo-Byzantine-style architecture is a beautiful sight to behold. Saint Mark's Basilica is absolutely splendid. The ceiling is completely covered in beautiful mosaic. It is a church made of marble and gorgeous design. It is a unique masterpiece! The tomb of Saint Mark is behind the main altar. According to Christian traditional story, in 828, relics and the body of Saint Mark were stolen from Alexandria by Venetian merchants and taken to Venice.

We attended Holy Mass. It was beautiful. The songs during Mass were very solemn and ethereal. Attending Holy Mass in various churches in Europe is one of my favorite things to do, in addition to visiting museums. I paused and reflected and felt the nearness of God. I was so spellbound.

In the Piazza San Marco, I enjoyed feeding the pigeons. God provides for the birds that gather nothing and store nothing in the barns. I bought the seeds from the street vendors for the birds.

There were several musicians situated all over the piazza. It was enthralling watching the musicians and listening to the music especially the song "Solamente Una Vez" (Only One Time). The piazza is the very heart of Venice. Centuries of history abound in this piazza. Napoleon Bonaparte called this piazza as the finest drawing room in Europe.

Listening to classical music at the Piazza San Marco made me remember my children in their growing up years. During their nine years of piano lessons, they performed on several piano recitals in Sacramento, California. My favorite piece William played in a piano recital was Beethoven's Sonata No. 20, "Grande Sonate Pathetique," in G major, Opus 49, No. 2, Allegro ma non troppo. My favorite piece Susana played in a piano recital was Beethoven's Fur Elise (For Elizabeth).

My grandson Logan played Beethoven's Fur Elise during a competition at Trinity Christian School in Sacramento, California and won fifty dollars. Wow! What an excellent performance!

It was blissful to have been in Venice. It was great attending Holy Mass, sitting in the piazza, feeding the pigeons, listening to calm, soothing, and fine classical music, relaxing, and letting the world go by. What a fascinating, spellbinding, and an extraordinary experience it was! I could live here in the Floating City.

The Dinner on My Birthday - In Venezia (Venice), the Floating City
We went to dinner on my birthday, 30 August. The musicians played classical

music. I was feeling ecstatic being in the Floating City, so splendid, so romantic, so breathtaking, the realization of a lifelong dream to travel to Venice. I could not believe I was there. We came early for dinner. The entree, the Italian food I ordered with all the trimmings was superb – food to die for. The grilled chicken, the unique salsa, the delicious fresh baked bread, the colorful vegetables cooked to perfection, the scrumptious, creamy, and rich tiramisu dessert made my birthday so memorable. The dining service was impressive. It was elegant! The waiter kissed me when Tom told him it was my birthday. Tom kept teasing me that I was kissed by an Italian guy. Thank God for the blessing of the excellent food and the lovely trip to Venice. I paused and reflected and thanked God for the blessing.

Saint Stephen's Cathedral (Stephansdom) - Vienna, Austria

At Saint Stephen's Cathedral, I lighted a votive candle in one of the altars, put a euro in the box, and prayed. I love lighting a votive candle whenever I visit a church I have never been before. The votive candle is a symbol of my prayer request.

We toured the Saint Stephen's Cathedral. Saint Stephen was the first martyr of Christendom. This is a Roman Catholic cathedral of the Archdiocese of Vienna. It is the city's most important and a well-known symbol. It is a leading feature of the Vienna skyline.

The church is magnificent. In the center of the main altar are a large crucifix and beautiful Blessed Sacrament Tabernacle. The majestic towers, the stained-glass windows, the life-size statues of many saints, angels, Stations of the Cross, huge golden glass chandeliers, candelabras, impressive organ, the architectures, etc. are all marvelous. There are eighteen altars in the main part of the church, and more in the various chapels. There are twenty-three bells. I marveled and gasped at everything in sight. Too sublime and absolutely divine!

Here, we attended Holy Mass on a Sunday twice. The Holy Mass was celebrated in Latin. It was like the Holy Mass when I was in Catholic school. I was able to pray in Latin without a prayer book. I still remember the prayers in Latin. The Mass brought me back to my parochial school days. The first reading, the second reading, the Gospel, and the homily were the only ones spoken in German during Mass. The solemn liturgy took my breath away.

I paused, reflected, and prayed in silent meditation and talked with the Lord God. I was filled with joyful excitement. I felt God's precious love and presence, and I loved it. It was another spellbinding experience. I was ecstatic.

Wolfgang Amadeus Mozart worked as an adjunct music director here in this cathedral. This was his parish church when he lived in Vienna, and he was married in this cathedral.

Saint Peter's Churchyard, Salzburg in Austria
It is the oldest Christian graveyard in Salzburg dating back to 1627. Many of the aristocratic families in Salzburg lie buried here, along with many other notable and prominent people. It is a worthy attraction, and many visitors come to see the place where the Von Trapp family hid out in the movie "The Sound of Music."

Saint Peter's Church in Salzburg in Austria
I prayed in the church. It is majestic. The Blessed Sacrament Tabernacle and the Crucifix on the main altar are celestial. The frescoes and stained glass windows are absolutely mystical. All basilicas, cathedrals, and churches in Europe are indeed magnificent. It is ineffable. I paused and reflected in constant prayer.

Saint Vitus Cathedral - Prague in the Czech Republic
Saint Vitus Cathedral is a Roman Catholic Cathedral in Prague in the Czech Republic, and the seat of the Archbishop of Prague. Tourists flock to Prague to see this famous Saint Vitus Cathedral. It is marvelous. The statue of Saint Wenceslaus I, Duke of Bohemia is in this Cathedral. It also contains the tombs of many Bohemian kings and Holy Roman Emperors. Prague was a part of the Holy Roman Empire, and so was Austria. The cathedral is an excellent example of Gothic architecture. It is the biggest and most important church in the country of the Czech Republic. An impressive sight to behold, I was in awe!

Saint Nicholas Church - Prague - Czech Republic
Johannes, the tour guide, told us the story of Saint Nicholas, a priest, a bishop, and a compassionate man who gave away a lot of his inheritance to the poor. It is the most famous Baroque church in Prague with lovely white façade. This church is magnificent as well, like any church in Europe.

In Salzburg, Austria

Ofelia standing in front of the Gothic Powder Tower in Prague in the Czech Republic

Saint John of Nepomuk - Prague - Czech Republic

The memorial statue, a stone curved figure of Saint John of Nepomuk is on the side of the Charles Bridge. There are many sculptures of saints on both sides of this bridge. According to Johannes, the tour guide, Saint John of Nepomuk is the national saint of Bohemia. He was a martyred saint. The king saw his wife having a confession. He suspected his wife of having a lover. The king compelled Father John to reveal the sins of his wife. Father John did not divulge her sins. He opted to die rather than reveal the sins of the queen. The king ordered the priest's death. The king's men threw the priest into the Vlatava River below the Charles Bridge. He was canonized and became Saint John of Nepomuk.

Saint John of Nepomuk is the first martyr of the Seal of the Confessional. He is also the patron saint against slander.

I continued pausing and reflecting, this time meditating on the stalwart men and women of faith who suffered martyrdom for their sincere and deep love of God.

Matthias Church - Budapest in Hungary

We toured Budapest. The Holy Trinity Column that was built between 1710 and 1713 is in the Holy Trinity Square. It stands majestically in the center of Budapest's Holy Trinity Square, and is a significant landmark.

On the right side is the Matthias Church. It is a Roman Catholic Church in the heart of Buda's Castle District. The church was the place for several coronations. Hungarian Habsburg kings were crowned in this magnificent church. There is an Ecclesiastical Art Museum in the church that contains sacrosanct relics, medieval stone carvings, and exquisite replicas of coronation precious jewels, and the lovely Hungarian royal crown.

The front of the church was closed. We had to enter at the side of the church. The Matthias Church is very impressive. The architectural style is Gothic. The church abounds in marvelous frescoes, stained glass windows, and sculptures. The Blessed Sacrament Tabernacle, the Crucifix on the main altar, the statue of the Blessed Virgin Mary, and several statues of saints adorn this celestial church.

I prayed in this church, paused and reflected on the exuberant blessings God has bestowed on us.

Statue of Saint John of Nepomuk in Prague in the Czech Republic

At The Matthias Church in Budapest in Hungary

Saint Peter and Saint Paul's Church - Budapest Hungary

The Saint Peter and Saint Paul's Church in Budapest is breathtaking and awe-inspiring. I lighted a votive candle. We had a marvelous tour. The cathedral is magnificent. A resplendent large pipe organ, amazing statues of saints, dazzling stained glass windows, a beautiful Blessed Sacrament Tabernacle, the big Crucifix are awesome. Tom wanted a coin of the church, so I bought one for him for twenty euros.

Many people of faith prayed, paused, and reflected in this beautiful place of worship.

Basilique de Notre-Dame de Genève (Basilica of Our Lady of Geneva) – Geneva, Switzerland

We visited the Basilica of Our Lady of Geneva, the principal Roman Catholic Church in Geneva. We attended Holy Mass in French. I got to say, "Paix" (Peace), to people around me. This is a beautiful and marvelous basilica. The architecture is Gothic revival style. The structure has similarities with the Notre-Dame Cathedral in Paris, France. I marveled at the main altar, the Blessed Sacrament Tabernacle, the Stations of the Cross, the Crucifix, the side altars, the votive candles (I lighted one for my prayer – safe travel, safe stay in Europe, etc.), the stained-glass windows, the statues of saints, the Blessed Virgin Mary's statue, etc. I was so spellbound attending Holy Mass in French.

La Cathedrale Saint-Pierre - The Saint Peter's Cathedral - Geneva, Switzerland

This is now a Protestant church. It was a Catholic church before the Reformation. It is magnificent. The several Romanesque columns in the façade of the cathedral are breathtaking. There is a museum near the Cathedral. It has the history of the Reformation.

Saint Francis Church - Lausanne, Switzerland

In Lausanne, after an orientation tour, we visited this medieval city. We entered Saint Francis Church. It was a Roman Catholic Church before the Reformation. In 1536, the Reformists came with the Bernese army and the church was closed. According to the tour guide, the reformists destroyed all of the sculptures inside the church. He also said the stone carvings on the side wall - the Assumption of the Blessed Virgin Mary, holy angels, and saints were not destroyed by the reformists. The reformists missed them. These marvelous original works were spared. I am happy they were spared, and we got to see them. It is now a Protestant Church.

I paused, reflected, and prayed in the Saint Francis Church.

The Cathedral of Our Lady in Antwerp in Belgium

The Roman Catholic Cathedral of Our Lady in Antwerp in Belgium is breathtaking! The Gothic architecture of the church is magnificent. The Cathedral is adorned with many beautiful and exquisite paintings by famous artists, some of them by Peter Paul Rubens. Paul Rubens was one of the most prominent and prolific European artists of the 17th century. This Flemish artist was born in Antwerp.

Several life-size sculptures of saints abound in this cathedral. What an awesome sight! I just marveled at the many captivating works of art that adorn one of the most resplendent cathedrals in the continent of Europe - centuries of history!

Notre Dame Cathedral in Paris, France

We attended Holy Mass in this cathedral twice, and toured it three times. The Holy Mass started with a vesper. Two ladies led the singing. They took turns singing the solo numbers. They were accompanied by an organist. Their soprano voices filled the whole church. The vesper was heavenly.

After the thirty minutes vesper, the Holy Mass began. It was celebrated in the French language, but most of the songs were in Latin. It was a beautiful Mass. It was heavenly like you are in Heaven on Earth. I was spellbound and felt God's presence. The Lord is near.

The Notre Dame Cathedral was started in 1163 during the reign of King Louis VII. According to the tour guide, Bishop Maurice de Sully initiated the construction, and invited the common people to help and work in the construction. It was completed over the course of 200 years. It is one of the most notable landmarks in Paris. The cathedral is magnificent. Several side altars with many sculptures of saints, exquisite paintings, huge and elaborate chandeliers, statues - the statue of Jesus, the Blessed Mother Mary, and saints are abundant in this cathedral. The stained-glass windows are breathtaking. I had a picture taken in front of the statue of Saint Joan of Arc.

Eglise de la Madeleine – Church of the Madeleine - Paris, France

The Church of the Madeleine, a Roman Catholic Church - The design was impressive. It is built in the Neo-classical architecture. There are fifty-two stunning Corinthian columns all around the entire church. Tom and I walked around the entire church and looked at the individual statue of each saint on the wall around the church. Each name of the saint appeared near their statue. In the interior of the church, the sculpture of the "Last Judgment" by Lemaire is strikingly impressive. There are three dazzling domes in the one nave in the interior. The sculpture of Saint Mary Magdalene showed her being gloriously lifted by angels. The many frescoes are mystifying. The large pipe organ is enthralling.

The Madeleine is a parish of the Archdiocese of Paris. Holy Masses and several other religious liturgies are celebrated here every day.

Several visitors sat down, paused, and reflected in this cathedral. I prayed for me, my family, relatives, friends, classmates, students, town mates, and people who have touched my life.

It rains a lot of the time in Paris. I bought a raincoat. It was raining on that day when we visited the Madeleine Church.

Sacre Coeur - La Basilique du Sacre Coeur de Montmartre (The Basilica of Sacred Heart in Montmartre) - Paris, France

This Basilica of Sacred Heart in Montmartre in Paris is a Roman Catholic Church dedicated to the Sacred Heart of Jesus. It is a popular landmark. It is located at the summit of the butte Montmarte. We took a lift to get here. Then, we had to climb more stairs to get to the church.

Christ in Majesty, a mosaic in the apse by Luc-Olivier Merson is one of the largest in the world. The church is majestic, awe-inspiring, and holy. The top of the dome is available to tourists and offers a resplendent panoramic view of the city of Paris.

We attended Holy Mass in French. It was a magnificent liturgy. The priest translated his homily in French to English. It was a beautiful homily about the Sacred Heart of Jesus, what Jesus is calling us to do as Christians. The large, fine pipe organ that provided beautiful music during Mass enhanced the liturgy.

I prayed for me, my family, relatives, friends, classmates, students, and town mates. It is indeed a divine place of worship to pause and reflect about the goodness of God and His exuberant blessings.

Sainte Chapelle – Paris, France

This chapel was built to house the King Louis IX's collection of relics. It was

At La Basilique du Sacre Coeur (Sacred Heart) de Montmarte in Paris, France

At the Sainte-Chapelle in Paris, France

meant to provide a place for several precious Christian relics including Jesus Christ's crown of thorns, fragments of the True Cross, Holy Lance, and some other items. It is a 13th century church. The upper chapel (the stairs going to the upper chapel are very narrow) has lots of exceptional and intricate stained-glass windows and a splendidly decorated ceiling. Descriptions of who are depicted on the stained-glass windows are available. I read some of them - Jesus, the Blessed Virgin Mary, and Biblical scenes, etc.

I enjoyed the grandeur of it all! It is another wonderful place to calm down, to pause and reflect.

Lourdes, France

Lourdes is in the foothills of the Pyrenees in Southern France. It is the site of the Apparition of the Blessed Virgin Mary to Bernadette. Each year about four to six million pilgrims from around the world come and visit the shrine of our Lady of Lourdes. Many sick and infirmed people come to be healed. There are many known miracles of people who were healed after coming to Lourdes and taking the healing bath.

Basilique de Notre-Dame de l'Immaculee Conception (Basilica of our Lady of the Immaculate Conception) – Lourdes, France

The Basilica of our Lady of the Immaculate Conception is grand and magnificent. The front of the basilica has the image of Pope Pius X holding the decree of November 13, 1907, by which the Mass of the Apparition of Our Lady of Lourdes was extended to the Universal Church.

In the lower level of the Basilica just above the entrance to the Crypt, there is an altar containing some of the relics of Saint Bernadette.

We attended Holy Mass three times at the Basilica of Our Lady of the Immaculate Conception. I noticed the beautiful mosaic of the Passion of Jesus. It adorns the main altar. I loved attending Holy Mass in this magnificent Basilica. It was ethereal, glorious, and sublime. It was just incredibly beautiful. The captivating music from the huge pipe organ enhanced the liturgy. It took my breath away. I was dazed feeling spellbound by it all.

In Lourdes, every hour, the bells of the Basilica play the Ave Maria of Lourdes.

The pilgrimage to Lourdes is majestic, blessed, and sacred. It is a marvelous place to pause and reflect and completely get absorbed by the holiness of it all. It is overwhelming; the whole body, heart, mind, and spirit are filled with indescribable ecstasy and euphoria feeling the closeness of the Lord God.

The Grotto - Lourdes in France

The Blessed Virgin Mary appeared to Saint Bernadette Soubirous in several apparitions in Lourdes in France. We stood in a long queue to visit the Grotto of the Blessed Mother Mary. When I got to the place of the Grotto, I touched the wall and the water on the wall. I put some water on my hands.

During the Apparition, the Blessed Mother Mary asked Bernadette to dig the ground. Bernadette dug the ground and mud came out. She ate the mud and spit it out. She kept digging until the mud became clear water.

The water from the well is holy and miraculous. Pilgrims from all over the world come to Lourdes to be healed. They drink the holy water, and take a miraculous bath.

There were chairs provided for people who would like to sit down and pray before the Grotto of the Blessed Mother. Many people including me prayed, paused, and reflected.

The Holy Bath – Lourdes in France

I stood in queue for the holy bath for women. There is a separate bath for men. I stood for two and a half hours. After two and a half hours of waiting, some people, including me, finally got to the place where we can sit down. In this place while waiting for our turn for the holy bath, we prayed the "Our Father," "Hail Mary," and "Glory Be To The Father." We also sang the songs *Ave, Ave Maria* and *Laudate Maria*. The prayers were said in several languages in Latin, French, Spanish, Italian, etc. The praying and singing continued on. When the women sitting ahead of us moved from the line to take their bath, we, the people sitting on the benches moved closer. We kept moving closer, and praying the prayers and singing the songs. I was getting very, very hungry. I was starving. I did not bring food with me. I did not think it would take that long. A lady sitting beside me shared her little cookie with me. Although I was reluctant to take it, she encouraged me, so I did. It gave me a little relief. After four hours of praying and singing, I finally got called in to take the holy bath. An attendant gave me a bathrobe and told me to undress, so I did.

You take all your clothes to take your holy bath. It was done in good taste. After giving me a bathrobe, I was directed to a room. There, I saw a big bathtub. Two women were there, and we prayed the "Ave Maria" (Hail Mary). We prayed in Latin. I am so happy I know the Hail Mary in Latin, so I could pray with them very well. We also invoked Saint Bernadette to pray for us.

The ladies said, "Sainte Bernadette, ora pro nobis" (Saint Bernadette, pray for us).

The two ladies, one on my right and one on my left, both held my hands. They submerged me in the deep water in the bathtub. The water was very cold. It was like being baptized. The two ladies helped me get out of the tub. Then, I put my clothes on. There was a lady standing there, and she gave me a French hug.

It took me six and a half hours of total waiting time in queue before I took the holy bath. Our priest friend recommended to me to take this holy bath, so I did. It was like a miracle. I was submerged in the very cold water, and when I came out, I was not even wet! I did not even need a towel to dry myself. I was given a big towel.

The holy bath was refreshing! It was absolutely divine! It was the most unforgettable experience of a lifetime. Thank God for the blessing!

Church of Our Lady, Amstedam - Amsterdam, Holland

Amsterdam is one of the most beautiful and unique cities in the world. It is also known as the "City of Canals" and the "Venice of the North." It is a marvelous place.

We visited and toured the Church of Our Lady, Amsterdam. It is a magnificent Gothic cathedral. We attended Holy Mass in this church twice. The Holy Mass was celebrated in Latin. I was at ease attending Holy Mass in Latin. I know Latin prayers – the Sign of the Cross, the Confiteor, the Kyrie, the Gloria, the Pater Noster, Ave Maria, Hosanna, etc.

I was so spellbound attending Holy Mass in several churches - basilicas and cathedrals in the countries of Europe. The joy of feeling God's love and presence is indescribable. It is marvelous to see people in the church in silent prayer pausing and reflecting in communion with the Lord God.

Saint Mary's Pro-Cathedral - Dublin, Ireland

Ireland, the Emerald Isle and the land of saints and scholars is a beautiful, fascinating, and spectacular country. The main religion of Ireland is Roman Catholic.

At the Saint Mary's Pro-Cathedral in Dublin, Ireland

We visited Saint Mary's Pro-Cathedral in Dublin. It is a Roman Catholic cathedral, and it is magnificent! Holy statues of several saints, the Virgin Mary, and the apostles, abound in the many side altars of the cathedral. The sculpture of the crucified Jesus Christ, the Lord God on the side altar is sublime. The main altar is ethereal!

I have lighted votive candles as a sign of my prayer invoking the good Lord to keep us safe in our travel. I put some euros in the box as charity donation.

We attended Holy Mass. It was ethereal! I felt God's love and presence. After attending Holy Mass in Latin, German, and French, we finally got to attend Holy Mass in the English language.

Saint Patrick's Cathedral - Dublin, Ireland

Saint Patrick is the patron saint of Ireland known to preach the Holy Trinity using a shamrock leaf. This cathedral was founded in 1191. After the English Reformation, the cathedral became an Anglican Church of Ireland. The main altar is magnificent and breathtaking. Everything is awesome! I just marveled at the beauty of the cathedral that was once upon a time a Roman Catholic cathedral.

I bought two Irish Rosaries in the gift shop. I have a large collection of Rosaries from several countries in Europe. This is another nice place of worship to pray, pause, and reflect.

Sankt-Hedwigs- Kathedrale (Saint Hedwig's Cathedral) - Berlin, Germany

We attended Holy Mass at Saint Hedwig's Cathedral in Berlin twice. The liturgy was in German. I am fascinated by languages and attending Holy Mass in different languages suits me just fine. There were four priests who celebrated Holy Mass. It was absolutely divine! God was near!

Saint Hedwig's Cathedral is a Roman Catholic Cathedral. It is the seat of the archbishop of Berlin.

Like the other cathedrals in Europe, it is beautiful and astonishing. The architecture is Neo-classical.

Sources on the Holy Gospel Readings: The Holy Bible

Sources on the Spellbinding Journeys: Guided tours by men and women tour guides, audio CD tour guides, pamphlets handed out on tours, and writings on the walls in some of the museums.

PART III

Reflections on the Advent Season

REFLECTIONS ON THE ADVENT SEASON

First Sunday of Advent

The first Sunday of Advent is the first season of the Christian church year. Advent means "coming." Every year during Advent, we reflect the coming of the Lord. It is a preparation for the coming of the Messiah, the Savior. We are called to be prepared, vigilant, watchful, and alert! It is now time to get organized. Mountains shake and the seas rage at the Lord's presence. Be ready any time!

During the first Sunday of Advent, the priest wears a purple liturgical vestment symbolizing penance. It is a time for repentance, renewal, and penance. Advent persuades us to look at ourselves clearly as being a sinner. We are called upon to take the fundamental step in going back to God.

The church is beautifully and richly decorated during the first Sunday of Advent. Purple wreaths with some greenery are mounted on the wall. The altar cloth is purple. The Advent wreath with the traditional three purple candles and one pink is resplendent. One purple candle is lighted before Holy Mass. The second purple candle is lighted on the second Sunday of Advent; the pink on the third Sunday, and another purple on the fourth Sunday.

Jesus comes to us bringing glad tidings and good news to all. He comes to set us free! Let us proclaim the good news of His upcoming birth, the beginning of our salvation. Will we receive Him gloriously in our hearts? Are we really ready?

Oremus (Let us pray). O God, may we truly prepare for your imminent coming, the Messiah, so when you come on midnight, Christmas Eve, we are fully prepared to embrace you. May we proclaim the Gospel, the good news, of your birth, the beginning of our salvation now and forever and ever. Amen.

Days Before Christmas

Some suggestions for the preparation of the coming of the Messiah:

Show extra compassion for the poor and give alms. Have a generous heart and give to charitable organizations that aid the poor in the U.S.A. and worldwide, especially during this time of the year, the Christmas season. Also, support your local church benevolently, and give your tithing or stipends. It is a Christian duty to assist your church financially.

Participate in feeding the poor in your local community. Contribute to this worthy cause. Volunteer your time, and get involved in preparing and cooking the food by helping in the kitchen. Support the Angel Tree program in your local parish, and give gifts to the poor children whose parents cannot afford Christmas presents for them. The angel tree is filled with paper angels. On each angel, it lists the age of the child, the gender, and the child's wish for Christmas. If you take one paper angel, you get the gift for the child, and you will grant the child's wish. Isn't that wonderful? You get to be the Santa Claus for the needy child. Generous parishioners give Christmas presents to many kids. It is a very worthy project to be able to give joy to poor children in the local community. The loving smile of a child when he/she receives a Christmas present is priceless.

Share your blessings the loving God has given you to your least brothers and sisters in Christ.

Keep Jesus Christ

Keep Christ in Christmas. He is the main reason for the season! Foremost of all, keep the holy in the holiday season. Shopping, holiday parties, and festivities, these are all fine, but should not be the central focus.

The heart of Christmas is Jesus who was born into the world primarily for the salvation of mankind. His name Jesus means "Savior" – save – Jesus is salvation. He is Christ, the anointed one. Some ideas we can do in preparing for the coming of the Messiah:

Spend more time in prayer and meditation and have a chat with God. Attend daily holy Mass, if work time allows you, in addition to Sunday Mass. Set aside quality time with your family, relatives, friends, et al. Attend the penance service, and go to confession. Forgive anyone who had offended you. Make amends and peace with them. Give thanks to God for the many blessings He has bestowed upon you. Encourage one another to reach out and touch someone, etc.

Sing

During this Christmas season, sing, although you can't carry a tune. Play your Christmas CD, and sing along with the soothing Christmas music. When you are shopping in the mall and Christmas holiday songs are played, sing or hum along. Music is an effective medicine for a very weary mind and an exhausted body.

Gaudate Sunday

Gaudate means "rejoice." The pink candle is lit during the third week of Advent. On this week, the church lightens the penance time. The first reading invites us to rejoice - Zephaniah 3:14-18a.

In the second reading, Saint Paul wrote, "Rejoice in the Lord always. I shall say it again: rejoice! Your kindness should be known to all. The Lord is near." - A Letter of Saint Paul to the Philippians 4:4-7.

Let us all REJOICE and proclaim the wonder, majesty, and greatness of the Lord! Play the trumpet, piano, harp, lyre, cello, trombone, violin, guitar, mandolin, clarinet, etc. Play them loudly in full blast. Sing praises and adoration to our God. Maranatha!

The long-awaited arrival of the Messiah is soon! It is beginning to look a lot like Christmas, everyone's favorite season of the year.

The Nativity of our Lord – Christmas Day

After preparing spiritually for four weeks for the coming of the Messiah, the inevitable day has finally arrived. The Lord, the Savior of the world has come. For today in the city of David a savior has been born for you who is Messiah and Lord. – Luke, Chapter 2:11

For a child is born to us, a son is given us; upon His shoulder dominion rests. They name him Wonder-Counselor, God-Hero, Father-Forever, and Prince of Peace. His dominion is vast and forever peaceful, from David's throne, and over His kingdom, which He confirms and sustains by judgment and justice, both now and forever. The zeal of the LORD of hosts will do this! – Isaiah 9:1-6.

GLORIA IN EXCELSIS DEO, ET IN TERRA PAX HOMINIBUS BONAE VOLUNTATIS! GLORY TO GOD IN THE HIGHEST AND ON EARTH PEACE TO THOSE ON WHOM HIS FAVOR RESTS. Luke 2:1-14

Reflection on the Book of the Prophet Isaiah 9:1-6:

The Lord Jesus Christ is the Messiah for whom the prophets had foretold. As we celebrate Christmas on this momentous day, may God renew His love for us. May He bless us, and make us holy! May we keep Jesus in the deepest core and warmth of our hearts, and let His loving light gleam brightly in us. May we recognize Christmas is the very essence of

Christianity, the hope for a peaceful world. May we be true and devout Christians in faith by making this significant day a marvelous day that it is - a day of kindness, charity, hope, peace, goodwill, joy, and love to all people no matter who they are!

The Savior is born! Venite adoremus! Come, let us adore Him! To Jesus Christ, our newborn king and salvation, the Messiah and Lord, let us sing a song of never-ending rejoicing! Alleluia! Let us all rejoice in the Lord, for Jesus, the long-awaited Messiah, our Savior, the Wonder-Counselor, God-Hero, Father-Forever, Prince of Peace has been born. Today, real peace comes down to us from heaven above! Hallelujah!

Let us glorify, praise, adore, thank, and love Jesus Christ our Lord, who was born into this world to save us. He is our light and salvation who brings peace into the world, now and always.

This is the day the Lord has made; let us rejoice and be glad. - Psalm 118:24

Let us pray. O God, help us to make each day of our life a Christmas day remembering every day to keep the true joy, share the genuine love and kindness, spread hope, lasting peace, happiness, and cheer to all. Daily, at the break of dawn when we wake up in the morning, may we feel an excitement and anticipation for Christmas.

GLAD TIDINGS TO ALL! May God continue to bless all of us – all the days of our life! Wishing everyone and your cherished loved ones a holy, jubilant, blessed, and glorious Christmas!

Christmas Blessing for You All - Cherished Loved Ones - Relatives, Classmates, Students, Friends, and Town mates:

> May the sweet baby Jesus smile lovingly on you,
> and give you prolific blessings from Heaven.
> May He give you countless joy and continued good health,
> and fill your heart, mind, and soul with His marvelous love.

> May there be sunshine, peace, tranquility,
> and profound hope in your heart now and always,
> and that's the heart-felt prayer I am praying to God
> for you, this jubilant and glorious Christmas day!

Saint Nicholas

I thought of sharing a story of Saint Nicholas' life, his overwhelming kindness and service for God and humanity for a spiritual meditation especially during the Advent season.

When we toured Prague in the Czech Republic, Johannes, the tour guide, told us a story about Saint Nicholas when we visited the magnificent Saint Nicholas Church in Prague. Here is the story.

Johannes said a poor man had three daughters, but could never afford the amount of their dowries. They may have to remain unmarried. Perhaps, if they were unable to find any work, they may have to become prostitutes. Nicholas, upon hearing the young ladies' serious problem, decided to help the three young women. He did not want anyone to know of his generosity, so he went to the house of the young ladies in the middle of the night, and threw three purses filled with gold (one for each daughter) through the window into the house. The father tried to find the kind, caring, and God-loving man who helped his daughters, but he had never found who he was.

Johannes continued his story of Saint Nicholas and said he used his inheritance from his affluent parents to help the poor, the suffering, and the sick. He became a priest, and he was made Bishop of Myra. He was well-known throughout the land for his kindness, compassion, and deep love for children.

May we emulate the good and the wonderful deeds of this generous Christian man named Saint Nicholas, or Santa Claus, especially during the Christmas season.

The Solemnity of the Epiphany of the Lord

A reading from the Holy Gospel according to Matthew 2:1-12:
When Jesus was born in Bethlehem of Judea, in the days of King Herod, behold, magi from the east arrived in Jerusalem, saying, "Where is the newborn king of the Jews? We saw His star at its rising and have come to do Him homage."

When King Herod heard this, he was greatly troubled, and all Jerusalem with him. Assembling all the chief priests and the scribes of the people, he inquired of them where the Christ was to be born.

They said to him, "In Bethlehem of Judea, for thus it has been written through the prophet: And you, Bethlehem, land of Judah, are by no means least among the rulers of Judah; since from you shall come a ruler, who is to shepherd my people Israel."

Then Herod called the magi secretly and ascertained from them the time of the star's appearance. He sent them to Bethlehem and said, "Go and search diligently for the child. When you have found Him, bring me word, that I too may go and do Him homage."

After their audience with the king, they set out. And behold, the star that they had seen at its rising preceded them, until it came and stopped over the place where the child was. They were overjoyed at seeing the star, and on entering the house they saw the child with Mary, His mother. They prostrated themselves and did Him homage. Then they opened their treasures and offered Him gifts of gold, frankincense, and myrrh. And having been warned in a dream not to return to Herod, they departed for their country by another way.

Commentary on the Gospel of Matthew:
The feast of the Epiphany is a fascinating time of the year. Three wise men in the East traveled to Bethlehem and followed a bright shining star that led them to the Christ child, the Messiah. They found the baby Jesus and offered Him their gifts of gold, frankincense, and myrrh. This is the Messiah we celebrate today. The Gospel reading today invites us to follow the bright shining star like the three wise men. God has called us out of darkness into His marvelous light. We are called upon to follow Jesus Christ, offer our gifts, and be a light of Christ for the world! It is also asking us to be wise like the three wise men; have a good judgment and wisdom in everything we do that we do not allow

ourselves to be separated from God, but open our hearts to the divine grace of the Lord God.

The Lord has come. O come, let us adore Him!

Oremus (Let us pray). O God, as we follow you with great joy, may you pour out your kindness and blessing upon us that our hearts may be filled with love, hope, charity, peace, and faith. May you make us a radiant light for our sisters, brothers, neighbors, et al and the world. Grant this prayer, O God, in the name of Jesus, Your Son, who lives and reigns with You in the unity of the Holy Spirit, one God forever and ever. Amen.

Feast of the Holy Family of Jesus, Mary, and Joseph
A reading from the Holy Gospel according to Luke 2:41-52:
Each year Jesus' parents went to Jerusalem for the feast of Passover, and when He was twelve years old, they went up according to festival custom. After they had completed its days, as they were returning, the boy, Jesus, remained behind in Jerusalem, but His parents did not know it. Thinking He was in the caravan, they journeyed for a day and looked for Him among their relatives and acquaintances, but not finding Him, they returned to Jerusalem to look for Him. After three days, they found Him in the temple, sitting amid the teachers, listening to them and asking them questions, and all who heard Him were astounded at His understanding and His answers.

When His parents saw Him, they were astonished, and His mother said to Him, "Son, why have you done this to us? Your father and I have been looking for you with great anxiety."

And He said to them, "Why were you looking for me? Did you not know that I must be in my Father's house?" But they did not understand what He said to them. He went down with them and came to Nazareth, and was obedient to them; and His mother kept all these things in her heart. And Jesus advanced in wisdom and age and favor before God and man.

Commentary on the Gospel of Luke
We celebrate the Feast of the Holy Family of Jesus, Mary, and Joseph. In the Gospel reading, we are called to imitate constantly the exemplary life of Jesus, Mary, and Joseph. Joseph, the good father who provided for his family; Mary, the good mother who took care of Jesus, her son and Joseph, her spouse. I think Jesus is a good kid. He is God, and I would think He is a perfect child.

He obeyed His parents. We are called to live up to our commitment and responsibilities to our family. Fathers and mothers have a magnitude of responsibilities to love, take care, and provide for their children. Be kind and be patient to your children. Do not nag your children. Don't torment them. Nourish them well, raise them up to be trustworthy, honest, law-abiding, and upstanding adults. Teach them love of God and help them grow in holiness, etc. Your family may not be an ideal family, and it is not perfect, but do your utmost best. Children, respect your parents. When they get older, make time for them. Look after them, help them, and be patient with them. Strive to be a better family, and reflect God's love to your family and other families as well. Make your home a haven of love, faith, joy, hope, and peace!

Sources on the Holy Gospel Readings: The Holy Bible

PART IV

Meditations on Lenten Journey

The Forty Days Lenten Journey

Meditation on Lent:

It is Lent. It is a time for contemplation, spiritual renewal, assessment, and repentance. Lent begins on Ash Wednesday when we receive ashes on our forehead.

During Holy Mass when the priest puts ashes on the forehead of each faithful Christian, he says, "Remember that you are dust, and to dust you will return. Turn away from sin and be faithful to the Gospel."

Lent is a journey for forty days. During the season of Lent, Christians are encouraged to pray, fast, abstain, give alms, and do works of piety and charity.

Making time to pray. Prayer is an essential part of Lent. In our prayer, we meditate, read Holy Scriptures, pray the Stations of the Cross, or the Rosary, or the Divine Mercy Novena, etc. It is good to attend the Stations of the Cross every Friday in Lent. Visit Jesus in the Blessed Sacrament and spend an hour with the Lord. Attend daily Holy Mass whenever you can. As we journey during these forty days, it is our hope as we encounter Jesus, we may feel very close to Him, and be cognizant of His love for us.

Time for fasting. Lent is a time for fasting. We fast on Ash Wednesday and Good Friday, or any day we wish. During all Fridays in Lent, we abstain from eating meat. We sacrifice, and eat fish, vegetables, etc. instead of meat. It is a time for giving up something. What are you giving up for Lent? Some people give up smoking cigarettes, watching movies and TV, Toblerone Swiss chocolate bars, ice cream, rich Italian tiramisu dessert, chocolate candies, beer, etc. Others fast from their favorite TV show or ballgame. Fasting is a form of penance. It helps us turn away from evil and focus our earnest attention toward Jesus Christ.

Almsgiving. It is a time for more sacrifice. Give to the poor what you give up for Lent. Sharing and giving some of what we have to the poor, the homeless, the impoverished, and the less fortunate brothers and sisters in Christ is profound compassion for those who are hungry. There are so many of them in the world. Make a difference in someone's life and reach out to others.

Let us remind ourselves of the inspirational words from the Holy Scriptures about the poor.

Jesus saw the rich putting their gifts into the treasury. He saw a poor widow putting in two small copper coins. He said, "Truly I say to you, this poor widow put in more than all of them; for they all out of their surplus put into the offering; but she out of her poverty put in all that she had to live on." - Luke 21:1-4.

The crowds asked John the Baptist, "What should we do?"

John replied, "Whoever has two coats must share it with anyone who has none; and whoever has food must do likewise." - Luke 3:10-11.

He will answer them, "Amen, I say to you, what you did not do for one of these least ones, you did not do for me." – Matthew 25:45.

Lent is a time for repentance. With humility, we ask for the forgiveness of our sins. Attend the penance service, and go to confession. Even though you don't have grievous sins, it is absolutely divine to go to confession. It is rejuvenating, comforting, and glorious. In addition, you get a blessing by God through the priest.

Reconcile with family members, relatives, or friends whom you have been estranged. End the alienation, and forgive them, if they have done you wrong. Remember what Jesus said to Peter about forgiveness.

Then Peter came and said to Him, "Lord, how often shall my brother sin against me and I forgive him? Up to seven times?"

Jesus said to him, "I do not say to you, up to seven times, but up to seventy times seven." – Matthew 18:22.

Let us accompany Christ to Golgotha, Mount Calvary to the foot of the Cross, as we follow Him, join in His poignant sufferings, and hope we may emulate His intense love for us, and love overwhelmingly our family, relatives, friends, neighbors, and mankind like He did.

As devout Catholics, we happily practice Lenten disciplines because we are disciples of Jesus Christ. We pray, give alms, and fast because we emulate Jesus Christ, who had loved us so much He gave His own life unselfishly for us – for our salvation, so we may have eternal life in the Kingdom of Heaven.

Oremus (Let us pray). O merciful and gracious Lord God, we turn to you with our whole heart, mind, body, and soul. A pure heart create for us, O God, in the name of Jesus Christ, your Son, our Lord. Amen.

THE STATIONS OF THE CROSS

Especially during this time of Lent, we would like to be nearer to God. In addition to doing penance, fasting, abstinence, and practicing works of charity that faithful Christians are encouraged to do, we pray more and spend quality time with the Lord God. We should keep growing in holiness, and hopefully achieve the piety, or the fervor of a saint.

The Stations of the Cross is one of the most beautiful Lenten prayers. There are several Stations of the Cross books available at Catholic bookstores.

For people who are very busy and don't seem to have time to pray the standard Stations of the Cross prayers, I recommend a shorter version from the Lenten Catholic prayers.

The following is said before each station:

> We adore you, O Christ, and we praise you, because by Your Holy Cross You have redeemed the world.
> Our Father, Hail Mary, Glory Be To The Father, and "Lamb of God who takes away the sins of the world, have mercy on us."

1. Jesus is condemned to death.
2. Jesus carries his Cross.
3. Jesus falls the first time.
4. Jesus meets His sorrowful mother.
5. Simon of Cyrene helped Jesus carry the Cross.
6. Veronica wipes the face of Jesus.
7. Jesus falls a second time.
8. Jesus speaks to the women of Jerusalem.
9. Jesus falls a third time.
10. Jesus is stripped of His garments.
11. Jesus is nailed to the Cross.
12. Jesus dies on the Cross.
13. Jesus is taken down from the Cross.
14. Jesus is laid in the tomb.

THE GLAMOUR OF EVIL

Excerpt from a reading from the Holy Gospel according to Mark 1:14-15:
Jesus came to Galilee proclaiming the Gospel of God: "This is the time of fulfillment. The reign of God is at hand. Repent, and believe in the Gospel."

Contemplation on the Gospel of Mark:
In this modern day and age, what is our challenge? During the season of Lent in this forty-day journey, many people give up something they love for penance, sacrifice, or to please the Lord God like good food high in calories, vices, etc., but what is the most important thing to give up during Lent?

SIN is the most important thing to give up during this time of Lent.

Be nice, and give up the glamour of evil. Give up gossiping, talking ill of others, making fun of other people, and grave sins.

God's reign is here, today and now! Keep silent, meditate, and listen to the voice of the Lord God. God beckons you to give up SINS. He asks for your conversion. Refrain from sins, especially grave sins. Also, pay your taxes, bills, and debts. Do not rob someone blind! God loves you! He does not condemn you! He just wants you to return to His fold. Like a lost sheep, or like the prodigal son, He will embrace you lovingly. He will take you in His loving arms!

Let us imitate Christ always, and renew our lives especially during this Lenten journey.

DAYS OF HOLY WEEK

During this time of Holy Week, the holiest week of the year, the faithful Christians are encouraged to continue to do penance through prayer, fasting, abstinence, and by practicing works of piety and charity.

Oremus (Let us pray). Merciful and gracious are you, O Lord God; may we turn to you with our whole heart, mind, and soul. May we pray to you fervently. O God, especially during this Holy Week, guide and help us create a clean and sympathetic heart. Lord, enlighten and illuminate our whole being with the grandeur of your grace that we may always contemplate what is pleasing to you, O God of majesty. May we love you always with utmost sincerity. O God, be merciful when in our frailties we fail, but may we be revived by the Passion of our Lord Jesus Christ, your only Begotten Son. May you protect us, O Lord, and keep us ever safe in your mercy that we may celebrate the Paschal Mystery with purity of heart and true contrition for our failings and weaknesses. Amen.

The Washing of the Feet

A reading from the Holy Gospel according to John 13:1-15:

Now before the Feast of the Passover, when Jesus knew that His hour had come to depart out of this world to the Father, having loved His own who were in the world, He loved them to the end. During supper, when the devil had already put it into the heart of Judas Iscariot, Simon's son, to betray Him, Jesus, knowing that the Father had given all things into His hands, and that He had come from God and was going back to God, rose from supper. He laid aside His outer garments, and taking a towel, tied it around His waist. Then He poured water into a basin and began to wash the disciples' feet and to wipe them with the towel that was wrapped around Him.

He came to Simon Peter, who said to Him, "Lord, do you wash my feet?"

Jesus answered him, "What I am doing you do not understand now, but afterward you will understand."

Peter said to Him, "You shall never wash my feet." Jesus answered him, "If I do not wash you, you have no share with me."

Simon Peter said to Him, "Lord, not my feet only, but also my hands and my head!"

Jesus said to him, "The one who has bathed does not need to wash, except for his feet, but is completely clean. And you are clean, but not every one of you." For He knew who was to betray Him; that was why He said, "Not all of you are clean."

When He had washed their feet and put on His outer garments and resumed His place, He said to them, "Do you understand what I have done to you? You call me Teacher and Lord, and you are right, for so I am. If I then, your Lord and Teacher, have washed your feet, you also ought to wash one another's feet. For I have given you an example, that you also should do just as I have done to you."

Commentary on the Gospel of John:

The Lord Jesus had one last supper with His disciples before He was arrested and condemned to death. As we celebrate the Mass of the Lord's Supper on Holy Thursday, here is my reflection on this Gospel reading. Jesus did not come to be served, but He came to serve. The Lord Jesus has given us a model to follow, so that what He has done for His disciples, we should also do - wash one another's feet. The Lord, who is God and Master, has manifested humility by washing the feet of His disciples. We are called upon to be humble servants to one another. We are called upon to serve. He also told His disciples to love one another as He has loved them. ("This is My commandment: love one another as I love you." - John, Chapter 15:12). Likewise, we are called upon to love one another.

May love, faith, and charity remain in us. By the love of Christ, we have been saved. May we all participate worthily in these mysteries. For whenever a Holy Mass is celebrated, we reenact the passion, the death, and the resurrection of the Lord, Jesus Christ. Let us all love our Lord Jesus, the living God, praise and revere Him forever and ever.

THE PASSION OF THE LORD · GOOD FRIDAY

Good Friday Reflection:

We commemorate the Passion of the Lord Jesus Christ on Good Friday. On this solemn and most Holy Friday, we Christians become more aware of our redemption, how Jesus died on the Cross for the salvation of mankind, our deliverance from sins. God willed Him, His only begotten Son, to submit to death on the Cross for our sake. Our Lord Jesus Christ was obedient to the Heavenly Father and was led to crucifixion like a meek lamb! By the shedding of his blood, our salvation is achieved. We are saved!

Can you imagine His love for you and me? "He emptied himself, taking the form of a slave, coming in human likeness; and found human in appearance, He humbled himself becoming obedient to death, even death on a cross." – Philippians 2:5-11.

Let us be more cognizant of the greatest love of our Lord Jesus Christ, who laid down His one and only life to bring us to God. The love of Jesus Christ for us is unparalleled. Let us hail, praise, and glorify the Lord Jesus for everything He has done for us.

Oremus (Let us pray). O God, have mercy on us all! Humbly, we ask you to forgive us - our sins, coldness, and indifference. Sanctify and strengthen us, O God, in faith, hope, and love. May we live the mystery of the Cross through Christ, Your Son, our Savior and Lord. Amen!

Wishing you all a very Holy Paschal Triduum (Holy Thursday, Good Friday, and Easter Vigil).

Dominus vobiscum! (The Lord be with you!)

Pax (Peace).

The Paschal Mystery

Commentary on the Paschal Mystery:

On Good Friday, we commemorate the Passion and death of Jesus.

Jesus Christ, while dying on the Cross, said: "Father, into your hands, I commend my spirit." - Luke 23:44-46. After saying that, He breathed His last and died on the Cross. This is the mystery of the salvation of mankind. We remember his ultimate sacrifice - death on the Cross to redeem humanity – thus opening the Kingdom of Heaven for all mankind.

On Easter Sunday, we celebrate His glorious resurrection. "Jesus Christ is risen from the dead! To Him be glory and power for all eternity." – Luke 24:34; cf. Rv 1:6

The Paschal Mystery – the dying and rising of Jesus (Passover sacrifice of Jesus from death to life) had been accomplished. May Almighty God who has given us rebirth by water and the Holy Spirit and bestowed on us great mercy for our transgressions, keep us forever by His grace in Christ Jesus, His only begotten Son.

Let us then sing hymns of triumphant praise to the Lord! Alleluia! Alleluia! Rejoice in the risen Lord! His death and resurrection allow us to enjoy eternal life with God. May we celebrate the joy of the Paschal Feast, and give profound thanks to the Lord for His goodness and His everlasting love.

"This is the day the Lord has made; let us rejoice and be glad!" – Psalm 118:24. Exult everybody! Enjoy and seize the delightful day!

May the ineffable joy of Easter be with all of us now and always. Wishing you and your family a holy, blessed, glorious, and happy Easter!

Oremus (Let us pray). Let us pray that the sufferings, dying, and rising of Christ in glory dispel the darkness in the world that we may all live in lasting peace. Amen.

God bless! Pax (Peace).

Sources on the Holy Gospel Readings: The Holy Bible

PART V

Prayers

Pray, Pray, Pray

The presence of God is magnificent and glorious. You can feel the nearness of God through prayer. Pray, pray, and pray. Jesus often withdrew from His disciples and prayed. After Jesus arrives in the garden with his disciples, he withdraws from them (Luke 22:41). He prayed earnestly in the Garden of Gethsemane. Prayer is a means of communicating with God and having a close personal relationship with Him. He wants us to converse with Him through prayer. What a marvelous privilege that is.

My prayer life. I spend time meditating and praying in my room. Praying in my room is not the only time I pray. The following are the other times and places where I pray:

- I pray when I go for a walk.
- I pray when I am in the doctor's clinic, or dental office waiting for my appointment.
- I pray when I am in queue at the bank waiting for my turn.
- I pray in the car when Tom drives to the big city (forty-five-minute drive) to see a Broadway musical, an opera, a ballet, a symphony, or a celebrity show like Tony Bennett, the Osmonds, Celine Dion, Sarah Brightman, Josh Groban et al. When we are headed for home while Tom is driving, I pray in the car.
- When Tom and I go out, and if I am not driving, I pray in the car while Tom is driving to get to the place where we are going.
- I pray whenever I have to sit down and wait like when I got my car inspected and prepared for winter driving.
- I pray when we are in queue at the grocery store waiting for our turn to pay for the groceries.
- When I am watching the TV news, I pray when it is time for commercial.
- On our way to Holy Mass on Sunday, I pray. On our way home after Holy Mass, I pray.

Honor, praise, glorify, and adore the sublime and great God in your fervent prayers. The more you honor the good and kind God, the more He will bless you, and the more you will find favor with Him. How awe-inspiring that is!

Loving Prayers to Our God

A Morning Prayer

Oremus (Let us pray). O gracious God, our loving Father, help us all through this day that we may help others. May we bring joy to you, to our family, relatives, friends, et al. Help us to be cheerful always, persevering when things don't go well, and calm when irritating things come in our path. Allow us to be helpful to those who are having difficult times, kind to those who are in dire need, and compassionate to those who are hurting and in pain. Help us to remain cool and never lose our tempers, that nothing may vanish our joy, nothing may ruin our peace and tranquility, and nothing may make us bitter towards anybody. O God, grant that those whom we work on a daily basis, and those whom we meet along the way may see in us as the reflection of you, our Lord and God. Shine your light through us, so those who see us may praise you. O Lord God, help us to do our best to seek you, to serve you, our neighbors, and our fellowmen/women. May we do all things for your greater glory and for the advancement of the Kingdom of Heaven through Jesus Christ, your Son, our Lord. Amen.

Calm Down

Oremus (Let us pray). O awesome God and Father, help me to slow down. Calm my rapid mind, relax my strain muscles, comfort my weary nerves, and appease my throbbing heart. Help me to learn to pause and take few minutes of vacation, get in touch with myself, hear and listen to your voice O God, and feel your loving presence that I may gain renewed strength, courage, light, and peace. Amen.

Prayer for Courage

Oremus (Let us pray). O God, there are times when we are not always strong. We turn to you for assistance. Bless us with courage and strength when life seems difficult to handle. Carry us on your loving and strong shoulder for in you, Lord, there is shelter and refuge. Keep us safe, O God. You are our hope and peace. We get our strength from you and your ever-omnipotent power. Hear our prayer, O God, in the name of Jesus, your Son, our Lord. Amen.

We Are Grateful O God

Oremus (Let us pray). O God, we are grateful to you for the gift of this wonderful new day. Be with us all as we go out and about doing our daily tasks faithfully. May we encounter other people joyfully and delightfully. May your real presence shine forth in all of us that we may continue to serve most steadfastly and most gladly. Restore our drooping spirit when we are weary. O Lord God, please be with us all today and every moment of our lives. Amen.

Shelter Us O God

Oremus (Let us pray). O God, shelter us; shield us against the intense heat of the Sun and the sometimes-inescapable tempests of our life. Assist us when we stumble. Pick us up like a child when we trip. Carry us on your shoulder when we could not seem to stand up. Grant us your guiding assistance firmly in our faith that we may be strong and always remain faithful to you our Lord and God. Hear our prayer, O God, in the name of Jesus Christ, your Son, our Lord. Amen.

Prayer Before Meal

Oremus (Let us pray). O gracious God and loving Father, you are compassionate and your kindheartedness is immeasurable. We pray you will provide us our daily bread, and furnish for the needs of all the poor hungry children worldwide. Hear our prayer in the name of Jesus, your Son, our Lord. Amen.

Another Prayer Before Meal

Oremus (Let us pray). Blessed are you Lord God of all creation, thank you for giving us our daily bread and these earthly presents. Merciful God and Father, we also thank you for the numerous blessings you have bestowed upon us. Bless us, and this meal for our nourishment and strength. Display your extra special care to those who are hungry and make us good examples of your compassion. Keep us forever thankful and generous to others. Help us to be lights of Christ for the world. May we also always remember the needs of others. We ask you, O God, in the name of Jesus Christ, your Son, our Lord. Amen.

Prayers from the Heart's Deepest Core

O Lord God, bless and protect us all the days of our life. May you keep us safe, and free us from harm and sin that nothing may ever separate us from your love. Hear our prayer, O God, in the name of Jesus Christ, your Son, our Lord. Amen.

The Living Water

O loving and marvelous God, you have unselfishly given us the water of life for our drink through Jesus Christ, our Lord and Savior. He is our great strength and solid rock. Help us, O God, to thirst for Christ, the living water in our daily life, and may we extend our thirst for Him to others. We pray in the name of Jesus, your Son, our Lord. Amen.

John, Chapter 4:14 – "But whoever drinks the water I shall give will never thirst; the water I shall give will become in him a spring of water welling up to eternal life."

God in Our Midst

O God, you are in our midst as we seek to do our daily tasks faithfully. May your presence shine brightly in all of us that we may serve most joyfully and lovingly. Renew our spirits when we feel downhearted. You have promised you will be with us all the time. Lord, assist us now, today, and all the days of our life. Amen.

O God, A Thousand Thanks

O God, you are the generous giver of all our precious gifts. You are the main source of everything we have beginning with your gift of our life. We are grateful and appreciative for everything we have and enjoy. A thousand thanks to you, O God! They come from your hands. May we treasure your gifts to us - our life, health, family, talent, and abundant opportunities. May we use our gifts to serve your people. O Lord, lead us closer to you. You are our hope and true joy! May we serve you with all our strength and lead others unto you by our good examples. By virtue of our Baptism, may we proclaim the Gospel, the good news, now and forever. We pray to you, O God, in the name of Jesus Christ, your Son, our Lord. Amen.

Endless Love

O Lord God, help us to make every minute of our life an act of endless love for you. Give us the grace to always be obedient to your laws. Help us to inspire and uplift everyone you put in our path. Grant our prayer, O God, in the name of Jesus, your Son, who is our savior and guide. Amen.

The Reflection of your Love
O God, help us that our words and actions all the days of our lives are always pleasing to you, and that they are always a reflection of your great love. O Lord God, hear our prayer in the name of Jesus Christ, your Son, our Lord. Amen.

The Awesome God
O God, you are a mystery. We don't understand everything about you, but we have faith, and we believe. You are great wisdom. You are love, and you are awesome! You are magnificent! Kindle the hearts of your people for you, and for your church, through the prayers and examples of your great saints. Grant this, O Lord, in the name of Jesus, your Son, our Lord. Amen.

The New Dawn
O God, we graciously thank you for the gift of this new dawn unique in its many opportunities, as well as difficulties, but it is always filled with your boundless love. Sometimes, we take your blessings for granted. We don't even see you are there. Give us joyful hearts and peaceful minds that we may use unselfishly our time and effort in the service of others. May we follow the exemplary life of our Lord, Jesus, who unselfishly served others. Amen.

Our World
Gracious and merciful God, you sent your only begotten Son to bring forth healing into our broken world that is severely ravaged by war, violence, crime, poverty, persecution, etc. In the name of Jesus through the Paschal Mystery – Jesus' dying and rising, O God, make this mangled world into whole that with one voice, we may joyfully sing our never-ending praise and glory to you! May there be hope for a true and lasting peace on Earth! O Lord, God, hear our prayer in the name of Jesus Christ, your Son, our Lord. Amen.

Let Us Pray
Prayer to the Holy Spirit:
O God, you have given us seven wonderful gifts - wisdom, understanding,

counsel, fortitude, knowledge, piety, and fear of the Lord (as listed in the Catechism of the Catholic Church, 1831) at our Baptism, and these gifts were strengthened at our Confirmation. O God, Holy Spirit, enable us to do good deeds, to give the best of ourselves, and to serve you and our neighbors. Thank you, O Holy Spirit, that you are present within us and helping us every day to live virtuous lives and proclaim the truths of our faith.

Shine Brightly

O God, we pray for the grace to let the light of your everlasting love shine through us brightly, so that those who see us may truly praise you! Work through us that your eternal glory may be known. Hear our prayer, O God, in the name of Jesus Christ, your Son, our Lord. Amen!

Our Home

O God, help us to make our homes a haven of faith, love, hope, joy, and understanding. Let us entreat to strengthen all families deeply, the foundation of our society. We pray to you, O God. Amen.

Thank You, O God

We thank you, O gracious and loving God, for your countless blessings, for our faith, for our church, for the priests, who are your representatives on Earth, for every moment we live, for granting us continued good health of mind and body, for the joys of life, for a home and shelter, for our daily bread, and earthly gifts. We thank you for our jobs, for the many material things for our sustenance, for the comforts of life, for the Sun that gives us warmth, for the air we breathe, for the spectacular moon and stars that illuminate the night, for the dazzling flowers of the fields, etc. We thank you for the unconditional love of our family, relatives, trusted, and treasured friends who brighten our lives and give us sunshine. Above all, we thank you especially for the great gift of Jesus Christ, your Son, whom you have sent for our redemption. Amen.

An Earnest Prayer

Lord Jesus, you opened the eyes of the blind and made them see. You touched the sick - the lepers, the paralytics, the mutes, the blind, the disabled, and the lames, and you healed them and made them well. You forgave Peter after denying you three times, yet you still showed him your profound love. Please, Lord, help us to open our eyes that we may see you in our less fortunate brothers and sisters – the poor, the homeless, the hungry, the naked, and the thirsty. Assist us that we may open our ears and hear the incessant cries of the poor, and do something about it. Lord, may we have tender hearts that we may love one another as you love us unconditionally. Help us to live in joyful unity with our fellow Christians and the whole human race that we may proclaim your saving love to all mankind. Lord, hear our earnest prayer in the name of Jesus Christ, your Son, our Lord. Amen.

Hear Our Prayer, O God
A Prayer During Difficult Times

Gracious Lord God of mercy and love, assist _____ (mention the name of the person you are praying for) in times of stress and anxiety. Ease his/her heavy burden. Increase his/her fortitude, one of the seven gifts of the Holy Spirit that you gave him/her. Elevate him/her trust and faith in your compassion.

Give _____ (mention the name of the person you are praying for) intrepid confidence he/she needs, O God, to face the difficulties ahead, knowing that with your protection, love, and your miracles in the hands of the doctors and medicines will restore his/her health, recover quickly, and make him/her whole again.

I pray for your healing graces and ask that you envelope _____ (mention the name of the person you are praying for) with your comforting love and healing hands. Watch over him/her, O Lord. Fill him/her with your everlasting love, deep hope, and profound peace that you will carry him/her through, and everything will be fine and well. Help his/her body, mind, and heart to stay calm. Please hear our prayer for _____ ,(mention the name of the person you are praying for) O God, in the name of Jesus Christ, your Son, our Lord. Amen.

The Name of the Lord

Blessed be the name of the eternal Lord God now, and always! From the breaking of the dawn to the end of the day, let the name of the Lord be highly praised forever and ever!

When We Are Tempted

O Lord God, when we are tempted to compromise our integrity and Christian values for riches and power, help, guide, and enlighten us.

O Lord God, when we are tempted to neglect our own families, relatives, and friends for selfish and personal gain, help, guide, and enlighten us.

O Lord God, when we are tempted to live more than our means and bite more than we can chew to show off, or measure ——up with others who have more than we have, help, guide, and enlighten us.

Hear our prayer, O God, in the name of your Son, Jesus Christ, our Lord. Amen.

Fill Our Hearts
Alleluia! Alleluia! O God, fill our hearts with joy and a profound love for you. Grant us light that we may always have the wisdom to remain faithful in your love. May we walk in your ways always, today, tomorrow, the next day, and all the days of our life. Hear our prayer, O God, in the name of Jesus Christ, your Son, our Lord. Amen.

Seek the Lord
O Lord God, help us to do our best to seek you, to serve you, our neighbors, and our fellowmen/women for love of you, for your greater glory, we pray through Jesus Christ, your Son, our Lord. Amen.

Glory to God
We give glory and praise to you, our God, who gives light to our life. Many are your blessings to us, if we but place our trust in you! Amen.

Alleluia
O God, we say alleluia, alleluia! The Spirit of the Lord is upon us. May we proclaim your Kingdom, your greater glory, and may we bring glad tidings to the poor. Alleluia! Lord, hear our prayer.

We Call Upon You, O God
A Prayer for Vocation
Lord Jesus Christ, you came into the world and became man. You showed us the profound joys of helping others and self-sacrifice. You served delightfully. Affectionately, instill in us the impassioned desire to devote our lives to you.

O God, give us many, many priests, deacons, and theologians to preach the words of the holy Gospel, the good news to all people. O God, grant us also holy nuns, sisters, and brothers to instruct the children and inspire young men and women to serve you, to attend to the sick, and oversee charity to everybody who may need it. May they emulate you in their hearts. Hear our prayer, O God, in the name of Jesus Christ, your Son, our Lord. Amen.

Consecrated Life
For an increase of vocations to the priesthood, deaconship and to the religious life, let us pray to the Lord. Amen.

The Rock
O God, you are the solid rock and stronghold on which we stand. Whatever we are experiencing in our lives, whether it is job related, family relationships, or uncertainties about our health, and a big tempest seems to be coming in our life, we put our deepest trust in you. O Lord, we know you will give us strength and deliver us from these trials, just as you have delivered David from the giant Goliath, the Philistine (First Book of Samuel 17:32-33, 37, 40-51). Hear our prayer, O God, in the name of Jesus, your Son, our Lord. Amen.

Hold Us
O Lord God, hold us firm that we may remain righteous and never be separated from your love for even the holiest of men/women slipped and fell into sins. We pray to you, O God, in the name of Jesus Christ, your Son, our Lord. Amen.

Protect Us Please
O God of mercy, power, might, love, and compassion, please protect us from all harm. Grant us liberty of spirit and continued health of body and mind to enable us to do your work in this world. Hear our prayer, O God, in the name of Jesus Christ, your Son, our Lord. Amen.

Lord Have Mercy
O God, you give us love and compassion. Lord have mercy.
O God, you give us kindness and forgiveness. Lord have mercy.
O God, you are the truth by which we live our lives. Lord have mercy.

Relationships

O God, in our relationships with our immediate family and loved ones, relatives, friends, neighbors, and even strangers, illumine our hearts with the shining light of your fervent love, let us pray to the Lord. Amen.

The Life

O God, guide everyone to recognize that each human being is a precious creation of you. We pray that from conception to death the life of each human being will be preserved and protected in our law. Hear our prayer, O God, in the name of Jesus, your Son, our Lord. Amen.

In All We Do

O God, in everything we do, in words, in actions, and in what we think, may we always seek your glory.

Religious Freedom

In the gentle and loving compassion of our God, we pray that all assaults on religious liberty will cease forever. May the high-ranking government officials of the United States of America and the leaders of the world have the courage, strength, grace, and wisdom to preserve conscience rights and uphold our fundamental human rights – free to worship you, O God, without fear all the days of our life. May the leaders of the United States of America and the leaders of the peoples of the whole world protect all people from being compelled to violate their beliefs, moral, and religious - Christian/Catholic convictions. Grant our prayer, O God, through Jesus Christ, your Son, our Lord. Amen.

World Peace

O God, may we have a lasting world peace, an end to violence, and religious persecution. O God, hear our prayer. Amen.

Hear Us O Gracious God

Lord, today, dwell in our midst in your compassion, forgiveness, and love. Hear our prayer, O gracious God.

Lord, provide comfort to your people who feel alienated from you. Hear us, O gracious God.

Lord, deliver the homeless, the poor, the impoverished, the unemployed, and the persons and children, who are being abused, from their pain with extra special favor and care. Hear our prayer, O gracious God.

Lord, show your healing power to those who are afflicted, and rescue them from their sickness. Hear our prayer, O gracious God. Lord, help and guide those people who left the Roman Catholic Church to come home, and let them know you are waiting for them with arms wide open. Hear our prayer, O gracious God.

A Prayer for His Holiness, Pope Francis (Jorge Mario Bergoglio)

At the Sistine Chapel in Vatican City, on March 13, 2013 was the day the College of Cardinals elected Cardinal Jorge Mario Bergoglio as the next Pope of the Roman Catholic Church.

Let us pray for Pope Francis.

For our Pope, Cardinal Jorge Mario Bergoglio, His Holiness, Pope Francis.

O Lord God, look with much favor upon Pope Francis. You have chosen him as the successor of Saint Peter. May you graciously guide him to be a beacon of hope and a shining example of a true disciple of Jesus Christ, and bear much fruit. May you bless and keep him, let your gracious face shine upon him, and grant him continued good health and enduring strength. May you fill him with much compassion, faith, grace, and wisdom. In his position as Supreme Pontiff of the Universal Church, may he tackle in an outstanding manner the duties, responsibilities, and challenges in his daily work. As he shepherds the Lord's flock of over 1.2 billion Catholics worldwide, we pray that he continues to follow in the footsteps of Jesus as the light of Christ for the whole world. May his strong leadership bring back to the fold the parishioners who have left the Catholic Church, let us pray to the Lord. O God, hear our prayer. Amen.

A Prayer for Priests

Almighty God, look with favor upon your priests and have compassion on them. Stir up in them the grace of their chosen vocation. Keep them close to your tender heart. May they remain exemplary priests always. Continue to give them a deep faith and an earnest love to shepherd your flock, light up their lives, and accomplish the demanding duties of their sacred calling. May they proclaim the Gospel, the good news, of faith, hope, peace, joy, and love eloquently. Grant them wisdom in their homilies/preachings that their parishioners will be inspired and be touched, be more cognizant of you, and love you more. Grant them good health so that they may continue to serve you with all their strength, lead your people to your glory, praise the majesty of your name, and love you sincerely and profoundly forever and ever.

May they always follow in the footsteps of Jesus as the light of Christ for the whole world. May their strong leadership bring back to the fold the parishioners who have left the Catholic Church. O God, keep them in your grace and bless them abundantly all the days of their life. Hear our prayer, O God, through Jesus Christ, your Son, our Lord and Savior. Amen.

A Prayer for a Chaplain Going on a Temporary Duty (TDY)

O God, source of all grace and blessing, we ask you to bless especially (mention the name of the priest) who will be going on a Temporary Duty (TDY) on a mission to _____(place where the chaplain is going). Please, keep him safe in all his travels. May he remain an exemplary priest as he has always been, a model of what a good priest should be. Continue to give him a deep faith and an intense love to shepherd your flock, light up their lives, and carry out the demanding duties of his sacred calling. Let him proclaim the Gospel, the good news, of faith, hope, peace, joy, and love. Grant him wisdom in his preachings and homilies. Keep him in your grace and bless him abundantly. O God, may you bless and protect him all the days of his life. Grant him good health so that he may continue to serve you with all his strength, lead your people to your glory, praise the majesty of your name, and love you profoundly forever and ever. O God, hear our prayer through Jesus Christ, your Son, our Lord and Savior. Amen.

A Prayer for All Mothers

O Lord God, we honor all mothers, and we give our thanks and appreciation to you for all mothers whom you have chosen, and have given the glorious gift of motherhood. May their profound love be a sublime inspiration for all of us. O God, grant all mothers the grace, wisdom, and daily enduring strength to carry on their magnitude duty in loving and caring for their children. O Lord God, we ask you to bless and protect all mothers, and free them from harm all the days of their life. May you let your face shine graciously upon them. May you always look upon them favorably, and grant them continued good health, much joy, and peace. Hear our prayer, O God, in the name of Jesus Christ, Your Son, our Lord. Amen.

Mothers are the sweetest and the greatest gift from God to us all. Motherhood is a twenty-four-hour job, but you can't resign, or retire from motherhood. God created a mother to bring enduring joy, endless love, and deep caring into the world!

A Prayer for All Fathers

O Lord God, we give our thanks and appreciation to you for all fathers whom you have chosen, and whom you have given the glorious and great gift of fatherhood! May their profound love be a sublime inspiration for all of us. O God, grant all fathers grace and wisdom, and strengthen them by your enduring love that they may be the loving and caring fathers they are meant to be. Guide and help them to carry on their magnitude duty in taking care of their sons and daughters the best way they can. Let their faith and love be exemplary for their children to emulate. O Lord God, we ask you to bless and protect all fathers, and free them from harm all the days of their life. May you let your face shine graciously upon them. May you always look upon them favorably, and grant them continued good health, much joy, and peace. Hear our prayer, O God, in the name of Jesus Christ, your Son, our Lord. Amen.

A Thanksgiving Prayer

Oremus (Let us pray). Loving and gracious God, we thank you for your countless blessings. On this Thanksgiving Day, we are here before you grateful for your loving mercy and kindness. O God, the giver of all good things, you are the main source of everything we have. May we open our hearts to your absolutely divine love today, and may we give our care and concern for others. May we lead others unto you by our good examples and do all things for your greater glory and for the advancement of your kingdom. May we earnestly serve you and your flock, the people of God. We pray to you, O God, in the name of Jesus Christ, your Son, our Lord. Amen.

On Thanksgiving Day, we thank you, O God, for all the countless blessings you have bestowed upon us:

For the love of God, for the Church, for our faith, we thank you, O God.

For calling us to serve you in our parish, we thank you, O God.

For the gift of life, for every breath and every moment we live, for continued health, strength and energy, for rest. We thank you, O God.

For our home and shelter, for our daily bread, good food, and earthly gifts that make us strong. We thank you, O God.

For successes, achievements, and accomplishments. We thank you, O God.

For safe travels to Europe and back to the U.S.A. We thank you, O God.

For generous gifts - talents, abilities, skills, honors, awards. We thank you, O God.

For entertainment, movies, Broadway musicals, operas, Shakespearean live theatre plays, ballet, concerts, and symphonies. We thank you, O God.

For joys, laughter, charities, and kindnesses. We thank you, O God.

For our nation, for the gift of freedom, for teachers who teach our youth, for educators, and college professors who lead our young people in the pursuit for higher education. We thank you, O God.

For the incredible wonders of creation, for the Sun that gives us warmth, the Moon that gives us light, the bright stars, the galaxy, and the whole Universe, and the gorgeous flowers, abundant trees with luxuriant foliage, vegetable plants and fruits, pristine rivers, lakes, vast seas and oceans, etc. We thank you, O God.

For the times we have helped other people, for the moments we made them happy, and for the times we made a difference in their lives. We thank you, O God.

For the people who inspire and give us wisdom for our enlightenment, and for everything that makes life good to live. We thank you O God.

For struggles, sorrows for the death of our departed loved ones, sicknesses, trials, and sufferings that you have helped us overcome: We thank you, O God.

For our heroes, our military men and women in uniform for their exceptional services and sacrifices for our freedom. We thank you, O God.

For our beloved pets – dogs, horses, cats, birds, monkeys, etc., and for all the animals of the world. We thank you, O God.

For the love of our precious family, treasured relatives, and trusted friends, especially our relatives and friends who brighten our lives, and put smile on our faces. We thank you, O God.

For a blessed, marvelous, and happy THANKSGIVING DAY with much food with all the trimmings on our fine table! We thank you, O Lord God.

The Resplendent God
O God, beyond all adoration,
we bow down and praise you today.
We sing to you a new song,
and let our song be sung from the highest
mountain peak.
O God, we can never thank you enough for
your never-ending mercy.
And every blessings and gifts you send
our way.

O dear, loving, and gracious Savior,
kindly accept the love we give you.
That we may serve you unselfishly as our mighty King;
to wonder at your breathtaking majesty;
and joy in your ways.
And create a glorious sense of duty
our offering of sacrifice of praise and thanksgiving!

Saint Frances Xavier Cabrini

Mother Cabrini was the founder of the Missionary Sisters of the Sacred Heart of Jesus. She had done a lot of good work. She had established schools, an orphanage, and prison ministry. She had also extended her wonderful and humanitarian work not only in the United States, but overseas as well - in Europe and Central and South America. She was the first naturalized American Saint and canonized in Rome on July 7, 1946.

When we toured Chicago, the Windy City, a very fascinating city in 2005, we visited the Sears Tower. On the very top floor, there is a section that features the charitable works of Mother Cabrini. She was a beloved figure in the Chicago area and around the world.

Oremus (Let us pray). O God, may we follow the examples of Saint Mother Frances Xavier Cabrini who had worked tirelessly to serve you gloriously. May we celebrate Jesus' work of boundless charity by the examples of Mother Cabrini. Teach us, O God, to have an intense caring for the sick, the poor, the homeless, and the stranger like Mother Cabrini. Help us to see Jesus Christ in all men and women we meet. May they see Jesus in us. May we be confirmed in our love for you and our neighbors. May we be of service to your people. O God, hear our prayer through your beloved Son Jesus Christ, our Lord and God. Amen.

Our Lady of Mount Carmel

On the celebration of the feast day of Our Lady of Mount Carmel, let us honor Our Lady of Mount Carmel by our prayers.

Oremus (Let us pray). O gracious and loving God, the generous giver of all good things, you have given us the Blessed Virgin Mother Mary as our own mother to pray and intercede for us. She was always the faithful handmaid of the Lord. Through her exemplary obedience and love of you, O God, and her maternal intercession, help us to hear your words. Empower us to love, and serve you loyally like her. Hear our prayer, O God, in the name of Jesus Christ, your Son, our Lord. Amen.

Prayer Before Holy Mass for Those Who Serve at Mass

O gracious and loving Father, we praise you, and we thank you for the many blessings you have bestowed upon us. Thank you for calling us to serve. Help us to make our church a haven of love, faith, hope, and joy. Let us seek to strengthen our church.

May we serve you with all our strength, lead others unto you by our examples, do all things for your greater glory, and for the advancement of your kingdom. May we be true disciples of Jesus and bear much fruit.

O God, show your special care to the poor and the hungry. Make us examples of your compassion, and keep us forever grateful in your loving service.

O God, grant us the grace to let the shimmering light of your everlasting love shine brightly through us all that anyone who sees us may glorify your majestic name.

May you bless us, keep us safe, and protect us from all harm. Grant our prayer, O God, through Jesus Christ, your Son, our Lord. Amen.

> A Grandmother's Prayer
> My Lord and God, look favorably on my two grandsons,
> Logan and Kaleb, so wondrously created,
> wrought together by you from their mother's womb.

Keep them safe everywhere they are,
that no one harms them, free them from trouble,
and any wicked persons who intend to hurt them.

And when life's violent wind and tempest may come,
give these grandsons tranquility,
as on a mother's loving arms and embrace.

In the unknown and mysterious future
that only you know,
grant these grandchildren strong faith for looking ahead,
hope that never dismays
and a safe place always near you.

O God, cherish Logan and Kaleb as the apple of thine eyes.
Grant them wisdom and grace as you have given to Solomon.
We are very grateful for these precious and
treasured gifts, and pray
Logan and Kaleb grow up fine and nifty.
May you bless them to be righteous
and virtuous men. Amen.

This prayer is one of my favorite prayers in praising the Lord God. It is refreshing to pray this prayer from the *Catholic Prayers*. I recommend it to everyone.

Te Deum Laudamus (Thee, God, We Praise)

You are God: we praise you;
You are the Lord: we acclaim you;
You are the eternal Father:
All creation worships you.

To you all angels, all the powers of heaven,
Cherubim and Seraphim, sing in endless praise:
Holy, holy, holy, Lord, God of power and might,
heaven and earth are full of your glory.

The glorious company of apostles praise you.
The noble fellowship of prophets praise you.
The white-robed army of martyrs praise you.

Throughout the world the holy Church acclaims you:
Father, of majesty unbounded,
your true and only Son, worthy of all worship,
and the holy Spirit, advocate and guide.

You Christ, are the king of glory,
the eternal Son of the Father.

When you became man to set us free
you did not spurn the Virgin's womb.

You overcame the sting of death,
and opened the kingdom of heaven to all believers.

You are seated at God's right hand in glory.
We believe that you will come, and be our judge.

Come then, Lord, and help your people,
bought with the price of your own blood,
and bring us with your saints
to glory everlasting.

One of my favorite Psalms in the Holy Bible is Psalm 23. I pray it all the time.
I find it very comforting and uplifting knowing God is there for me especially
during difficult times. From the Holy Bible, here is Psalm 23.

Psalm 23
The Lord is my shepherd; I shall not want.
In verdant pastures He gives me repose;
Beside restful waters He leads me;
he refreshes my soul.

He guides me in right paths
 for His name's sake.
Even though I walk in the dark valley
I fear no evil; for you are at my side
With your rod and your staff
that give me courage.

You spread the table before me
in the sight of my foes;
You anoint my head with oil;
my cup overflows.

Only goodness and kindness follow me
all the days of my life;
And I shall dwell in the house of the Lord
for years to come.

PART VI

The Great Travel Adventures

Anything Under the Sun

Dawn Will Come – A Short Story

The Great Travel Adventures

Saint Augustine said, "The world is a book and those who do not travel read only one page."

I agree with Saint Augustine. Traveling is great! It is fun, exciting, and glorious. It is delightful to visit fascinating and amazing places, especially awe-inspiring and absolutely divine places of worship where pilgrims go and visit. I am writing our travel adventures to inspire, move, invite, and encourage. I have some friends who told me, "I will travel one day. I would like to go to the places you have been. They are in my bucket list. I have learned a lot just listening to you and telling me about your travel experiences." But, they have not traveled yet until now. They keep on waiting and waiting, and it looks like that day will never come. I would like to say, "Please, travel now while you are still healthy and can walk. Don't take too long to decide. Time flies very fast."

Journey with me to the fascinating places we have visited. If you have already visited these places, you can recall the wonderful memories and imagine them beautifully. Remember the splendid time you have spent there. To those who are lingering, perhaps, you will take the necessary steps to take a leap, and make your airline and hotel reservations, and go now, today, the next day, or soon.

Italy

Buon giorno (Good morning/afternoon). The glory that was Rome, the Eternal City, is the capital of Italy. This cosmopolitan city is one of the most visited cities in the world. Vatican City is a small, independent country with the Holy Father, the Pope, as the head of the country. We visited Rome, Vatican City, and several other places in Italy twice, years before and last year in August 2015.

Amo Roma e il Vaticano (I love Rome and the Vatican). The first thing to do when you are in Rome is to take the tour of Rome on the Rome Hop-On Hop-Off sightseeing tour. This bus will take you to the most important tourists' places in the city of Rome.

We toured the following places in Rome and Vatican City:

The Papal Basilica of Saint Peter in the Vatican. It is the largest Roman Catholic Church in the whole world. It is magnificent. You will see the famous dome of Saint Peter and the tomb of Saint Peter, sculptures of many saints, fresco paintings, and much more. We attended Holy Mass in this great Basilica. It was divine.

Remember, the dress code is very strict. No shorts, sleeveless shirts, or miniskirts. If you happen to wear a shirt that bares your shoulders, you can buy a scarf and cover yourself.

The Papal Basilica of Saint Paul Outside the Walls - It is sublime, and it is splendid. In front of the Basilica is the memorial statue of Saint Paul. He is holding a sword and book. All of the popes' pictures are displayed on the wall, in a higher place close to the ceiling. Saint Paul's tomb is in this Basilica. We attended Holy Mass. It was ethereal.

The Papal Basilica of Saint Mary Major - It is another of the four major Basilicas in Rome. It is majestic. It is richly decorated. It is filled with many fine sculptures of saints, fresco and mosaic Christian paintings. The nice painting of the Blessed Virgin Mary and her infant son, Jesus adorned the high altar.

The Papal Archbasilica of Saint John Lateran (Arcibasilica Papale di San Giovanni in Latereno) – This is the Cathedral of Rome. It is the Pope's Cathedral. It is the official Episcopal seat of the Bishop of Rome. His Holiness, the Holy Father, Pope Francis, is the bishop of Rome. This is where the Pope's cathedra is – where his cathedra (chair) symbolizing his teaching authority rests. Constantine, the Great, the first Christian Emperor in Rome, ordered the construction of this Basilica. The design of the structure is Baroque style. The interior is filled with many massive marble statues of saints, exquisite Christian paintings, elegant, huge rich gold color chandeliers, etc.

This cathedral is the earliest in Christendom. It was also the residence of the popes for about a thousand years.

It is dedicated to Saint John the Baptist and Saint John the Evangelist. It is beautiful. We attended Holy Mass in this resplendent Basilica twice. It was enthralling.

The Marble Statues - The more than life-size marble statues of the twelve apostles of Jesus – Saints Peter, Andrew, James the Great, son of Zebedee, John, Matthew, Bartholomew, Thomas, Philip, James, the Less, son of Alphaeus, Thaddeus, Simon, the Zealot, and Matthias in the Papal Archbasilica of Saint John in the Lateran are so huge and marvelous. I stood in front of these statues and wondered in awe how they were curved. Saint Paul also has a more than life-size marble statue in this church.

Capella Sistina - Sistine Chapel in Vatican City - When we arrived in Vatican City to tour the Capella Sistina, the queue was long. Someone approached us and offered the "Skip the Line Tour," if we would tour with his company.

Tom and I took the opportunity. The tour guide took all the tourists who opted for this tour to the back door of the Sistine Chapel. The line for the security check was short. We still had to go through security check. How wonderful it is to have seen the Sistine Chapel for the third time, twice years earlier.

We paid three times more than the cost of regular tickets to skip the line, but it was well worth it. We did not have to be in queue for more than three hours. The tour guide was very knowledgeable. She described in detail to us all the things we were seeing.

The picture gallery was breathtaking, and the many exquisite paintings, tapestries, statues from antiquity, the frescoes, etc. are astounding and majestic. The tour guide said Michelangelo never wanted to paint the Sistine Chapel, but the Pope at that time wanted Michelangelo to do it; if Michelangelo did not come to Rome to do the work, he would wage a war against Florence (Michelangelo was a resident of Florence). Reluctantly, Michelangelo went to Rome to do it. It took him more than two years to complete the painting on the ceiling of the Sistine Chapel. He did fresco painting. It was a very difficult process – using sketches, heat, glasses, etc. The tour guide said Michelangelo painted the ceiling standing up! Not lying down, as I thought!

The Scala Santa - The Holy Stairs - According to the tour guide, Jesus Christ climbed these steps when he was interrogated by Pontius Pilate. There is a small, but beautiful, chapel on the right side above the steps. I prayed for my family, relatives, friends, classmates, students, town mates, former co-workers, supervisors, and directors.

The Pantheon - It is a Roman temple. When Christianity became the official religion of the Roman Empire, it was converted to a Roman Catholic Church dedicated to the martyred saints. I prayed in front of the main altar.

Basilica di San Pietro in Vincoli (Saint Peter's Basilica in Vincoli) - There is a big statue of Moses in this church curved by Michelangelo. I enjoyed looking meticulously at the marble statue of Moses.

Mamertine Prison - Saints Peter and Paul were imprisoned in this prison.

The Trevi Fountain - The fountain was initiated by Pope Clement XII. In the center of the fountain is an impressively carved marble statue of the Greek sea god, Oceanus, riding in a sea-chariot pulled by two Tritons. The basin below symbolizes the sea.

The legend says if visitors throw a coin over their left shoulder into the water, they are guaranteed a return to Rome. When I was in Rome for the first time a few years ago, I threw a coin over my left shoulder into the water. I returned to Rome for the second time last August 2015, so the legend must be true. I enjoyed our stay for the second time. The fountain is the largest Baroque fountain, and the most beautiful in the world.

There are about 3,000 euros (coins) thrown into the fountain every day.

Remember the movie "Three Coins in the Fountain?" Some of the scenes in the movie were filmed near the world-renowned Trevi fountain.

I sat near the fountain, paused, reflected, and relaxed. I enjoyed looking at the awesome Trevi Fountain and watched the world go. I was feeling dazzled and ecstatic by the beauty and wonder of it all.

The Roman Soldier - Near the Trevi Fountain, there was a man who was nicely dressed as a Roman soldier. He asked me if I would like a picture taken with him for five euros; that is equivalent to $6.35 American dollars. Tom encouraged me to have a picture taken with him. So, I did. After the first picture, this Roman guy told me to put the plastic sword on his neck and, in broken English, to kill him. I put the plastic sword on his neck and pretended I was stabbing him. He pretended he got stabbed and was dying. I paid him ten euros, equivalent to $12.70, for the two pictures he posed with me. That was one of the fun experiences near the Trevi Fountain. That was all right; he was earning an honest living.

Villa Borghese - We walked a long way to get to the Villa Borghese to see the museums and attractions. Pauline Bonaparte, the sister of Napoleon Bonaparte, married Prince Camille Borghese and lived in the Villa Borghese. The Galleria Borghese is an art gallery. Exhibited in the spacious galleries are abundant collections of precious works of art, such as sculptures, paintings, etc. There is an awesome sculpture of Pauline Bonaparte reclining on a chair in the gallery. She was half naked. It is a fascinating place to visit in Rome. And oh, the vast gardens are dazzling and spectacular.

The Castel Sant' Angelo (Castle of the Holy Angel) - It is a towering building in Rome. The bronze statue of Saint Michael, the Archangel, stands on the roof of the Castel Sant'Angelo. It has been a prison and the residence of many popes. There is a passage that links to the Vatican for the pope to escape in case of trouble or invasion.

Vittorio Emanuele II Monument, Rome - One of the most important landmarks in Piazza Venezia is the Victor Emmanuel II Monument. Tom and I toured this astonishing landmark dedicated to King Victor Emmanuel II, the first king of Italy, twice. He was the King of Sardinia and became the first king of a united Italy. It is a white marble monument. From this place, you can walk to more fascinating and tourists' places to visit such as the Roman Forum, the Pantheon, and the Capitoline Hill. We got on the elevator that took us to the higher story of the building. What a magical experience! We could see the aerial view of Rome.

The National Roman Museum - Sculptures, frescoes, and mosaics, coins, precious jewels and unique gems, portraits etc. are housed in this museum. There are plenty of marble statues, including that of Julius Caesar, etc.

In Rome, we kept touring till we dropped dead. I was so tired, and, in this place, I accidentally backed up on the statue of Julius Caesar and almost fell on it. That statue is priceless. Thank God nothing bad happened to the statue. Tom told me to be very careful, that I might be put in jail! God is kind. I was fine, and so was the statue of Julius Caesar!

The Capitoline Museum - The Capitoline Museum is in the heart of Rome in the Piazza del Campidoglio on Capitoline Hill. It was great to have visited this museum for the second time. There was an exhibition when we visited the museum. On exhibits are the busts of several Roman emperors such as Constantine, Augustus, Tiberius, Hadrian, Nero, Marcus Aurelius, et al.

More collections are a sculpture of Romulus and Remus, legendary founders of Rome being nursed by a wolf, the Dying Gaul, etc. The picture gallery includes masterpieces of Tintoretto, Titian, Caravaggio, and Rubens, et al.

I took a picture of the bronze statue of Constantine, the first Christian Emperor of Rome, displayed in this museum. His mother, Saint Helena, was a devout Christian.

The Roman Forum and Imperial Fora - It displays a collection of historical monuments – temples and tombs of past emperors, etc., including Julius Caesar. Julius Caesar's tomb is in the Roman Forum. It was the center of politics and business during that time. The tourists can see many ruins of ancient government buildings. There are sculptures of Vestal Virgins guarding the eternal flame.

Piazza del Popolo - It is the Square of the People. The Santa Maria del Popolo Church is beautiful. There is an obelisk in the piazza and some statues.

Piazza Colonna - Piazza Colonna is in the historic heart of Rome in Italy. The Palazzo Chigi, the official residence of the prime minister of Italy is in this square. In the centre of the square, there is a tall obelisk Colonna di Marco Aurelio with the statue of Marco Aurelio (Marcus Aurelius) that was on top of the obelisk as an honor to him for his military victories. The bronze statue of Saint Paul replaced the statue of Marcus Aurelius in 1589 by order of Pope Sixtus V.

Tom, my spouse, told me to pose for a picture with two young Italian men, members of the Italian Polizia who were guarding Piazza Colonna, the political centre in Roma. They were handsome, suave, and dashing young men. They looked chivalrous. I think they were. They were very polite and posed for a picture with me.

We walked a little bit further and found the Italian Parliament. It was a colossal building and impressive. Politics, government matters, etc. are conducted in the Parliament.

The Colosseum - Another name for the Colosseum is the Flavian Amphitheatre. It was a place for entertainment such as gladiatorial combats and animal fights. The arena was spectacular and huge. It was an amazing building. Nearby is the Arch of Constantine.

Today, the Colosseum is one of Rome's most popular tourists' attractions. Millions of visitors come to Rome to see this Amphitheatre. Approximately, forty billion lire ($19.3 million) was spent for the restoration of this building. The windows on the top level are provided for tourists to see the beautiful view of the City of Rome.

Piazza di Spagna - It is one of the most popular squares in Rome. The church of the Santissima Trinita Dei Monti (Most Holy Trinity of the Mountains) is at the top of the Spanish steps. It is another beautiful church in Rome. In line in front of the Fontana della Barcaccia were many people cooling themselves by taking the water from the fountain and putting it all over their faces and necks. It was very hot in Rome on that day. A man, a stranger, gave me a beautiful red rose. I did not want to take it. I was surprised. Tom told me to take it and smile, so I did. Then, he asked some money from Tom. Tom gave him some euros.

I went shopping at the Christian Dior Store in Piazza Di Spagna. I found a beautiful dress for 5,000 euros. I did not buy it. It was too much to spend that kind of money for a dress. Look at how many poor people you can feed with that money for one dress. I bought a pair of Christian Dior sunglasses.

The pretty mannequin in the dress department of the Christian Dior store revealed the epitome of sophistication, class, elegance and good taste. Everything in this store is elegant and beautiful. The fabulous designer dresses, blazers, shirts, skirts, pants, and evening gowns on display made me think of my artistic and very talented Momma. She made dresses as beautiful as the ones on display in this designer store. Her creative work is truly splendid.

The architectural style of the Piazza di Spagna is Roman Baroque with an impressive butterfly plan. The Fontana della Barcaccia was designed by Bernini and his son Gian Lorenzo.

Tourists can find impressive and attractive stores that carry big name designers such as Dolce & Gabbana, Christian Dior, etc. in the Piazza di Spagna. They are trendy. The Spanish Embassy is nearby. In this place are elegant hotels and residences.

Piazza Barberini - We took a stroll in the Piazza Barberini. It was just fun.

Via Veneto - We took a stroll in Via Veneto. It is one of the most expensive, luxurious, and elegant streets in Rome. It is the ritzy part of the city of Rome. We saw the United States Embassy. I told Tom if we ever lose our passports, that is where we go. When I am abroad and I see a U.S. Embassy, I always feel a sense of security there are some people who could take care of us in case we need help.

We visited the Palatine Hill, Janiculum Hill, the Circus Maximus, and the Roman baths.

The Best Western Hotel President – Roma, Italia. Address: Via Emanuele Filiberto, 173-00185, Roma, Italia

In Rome, we stayed at the Best Western Hotel President. It is a very nice and comfortable four-star hotel. The suites offer free Wi-Fi and a large, flat screen TV. There was a refrigerator in the room filled with soft drinks and beer. You'd pay for the soft drinks if you need a drink. Coffee and tea are provided. There was a coffee maker the guests could use. A table, sofa, chairs, and another rectangular table for suitcases were in the room. There was a twenty-four-hour room service. Laundry was also available. Other amenities included a lounge bar and massage services. The lounge bar was also a restaurant that served Italian food for dinner. We dined there often and savored superb Italian food - food to die for.

This hotel was in walking distance to the Holy Stairs, The Papal Archbasilica of Saint John Lateran, and the Colosseum.

The hotel also provided scrumptious breakfast. It was a brunch (combination of breakfast and lunch). It was included with the cost of the suite. There was so much food served for breakfast – hams, salamis, sausages, beef, boiled and scrambled eggs, different kinds of cereals, cakes, croissants, tiramisu, cheeses, various kinds of fresh bread, variety of fruits, several kinds of marmalades, soft rice, veggies, fruit juices, coffee, English tea, milk, chocolate milk, etc.

Someone knocked at the door one day, and when I opened it, there was a young man giving me a basket of fruits – bananas, apples, oranges, and pears. He said they are courtesy by the hotel. How sweet of the people managing the hotel!

The members of the hotel staff were extremely friendly and courteous, especially a nice guy named Ubaldo. When I thanked him for helping me with my needs, he kissed my hand. What a fine gentleman! He was a knight in shining armor! I blew him a kiss when we finally left the hotel for a trip to Pisa to see the Leaning Tower of Pisa, etc.

Everyone at this hotel was so polite, and they addressed me as "Madam" all the time. I promised Ubaldo I would recommend this hotel, the Best Western Hotel President, Via Emanuele Filiberto, 173-00185, Roma, Italia, to everybody.

The Ristorante at the Presidente Hotel - Part of the fun in traveling to foreign countries on vacation is sampling the best food in the world and trying various kinds of food. At the restaurant of the Presidente Hotel in Roma, I sampled Roman food. One night, I had a Roman meal, Pollo alla Romana (Roman-Style Chicken) - chicken leg and thigh with red sauce, small purple potatoes, yellow bell peppers, carrots, purple cabbage, endive, cherry tomatoes, and green veggies. The dinner was superb – a meal to die for. One day, the taxi driver told me to try Carbonara (pasta noodles) with tomato sauce, cheese, etc., so I did. The sauce was very delicious. I savored the food and ate slowly, so I could taste it better. I loved the tiramisu, one of the most delicious desserts in the world. It is rich and creamy. There were times when I closed my eyes while eating to concentrate on the taste. Thank God for the blessing of good food.

Italia (Italy) has it all. Fine culture, incredible history, and sumptuous food to die for. Italian food is the envy of the world. Several restaurants in Italy provide gastronomic specialties that are memorable.

When you are in Europe, and you would like to ask for a jelly, say you would like marmalade. They know marmalade better than jelly. If you would like a Kleenex, say "tissue."

La vita e bella. (Life is beautiful). Thank God for the blessings we returned to Rome for the second time. Tom was born on 22 July, and I was born on 30 August. The second trip to Rome, Vatican, etc. was a birthday present from the Lord God. I paused, prayed, and reflected on the kindness of God to us.

We visited more places in Italy that are frequented by tourists:

Tivoli - We took the excursion to Tivoli and visited several ruins of Emperor Hadrian's Villa. He preferred Tivoli. This is a large Roman archaeological site. The buildings cannot be destroyed or modified. They can only be repaired to preserve the complex. This place is a World Heritage of the United Nations Educational, Scientific and Cultural Organization (UNESCO). It was a long walking tour. We kept walking from one place to the other to see the whole complex. The tour guide said walking was the only way to tour this site.

The compound had several more buildings for the members of his family and the many staff and workers of the emperor. Tivoli has a cooler climate than Rome. Many affluent Romans have summer residences in Tivoli. Then, the bus driver and tour guide took us to Villa d'Este. There were a hundred dazzling and beautiful fountains, gorgeous, and elaborate gardens in the Villa d'Este. The lovely grottoes, water sculptures, and nymphs abound in the world-renowned and awesome gardens.

Assisi, Umbria, Italy - In Assisi, we toured the Basilica of Saint Francis of Assisi. The tour guide told us the story of Saint Francis, the founder of the Franciscan Order and the construction of the church. The medieval arts on display were splendid. It was so great that when we arrived, a mass was being celebrated, so we were able to attend. We received Holy Communion.

Naples, a big city in southern Italy is on the Bay of Naples. The significant landmark is the Naples Cathedral. We enjoyed the historic center of Naples. The buildings have shops and apartments that are unique. Sophia Loren, the famous Italian actress used to live in the neighboring town of Puzzuoli.

Capri - We boarded a big boat in Naples that took us to the island of Capri. This is an island paradise, an enchanting place. According to the tour guide, Roman Emperor Tiberius loved Capri. He lived in Capri, and he had beautiful villas in Capri. The driver of the tour bus took us to Anacapri located at a much higher elevation. We stepped out of the bus to see the panoramic view. It was breathtaking! It was a beautiful sight to behold. We could see the vast sea, the many boats, the harbor, the pristine meadow, the lush trees, the villas, and the breathtaking beauty of nature. The scene was totally astonishing and fabulous. You can just marvel at the creations of God.

I went to Capri because I read an advertisement about a stunning model, a woman who went to Capri. She said she went to Capri and never returned.

I would like to find out why this sophisticated lady never came back to her home. Now, I know why. I saw why. She was totally captivated by the place and made it her permanent home.

This place is trendy. Designer clothes, purses, bags, shoes, sunglasses, etc. - merchandise by famous designers such as Christian Dior, Gucci, Versace, Louis Vuitton, Chanel, et al are abundant in Capri. Seeing the Blue Madonna was another highlight of the tour in Capri. Amo Capri (I love Capri).

Sorrento - We visited this coastal town in southwestern Italy. The Sorrentine coastline was captivating. The tour guide took us to a store that made beautiful jewelries. They had a Cameo jewelry sale. Cameo jewelries are exquisite and delicately made. My husband Tom was very kind. He encouraged me to buy a Cameo necklace, but I declined. I did not need it. I have enough. I also inherited a lot of jewelries from my Momma Librada.

Pompeii - We explored Pompeii. It was very hot when we got there. When Mount Vesuvius, a volcano erupted in the year 79 A.D., this ancient Roman city of Pompeii was terribly buried with volcanic ashes. We looked at the replicas of the people who died. There was a man sitting down and covering his eyes. The others were trying to shield their faces and their bodies. The eruption was indeed catastrophic. It must have been painful to have perished that way!

Mt. Vesuvius is still an active volcano. When we were there, my husband, Tom teased and told me the volcano would erupt. YAY! It didn't! I prayed it would never erupt again!

Firenze (Florence) in Italy

Florence, the capital of Italia's Tuscany Region, is the birthplace of the Renaissance. It is known as the "Renaissance City." It is in the Tuscany Region. Florence is home to abundant masterpieces of exquisite arts and marvelous architectures. It is a very enchanting city.

We visited the following tourists' places in Florence:

Galleria dell'Accademia - We visited the Galleria dell'Accademia in Florence. It is an art museum. The marble statue of David is housed in this museum. It is the original statue of David by Michelangelo. The sculpture of David is amazing. It is a wonder how Michelangelo curved it in such a way that anyone who sees the figure - his body, the head, face, eyes, nose, lips, curly hair, veins in his body, arms, and feet will have a lasting impression and will leave an indelible mark on their mind. The image will linger on for quite a while long after they have seen this incredible sculpture. The tour guide said the highest compliment you can give an Italian man is to compare him to David. There is a replica of the statue of David outdoor in the Piazza della Signoria.

Some of the works on display at the Galleria dell'Accademia are by Sandro Boticelli, Domenico Ghirlando, et al. There is an amount of Florentine Gothic paintings in the collection in this museum.

Basilica di Santa Croce (Basilica of the Holy Cross) in Florence - It is one of the most famous landmarks in Florence. It is a Franciscan church of worship. It is magnificent and strikingly beautiful.

The Florence Baptistery - It is called the Baptistery of Saint John. It is one of the oldest buildings in the city.

Loggia dei Lanzi or Loggia della Signoria in Florence. It is made up of wide arches. Renaissance and Gothic architectures are the architectural styles of this open building. This sculpture gallery consists of several Renaissance arts.

Pisa in Italy - In Pisa, we visited the following:

We hopped on a horse-drawn cart, and the tour guide took us around the City of Pisa. He took us to the highlights of the city – the Piazza dei Miracoli, Piazza del Duomo, downtown Pisa, the home of Galileo Galilei, Italian astronomer, physicist, engineer, philosopher, and mathematician, the church where Galileo presented his invention, the telescope, the university where he studied, oldest buildings, the nice stores, busy shopping places, historical landmarks, and many more.

Piazza dei Miracoli (Square of Miracles). It is splendid. It is crowded with many tourists. In the Piazza dei Miracoli are the Leaning Tower of Pisa, Cathedral of Pisa, Baptistery of Pisa, Museum of Sinopie, Monumental Churchyard, and the Museum of the Cathedral.

The Leaning Tower of Pisa - It is a campanile, a bell tower in Pisa in Italy. It is resplendent. Many tourists flock to Pisa to visit the Leaning Tower of Pisa. The incline is what makes this tower one of the most favorites of tourists around the world. The Italian government spent several million liras to fix the tower to save it from leaning further.

Tom and I chickened out. We did not climb the more than 265 steps! No elevator! I got my euros back. I returned the tickets after I found out there was no elevator.

The Abitalia Tower Plaza Hotel in Pisa, Italia.

In Pisa, we stayed at the Abitalia Tower Plaza Hotel. When we got in our room, I put on the computer/TV. A welcome statement appeared on TV: BENVENUTO WOODRING OFELIA (WELCOME WOODRING OFELIA). How cool. The Abitalia Tower Plaza Hotel is a five-star hotel. It is described as a luxury and elegant hotel with lots of amenities, nice, spacious, and clean rooms, beautiful bedsheets, pretty lamps, a computer and TV, fridge with sodas, juices, beer, large swimming pool with whirlpool zone, relax room with Turkish bath, comfortable shower, massage room, and exercise facilities, etc. Near the swimming pool is a solarium conveniently provided for guests who wish to have lunch or dinner. The hotel is popular for hosting business conferences.

The lobby was magnificent, richly decorated, and there was a grand piano. The dining area was elegant, and the bar was neat. The dining area served five-course meals for dinner. The breakfast was included with the cost of the room. There was so much food served for breakfast – meat – hams, salamis, sausages, beef, boiled and scrambled eggs, cereals, cakes, croissants, tiramisu, cheeses, various kinds of bread, fruits, several kinds of marmalades, fruit juices, coffee, English tea, milk, chocolate milk, etc. Breakfast is a brunch (a combination of breakfast/lunch).

The elegant and luxurious dining room at the Abitalia Tower Plaza Hotel is a five-star restaurant that offers a five-course-dinner every night at 7:00 P.M. During dinner, I often ordered the Mediterranean diet of fish cooked in olive oil, marinated olives, veggies – squash pilaf, eggplants, or protein-rich legumes. Some beans with cumin and herbs, fruits, and whole grain are good as well. The food is superb and heart-healthy. You are less likely to develop high blood pressure and high cholesterol, if you prefer a Mediterranean meal. Olive oil is very good for the heart. Most Europeans prefer Mediterranean meals.

It is a nice accommodation Jan B., the American Automobile Association travel agent, has reserved for us. She took care of us very well. I gave her the number of my Master Card visa, and she paid for all the airline tickets, train fees, and hotel reservations. I wrote a nice letter to Jan's supervisor, praising Jan, and told her what a great employee and asset she has in her company.

Thank God for this five-star hotel. I truly enjoyed staying here. If you plan to visit the Leaning Tower of Pisa, I recommend this cozy and elegant hotel.

Living la dolce vita (Living the sweet life) in Roma, eh. It is God's blessings. I prayed, paused, and reflected on the many blessings God has bestowed on me and Tom.

The Eurostar. The Eurostar train is a high-speed railway transport service in Europe. The travel agent who arranged our private trip told me it is a luxury, elegant, and a first-class train in Europe.

She said to me, "You will be traveling in style on this train." Oh, well, whatever the travel agent said. She is nice.

We boarded the Eurostar train from Rome to Venice. It was indeed a comfortable ride. It took four hours from Rome to get to the City of Venice. We had lunch on the train. I savored bow tie pasta. It was superb. The bowtie noodles are beautifully made. They would make a stylish decoration in your kitchen. Italian food is one of the best cuisines in the world. I read that Sophia Loren, the world-renowned Italian actress, is a gourmet cook. The attendants on the train were well-dressed. They were courteous, stylish, and very well-groomed.

We met an Italian Admiral, his wife, and granddaughter on the Eurostar train. He was stationed in the U.S.A. for a few years. We socialized with them, and they invited us to visit them, if we would return to Italy again. We correspond with them.

Venice, the Floating City in Italy. We toured the following in Venice:
The Basilica of Saint Mark - The style is Italian gothic and byzantine architecture. Saint Mark's Basilica is splendid. It is a masterpiece!

Piazza San Marco (Saint Mark's Square) in Venezia (Venice) – Italia (Italy) – It is a resplendent square, a place to relax, take a deep breath, and calm down.

The Doge's Palace. It was the seat of the government of Venice for many centuries. It is the residence of the Doge, the ruler of Venice. We toured the gothic-style palace and museum. Art works - many paintings abound in the palace. It is fascinating how these artworks were created.

Ponte dei Sospiri or Bridge of Sighs - The world-renowned Ponte dei Sospiri or Bridge of Sighs – A popular legend says if lovers kiss under the bridge when drifting below on a gondola (boat) at sunset, they will truly have an everlasting love. The sighs are said to come from the beguiling lovers who are deeply engulfed by the panoramic and romantic scene.

In romantic Venice, we took the gondola ride. It brought us to the canals of Venice. When we got under the Bridge of Sighs, we forgot to kiss. I guess we were just overwhelmed by the enchantment and splendor of it all.

We boarded a bigger boat and went on a cruise – We went on a cruise in the Grand Canal, a popular canal with water taxis. We saw classical buildings. The Rialto Bridge was incredible.

It was delightful cruising in the Grand Canal, and other major canals in Venice. I did not see any cars in Venice.

Gallerie dell'Accademia in Venice - This museum contains a vast collection of Venetian paintings and works of art, such as religious and Christian paintings. Christianity was also spread through works of art. The works of the Renaissance artists on display were done by Bellini, Veronese, Tintoretti, Tiziano, Giorgione, et al.

Piazza San Marco (Saint Marks Square) - It is said Napoleon Bonaparte called this square as the drawing room of Europe. I love Venice, the Floating City. It was refreshing and relaxing watching the band at the Piazza San Marco while they played "Solamente Una Vez" (Only One Time). They also played arias such as "Torna A Surriento" (Return to Sorrento), "Granada" (Granada – a place in Italy), "E lucevan le stele" (And the stars were shining, an aria in the opera Tosca), etc. I love these arias. The gorgeous melodies are soothing and rejuvenating for the mind and heart. I was totally captivated by the melodies, and I felt spellbound. I love the classics! Bella! (Beautiful!)

The Saint Mark's Campanile (The Bell Tower of Saint Mark's) Basilica. It is one of the most famous landmarks of the city. It is in the Saint Mark's Square. The belfry shows the Lion of Saint Mark. We took the elevator that brought us to the top of the tower. We could see the whole City of Venice. It was astounding. I paused and reflected, thinking of the magnificence of God in the beauty all around me.

Come sta? Come va la vita? Bene? (How are you? How is life? Fine?)

Arrivederci Italia. It was time to move on and fly to France.

France

J'aime Paris (I love Paris). Bonjour (Good morning/Good afternoon) - In the fabulous country of France, we toured Paris, Versailles, and Lourdes in France. We visited the following places:

The first thing to do in Paris, the City of Lights, is explore the city by buying a bus ticket to get on the Paris Hop-On Hop-Off Bus Tour. This tour

The Five Star Abitalia Tower Plaza Hotel in Pisa, Italy

Inside the Abitalia Tower Plaza Hotel in Pisa, Italy

The Leaning Tower of Pisa in Pisa, Italy

The Trevi Fountain in Rome, Italy

At the Christian Dior Department Store near the Piazza di Spagna, Rome, Italy

The Papal Basilica of Saint Mary Major in Rome, Italy

The Bocca della Verita (Mouth of Truth)
at the Basilica of Saint Mary in Cosmedin, Rome, Italy

will take you around Paris and tell you the highlights of the city that are a must to see and are frequented by tourists.

Notre-Dame (Our Lady) Cathedral in Paris - It is a historic Roman Catholic Cathedral in the heart of the city. It is one of the most exquisite of French Gothic architecture. It is also one of the largest and famous churches in the world. The church contains many works of art - amazing sculptures, stunning stained glass windows, and many side altars. The reliquary in the cathedral precious treasure contains some of the most significant relics of Catholicism.

At the Notre Dame Cathedral, I had a picture taken in front of the statue of Saint Joan of Arc with my hands clasped together in prayer. Joan of Arc was the Maid of Orleans. She was a heroine of France during the Lancastrian phase of the Hundred Years' War. She fought for France. To make a long story short, in the end, she was captured. She was turned over to church officials. She was charged with witchcraft, heresy, and dressing like a man. She was burnt at the stake. She was only nineteen years old.

Years later, a thorough investigation of Joan's death was conducted. She was cleared of all charges. She was innocent. She was praised as a martyr. She was canonized as a Roman Catholic saint.

In front of the Notre Dame Cathedral is the Equestrian Statue of Charlemagne. I looked at the amazing statue meticulously. He was King of the Franks and Emperor of the Romans. At the Vatican, Pope Leo III crowned him as head of the Holy Roman Empire on December 25, 800. He was one of the most important leaders of Europe.

How wonderful it is I celebrated my birthday last 30 August 2015 attending Holy Mass in Notre-Dame Cathedral in Paris. The trip was my birthday present from the Lord God. I prayed, paused, and reflected on the gift of life God continues to bless me and the members of my family. I thanked God many times, and I am eternally grateful!

Tourists from around the world flock to see the Notre-Dame Cathedral in Paris. I was so happy I toured the church three times trying to remember the many mystical things I have seen.

La Basilique du Sacre Coeur de Montmarte (The Basilica of Sacred Heart in Montmarte) – Paris. It is sublime. The church is dedicated to the Sacred Heart of Jesus Christ. I was ecstatic feeling God's presence when I attended Holy Mass and toured the church.

The funicular carried us passengers to the foot of the hill to reach Sacre Coeur. There are about 300 steps to climb to get to the church.

Eglise de la Sainte-Trinite (Church of the Holy Trinity) is another Roman Catholic Church we visited in Paris. On the last day, we were in Paris before returning to the U.S.A., this was the last church we visited. It was magnificent like the other churches we had seen, just a little smaller.

The Eiffel Tower in Paris - This is an engineering and an architectural wonder.

We arrived early in the morning and got in queue for security check. No knives, scissors, sharp objects, etc. were allowed. After getting our tickets, we got in queue for the elevator ride. The elevator took us to the top level, but we had to take another elevator to get to the very top of the tower. Once we got to the very peak, it was breathtaking. I enjoyed being at the top of the Eiffel Tower looking at the breathtaking and panoramic views all over Paris. It was astonishing how the engineers and architects had built such a stunning and awesome landmark. We could see the panoramic and spectacular views overlooking the Trocadero part of Paris. We could also see the River Seine, high hotels, skyscrapers, and other landmarks. Euphoria filled my heart and mind, thanking God for this awesome blessing I was there at the top of the Eiffel Tower. I paused and reflected on the blessings of God.

The Eiffel Tower is resplendent, and it is world-renowned. It is one of the famous landmarks in Paris. It was named after the engineer Alexandre Gustave Eiffel. His company designed and built the tower. The tower is 1,063 ft. tall. It is the tallest building in Paris. It is a much-visited place. Many people flock to Paris every year to see this wonder.

The tower has three levels with restaurants on the first and second level. The Alain Soulard's 58 Tour Eiffel restaurant is elegant. The third level is the observatory's higher platform. The food in the restaurants is sumptuous. When you are touring, dining in elegant restaurants is all right. Sampling and savoring superb food in various countries in Europe is a part of the adventure and fun.

In the evening, when all the lights of the Eiffel Tower are on, it is magical, sensational, enchanting, and spectacular. It is a very romantic scene. I thought I saw an abundance of gold glittering and illuminating the nocturne scene.

Paris is known as a romantic city. Many men take their brides to Paris and propose in the City of Lights. How romantic, eh?

Jardin des Tuileries (The Tuileries Garden) – Paris. I had a picture taken in the carousel at the Tuileries Garden in Paris. Catherine de Medici created the garden. It was the garden of the Tuileries Palace in 1564. After the French Revolution, it became a public park. There are so many dazzling statues curved by famous artists, fountains, several fabulous flower gardens, lush trees, and many more. It is a humongous place to walk and walk!

The River Seine Cruise - Touring more of Paris via the River Seine Cruise - From the dock, we boarded a boat and saw more of the tourist spots in Paris.

It was a guided tour through the very heart of historical Paris. It shows the beautiful banks of the Seine, the Eiffel Tower, the Louvre, the Notre Dame Cathedral, bridges, several other Paris landmarks along the banks of the river. A Seine cruise gives a calm and relaxing way to tour Paris sitting down comfortably on a chair without having to walk a lot. You can gaze at the marvelous architectures and splendid city views of Paris, including the busy and crowded café lined boulevard, and promenade along the way as well.

Mom and I took the cruise when I took her on a nice European tour a few years earlier. I miss my mom, and I wish she was here with me at this very moment. She was my security blanket. We were always together just about everywhere we went.

Les Invalides – Paris, France - Les Invalides, or L'Hotel des Invalides is made up of a set of buildings built by King Louis XIV. It has museums and monuments about the military history of France.

It was also a hospital and a home for injured war veterans. The Musee de l'Armee, the military museum of the Army of France, the Musee d'Histoire Contemporaine and the Dome des Invalides are in this building complex. Marvelous!

Napoleon's Dome, Paris - Napoleon Bonaparte's tomb is in the Napoleon's Dome. His casket is big and in the middle of a circular structure. There are several life-size sculptures around the circle.

According to the tour guide, Napoleon passed away on the island of Saint Helena. He had been in exile since 1815. Years later, his body was transferred to Napoleon's Dome. The greatest conqueror of much of Europe met his crushing defeat in the Battle of Waterloo.

La Musee du Louvre (The Louvre Museum), Paris - The Louvre is a royal palace, the home of King Louis XIV. What an incredible, grandiose, and spectacular tourist attraction. Later, the King moved to Versailles. I toured the Louvre Museum before with my mom when I took her on a tour of Europe.

Tom and I chose the skip the line guided tour to see the Louvre Museum. It costs three times the cost of regular tickets, but it was well worth it. We did not have to stay in queue for more than two hours at least. Having a tour guide with us after the security check, we just followed the guide and the tour began.

According to the petite and pretty young French lady tour guide, the Louvre Museum houses more than 380,000 objects and displays 35,000 works of art in eight curatorial departments. The Louvre exhibits are exquisite paintings, sketches/drawings, and archaeological discoveries. It is the most visited museum in the world, 8.6 million visitors in 2015. Masterpieces on display are works by Michelangelo, Raphael, Leonardo da Vinci, Caravaggio, Delacroix, Peter Paul Rubens, Paolo Veronese, Johannes Vermeer, Hieronymus Bosch, and many, many more.

Venus de Milo—at the Louvre, it was nice to see Venus de Milo for the second time. It is a famous sculpture. The tour guide said it was an ancient Greek statue known as Aphrodite of Milos. Aphrodite is the Greek goddess of love and beauty. In Roman mythology, she is Venus. It is made of marble. The arms were lost when it was found. It was found in the Greek island of Milos, and named Venus de Milo (Venus of Milo).

There were so many people taking pictures of this statue. Figure out for yourself why many tourists flock to the Louvre Museum to see this statue, eh? My own opinion is it's a radiantly stunning work of art. It is incredible. In the English language, figures of speech – personification - to personify the statue, Venus de Milo is a strikingly beautiful and captivating maiden. There is something mystical about her.

Winged Victory of Samothrace - It was also nice that I got to see the "Winged Victory of Samothrace," another world-famous sculpture for the second time. It is a Hellinistic sculpture of Nike, the Greek goddess of strength and victory. It is made of marble.

Mona Lisa - At the Louvre Museum, there were many people crowding the painting of Mona Lisa by Leonardo da Vinci. The tour guide said the Mona Lisa painting was a request from Francesco del Giocondo, a close friend of Leonardo. Francesco asked Leonardo to paint his wife, Lisa

Gherardini del Giocondo. Leonardo obliged and did the painting, but when it was completed, he never gave it to his friend. He kept it. The Mona Lisa is world famous, the most visited, and the most talked about lady in the world. Several lovely songs were written about her. The painting is now the property of the French Republic. It is on permanent exhibit at the Musee du Louvre.

What is the fascination about this acclaimed portrait? There is something mysterious and magical about this painting. They say if you look at Mona Lisa's eyes and walk away slowly, her eyes seem to follow and tell you, "Hey, I know all about you."

I focused my eyes on her eyes and slowly walked away, and yes, indeed, it seemed like her eyes were following me.

Is it unfathomable, or enigmatic? Yes, indeed, go for it, and see this most famous painting, and experience the thrill of seeing Mona Lisa (La Giocondo)!

Mom and I visited the museum years earlier, and we did the same thing; looked at Mona Lisa's eyes and experienced the mystery. I truly enjoyed the first and second visit at the Louvre. I told Tom to look at Mona Lisa's eyes to experience the magic, if her eyes were following him.

Many religious paintings, such as the "Nativity of Jesus," the "Passion of Jesus," his life, etc., the Blessed Virgin Mary, the saints, and Biblical stories, abound in the picture gallery. One of my favorite paintings is the life-size painting of the "Wedding at Cana" by Paolo Veronese. I was able to take a picture and captured the merriments at a wedding.

Jesus was a guest sitting in the middle of a large table. The wine ran out. Jesus' mother told him there was no more wine. It was the first time He performed a miracle, converting water into wine. The head waiter tasted the water, made wine, and did not know where it came from - John 2:3, 5, 7a, 9.

I paused and reflected on the beginning of the many miracles of Jesus.

The stunning glass pyramid in the front of the Louvre was designed by Chinese architect I.M. Pei, and was finished in 1989. I am a museum buff (enthusiast). Everywhere I went, visiting historical and art museums are a must-to see. It is essential for me.

The Place de la Concorde (The Place of Peace), Paris - The Place de la Concorde is one of the main public squares in Paris, France. During the French Revolution, this place was given a new name – Place de la Revolution. Many people were beheaded in this square.

The tour guide said after the bloody French Revolution, this place was renamed Place de la Concorde – Place of Peace – as a manifestation of peace and reconciliation.

The Parlement Francais (French Parliament) in Paris – The architecture of the building is impressive. Tom took a picture of me in front of the Senat (Senate) building.

The Musee d'Orsay, Paris - The Musee d'Orsay is a large museum that houses so many works of art. It is the second largest art museum in Paris, second to the Louvre Museum. On exhibitions are the collection of impressionist and post- impressionist masterpieces by well-known painters/artists such as Manet, Renoir, Cezanne, Sisley, Gauguin, Seurat, Van Gogh, Monet, Degas, and Sisley. Paintings, sculptures, furniture, photography, and many statues in addition to the exquisite paintings are abundant in this museum.

I have the painting of "A Celebration" of Renoir's "Luncheon of the Boating Party" (copy only), "The Starry Night" by Van Gogh (copy only), and "Sunset in Venice" by Monet (copy only).

Petit Palais (Small Palace), Paris - The Petit Palais is an art museum. It houses enormous collections of works of art – exquisite paintings, marvelous statues, fine sculptures, and many, many more stunning and various collections from antiquity to present. It is the City of Paris Museum of Fine Arts. Several sculptors, whose works are displayed in there, are Convers, Ferrary, Hugues, Peynot, Desvergens, Injalbert, et al.

Nearby, on the lawn, was the memorial statue of Sir Winston Churchill, my favorite statesman.

The Grand Palais, Paris - It is an enormous building used for exhibitions, etc. There is an elegant restaurant in this building that serves scrumptious food.

La Conciergerie, Paris - The Palais de Justice, the Conciergerie, and the Sainte-Chapelle consists of the Palais de la Cite (Palace of the Cite). We toured the Conciergerie. This is the place where the concierge lived. The King, in his absence, appointed a concierge responsible to run the palace. It was a very high-ranking appointment, and he was the head housekeeper for the King.

During the French Revolution, many prisoners were imprisoned in the La Conciergerie before they were executed. Marie Antoinette was imprisoned in the La Conciergerie before her execution.

There is a replica of Marie Antoinette wearing a black dress. She was confined in a little cell with replicas of two guards outside her cell.

The Place St. Michel (Michael), Paris - Saint Michel's Place is a very popular spot in Paris. Fontaine Saint Michel (Saint Michael Fountain) was constructed in 1855-60. You can see the statue of Saint Michael, the Archangel, holding a sword and fighting the cunning devil. This angel is the protector of the church. He is the right hand of God. He is like the general of God in battling evil.

You can also see statues of the four classical cardinal virtues - prudence or wisdom, justice, temperance, and fortitude. There are two dragons that spout water into the beautiful fountain.

At Saint Michel's Place, there was a man standing on a small platform wearing a bright gold color outfit. I thought it was a statue till I got closer and checked on him. He was alive, not a statue. You can have a picture taken with him, and give him some Euros. It is an honest living.

Tom and I sat in one of the restaurants, ordered food, and took a break from touring. We had a great time.

Sainte-Chapelle (Holy Chapel) in Paris - The architectural design of the royal chapel is Gothic. The chapel served as a parish church for all the residents of the palace. It is located at 8 Boulevard du Palais, 75001, Paris. It is in the heart of the city. I looked at the chapel meticulously and saw the grandeur of it all.

Arc de Triomphe, Paris - One of the most significant of all triumphal arches is the Arc de Triomphe. It is located at the centre (that is how they spell "center" in Europe) of the Place Charles de Gaulle. It was built in honor of the valiant men who fought battles for France, especially during the Napoleonic Wars when Napoleon conquered much of Europe. Written at the top of the arch are the names of the generals, war-fighting men, and wars they fought. There is a Memorial Flame that burns all the time in loving memory of those who perished during the wars. This is a highly regarded place in honor of the men who lost their only lives fighting for their cause.

It seemed forever to get to this place. From Champs-Elysees, we could see the Arc de Triomphe, but we couldn't cross the street from the Champs-Elysees to get there. There was a road, but no road for pedestrians. We kept walking, crossing several intersections before we finally found an underground. Speaking in broken French, I asked a man how to get to the Arc de Triomphe. He pointed to the underground. Lo and behold, we walked down the stairs and descended to the underground, kept walking and walking till we found the stairs to ascend. We climbed up the stairs, and there was the Arc de Triomphe in front of us. All the things you should do when touring places. God was always with us. We always found the places we wanted to see.

Champs Elysees - The Champs-Elysees is an avenue in the 8th arrondissement of Paris, also known as Elysian Fields. It is one of the most famous avenues in the world. In this fabulous street, you will find cinemas, theatres, café, and abundant stores, i.e. elegant and sophisticated designer merchandise, etc. The boulevard is lined with beautiful trees with luxuriant foliage and nicely arranged exuberant flower gardens.

Tom and I took a stroll and enjoyed this very impressive promenade. Then, we walked to see the Arc de Triomphe.

I had a picture of me pointing at the Victor Hugo station inscription on the board in Champs Elysees. Victor Hugo is the author of *Les Miserables*, one of my favorite plays.

Palais Garnier, Opera National de Paris - It is an architectural masterpiece, magnificent, and gigantic. This opera house seats 1,979 people. We took the tour by using a CD guide. This is a symbol of opulence - large glittering chandeliers, fine paintings on the ceiling that reminded me of the paintings on the Sistine Chapel, marble staircases, lovely sculptures, etc. The painting by Chagall in the main auditorium is marvelous to enjoy and look at. On the facade of the opera building, the names Beethoven, Mozart, Rossini, et al are engraved.

Pont Alexandre III - It is the most elegant, lavish, and elaborate bridge in Paris. The bridge symbolized the Russian-French friendship. It was named after Tsar Alexander III. We walked on this bridge twice and took pictures of the River Seine below.

The Moulin Rouge - It is a Parisian night club. Extravagant can-can dances are staged at the Moulin Rouge. You can see ostentatious displays of glamorous women wearing exquisite, elaborate, and glittering costumes.

Centre Georges Pompidou - Centre Georges Pompidou is an art gallery and a cultural hub. The pipes and air ducts are exposed. This makes this place unique in appearance. People flock to see this building complex in Paris.

Ecole Militaire - In this place, there are several big buildings that are used for different kinds of military training in Paris, France.

Fragonard Perfume Factory - We went on a tour to the Fragonard Perfume Factory in Paris. How to make perfume was demonstrated. Perfume is made of flowers with a combination of some alcohol, citral, aqua, etc. The demonstrator said some of the flowers used are imported from Latin America. One of the most valuable elements of an exquisite perfume is the rose flower. It is known as the queen of all flowers. Ylang ylang, Jasmine, Tuscan Iris, etc. are also favorite flowers for making perfume.

The factory offers the best perfumes in the world. The bottles of the perfumes come in different alluring designs.

No. 5 Chanel Paris and J'adore by Christian Dior are my favorite perfumes. They smell so good – fresh, zesty fragrance. I love perfumes and flowers. Flowers are a reminder of one of the most beautiful creations of God. Wearing perfume is one way to wear flowers. Flowers also brighten my life.

It was a must for me to see the Sorbonne University. One of my favorite operas is *La Boheme*. The score was composed by Giacomo Puccini and the lyrics were written by Luigi Illica and Guiseppe Giacosa. It is the story of the lives and loves of four Bohemians who lived near the Sorbonne University namely: Marcelo, the painter, Rodolfo, the poet, Schaunard, the musician, and Colline, the philosopher. They lived in the Latin Quarter. I was happy I got to see this institution for higher learning that reminded me of the opera *La Boheme*. It must have been so nice to have attended the Paris Sorbonne University.

The Palace of Versailles, or Chateau de Versailles in France - We boarded a tour bus and visited the Palace of Versailles. King Louis XIV moved his royal court from Paris to Versailles. Versailles became the seat of political power in the Kingdom of France. This palace is elaborately decorated, and it displays opulence. It is filled with many marvelous sculptures, exquisite portrait paintings of members of the royal family from generation to generation, historical and Christian paintings, etc. The Hall of Mirrors is stunning. In this hall are immense, beautiful mirrors, stupendous and elegant chandeliers. The opera house is sizable. All palaces in Europe are impressive and extravagant. They display luxury at its best, and obviously power and glory.

The Grand Trianon is another palace in the compound, but it is smaller. It was used by Marie Antoinette, wife of King Louis XVI.

One of the many paintings on display in this palace is of Jacques-Louis David. The painting shows Napoleon crowning his wife, Empress Josephine. On the day of the coronation, it had been intended that Pope Pius VII perform the ceremony and crown Napoleon. The Pope is sitting down holding a cross and waiting to crown Napoleon, but Napoleon decided to crown himself as Emperor before the Pope. According to the French tour guide, the Pope was miffed by Napoleon's actions.

Ludwig van Beethoven had dedicated his Third Symphony to Napoleon Bonaparte. He admired Napoleon. He named the symphony Bonaparte. When he heard Napoleon crowned himself as emperor, he took out the dedication. He renamed the title page to Eroica. It is a beautiful symphony. Beethoven wrote nine symphonies. I have all of the CD recordings of the nine symphonies by the Wiener Philharmoniker (Vienna Philharmonic) Orchestra.

The gardens of the Palace of Versailles are filled with gorgeous flowers and decorated with several resplendent fountains, many amazing white marble statues and much more. Louis XIV commissioned the white marble statues. In one of the fountains are bronze sculptures of a half-naked nymph and a young triton. The gardens are huge, and walking in this place seems endless. We walked, enjoying the fountains, the trees, the statues, and the many flowers in the flower gardens. We walked to a wooded garden, and I heard an opera aria being sung. It was the voice of Maria Callas, an American-born Greek soprano diva, and one of the most renowned and influential opera singers during her time. She was a beloved performer. The aria was enchanting.

Lourdes, France—Lourdes in the Pyrenees in Southern France - We went on a pilgrimage to Lourdes. This is the place where the Blessed Virgin Mary appeared to Bernadette Soubirous. It is an absolutely divine place to visit.

Take the Petit train tour around Lourdes, and see the highlights for the must-see tourist places to visit in Lourdes.

Things to do in Lourdes: Stay in queue to see the Grotto in Lourdes. Touch the water flowing freely on the wall from the well, and pray in front of the Grotto. Attend Holy Mass in the Basilique de Notre-Dame de l'Immaculee Conception (Basilica of our Lady of the Immaculate Conception). Take the holy bath, and tour the whole compound.

There is a statue of Saint Jean-Baptiste-Marie Vianney in the compound (Jean is French for "John") of Lourdes. He was a French priest, and he is the patron saint of parish priests.

Hotel Christina – Lourdes, France - In front of the hotel where we stayed, I sang *Que Sera, Sera, Dahil Sa Iyo* (Because of You), and *That's Amore* (That's Love). Tom accompanied my singing and played the rented guitar (we paid the owner ten Euros ($11.29 US dollar per day for the guitar rental). Can you imagine? People stopped, took the time to listen to my singing, clapped their hands, and raised their thumbs up; they liked my singing.

The Hotel Christina is a very nice hotel in Lourdes in the Pyrenees in southern France. It is centrally located. It is near the Basilica of our Lady of the Immaculate Conception, the Sanctuary of our Lady of Lourdes, and many stores. It has a nice restaurant that serves four-course meals every day, a fitness center, and a bar/lounge. Wi-Fi in public areas is free. There is a coffee shop and a sauna, and there is a terrace on the rooftop.

The hotel features 163 rooms with amenities such as premium bedding, satellite TV, refrigerators, hair dryers, and coffee makers. We enjoyed the place – comfortable and cozy. I recommend this hotel if you would visit Lourdes.

Daily, the hotel provides delicious breakfast with lots of food – various kinds of pastries, desserts, variety of fresh baked bread, boiled whole eggs, scrambled eggs, sausages, bacons, hams, beef, variety of marmalades, several kinds of fruits, juices, chocolate milk, regular milk, creamy French food, etc. The breakfast is a brunch. We dined in the elegant hotel restaurant often during our stay in Lourdes. The food was superb French food, creamy, rich and tasty.

The Elegant Dining and Food to Die For - One of my favorite things I love doing on vacation is dining in a four or five-star restaurant savoring the best food in the world. Elegant dining in the restaurant of the Hotel Cristina in Lourdes in the Pyrenees in Southern France is excellent. We dined here mostly during our stay in Lourdes. I enjoyed the full four course meal every night at dinner. The first course is soup with bread and butter. The second course is salad. The third course is the main entree the guest orders and the fourth course is the dessert.

On the first day, we had dinner at the Hotel Christina Hotel Restaurant, we had cauliflower soup for the first course. It was superb.

Tom said to me, "If you fixed this cauliflower soup for me, I would eat it."

I said to him, "Tom, do you realize this cauliflower soup was probably prepared by one of the best French cooks in the world who may have a degree in culinary art, or have been influenced by Julia Child? I am sorry, but I can't possibly cook this cauliflower soup for you. The cook will not tell me the recipe for cauliflower soup."

The second was salad – ham, lettuce, carrots, corn, tomatoes, beans, jicama, cheese, and red pepper with a dressing of your choice – Mediterranean dressing was one of the choices. That salad was sumptuous. The third course was the main entree I ordered - a juicy chicken breast with all the trimmings. It was superb. The fourth course was the dessert. Cake with chocolate, cheese, not sure what the dripping yellow cream was, maybe butter with syrup? The dessert was so beautiful! It was scrumptious. It tasted something like tiramisu. It melted in my mouth. It was a dessert to die for. The yellow cream on the plate was so delicious, and if I were at home, I may have licked my plate. No, I am only kidding!

I savored every bite, enjoyed the sumptuous food to die for that lingered on my mind for a while. Thanks be to God for the blessing! The Lord is kind. I prayed, paused, and reflected before dinner.

La vie est belle – Life is beautiful. Bonsoir – Good evening. Au Revoir (Bye).

In front of the Basilica of Our Lady of the Immaculate Conception in Lourdes in France

At the Notre Dame Cathedral in Paris, France

At the Palace of Versailles in France - Ofelia,
the tireless and enthusiastic tourist enjoying tourists' places.

The Paris-Sorbonne University – Paris, France

The Palais Garnier Paris Opera House in Paris, France

The Palais Garnier Paris Opera House in Paris, France

The Arc de Triomphe in Paris, France

In the Courtyard of the Petit Palais in Paris, France

The Eiffel Tower – Paris, France

Ofelia and her Momma in Paris, France

Vienna, Austria.

Ich liebe Wien und Salzburg (I love Vienna and Salzburg). Vienna is the music capital of the world, and it is also the capital of Austria.

We bought our bus fares and took the Hop-On Hof-Off Bus tour in Vienna. The bus took us to the best sights in Vienna. The lady tour guide mentioned all the places we should visit.

The following tourist spots we visited in Vienna were:

The first place we visited in Vienna is the Saint Stephen's Cathedral in Vienna. It was awesome. Holy Masses in Latin are held in this Cathedral.

The Schonbrunn Palace in Vienna in Austria. The palace is majestic. The tour guide told us the history of the Schonbrunn Palace. She said Schonbrunn means "beautiful fountain." The palace was the home of Maria Theresa, Empress of Austria. It is magnificent. The Schonbrunn was a gift from Maria Theresa's father. She was a devout Roman Catholic. She had sixteen children. One of them was Marie Antoinette, Queen of France, who was beheaded during the French Revolution.

This baroque palace is one of the most significant cultural landmarks in Austria. It contains 1,441 stupendous and elegant rooms. The opulent interiors display amazing frescoed ceilings, opulent and glittering crystal chandeliers, huge mirrors, and gold leaf ornaments. Six-year-old Mozart, a child prodigy, performed in the Hall of Mirrors in 1762. In the Grand Gallery, there is a painting of the members of the 1815 Congress of Vienna who celebrated joyfully by dancing after dividing up Napoleon Bonaparte's crumbled empire. On the ceiling are several paintings – one of them is Maria Theresa in a pink outfit. Beautiful portraits, Christian and landscape paintings, etc. by great artists also abound in the palace.

The tour guide also said the last of the Habsburg monarchs was deposed in 1918 and exiled to Portugal. An Austrian republic was established. No more kings in Austria, she said.

Today, this palace is used for concerts. The world-renowned Vienna Philharmonic Orchestra performs concerts in this palace. Thousands of tourists visit this place every year. The revenue from the tourists maintains the upkeep and splendor of the palace.

The Hofburg Imperial Palace in Vienna in Austria - We toured the palace using an audio CD guide. It narrated the history of the palace as we walked in each room. This was the home of Empress Elizabeth of Austria, who married

Emperor Franz Joseph I. She was a Bavarian princess. She was called "Sisi" by her family and friends. She was stunning and ravishing. She was both Empress of Austria and Queen of Hungary. She also held the title of Queen of Bohemia and Croatia. (We visited Bohemia and Moravia as well).

Life-size paintings of Emperor Franz Joseph I, the beautiful Sisi, their children, and many more exquisite paintings by world-renowned artists are displayed in the gallery and many rooms. Sparkling silver plates, silver spoons, marvelous porcelain dishes/bases, elegant golden chandeliers, unique crystals, opulent pieces of furniture, grand tables, wing chairs, etc. owned by the Imperial family are also displayed. Several things in this palace were gifts from France and other countries. The memorial statue of Sisi wearing an elegant ballroom gown looked so real. Impressive frescoes on the ceiling are abundant in the palace. The different wings of the former imperial residence portray the architectural periods of Gothic, Renaissance, and Baroque.

Elizabeth withdrew from public life after the death of her thirty-year-old son, Rudolf. She was depressed. She was murdered by an anarchist in Geneva, Switzerland in 1898.

The Memorable Concert at the Wiener Musikverein - One evening in Vienna, Austria, Ms. Silvana, the employee of the hotel, arranged a taxi for us. The taxi was to take us to the Musikverein Goldener Saal (Golden Hall) in Vienna. This place was listed as one of the "1,000 Places You Need to See Before You Die." The taxi driver showed up in the lobby and escorted us to the car. What a surprise! Silvana arranged for a Mercedes-Benz to take us to the concert. It was a big luxury car and very beautiful.

I told Tom, "See, we are going to attend the concert in style, in a luxury car." WOW! We arrived to the Musikverein in style. After the show, another big Mercedes brought us back to the hotel. Silvana took care of us so well. This Musikverein Concert Hall was magnificent, marvelous, and magical! It was ostentatiously rich, luxurious, and incredible. The mesmerizing decorations on the walls on the stage, the many beguiling statues on both sides of the hall, the ceiling, the huge chandeliers, etc. were all in rich, gold color. The elegance of the place was indescribable.

We attended the Wiener Mozart Orchester Concert (Vienna Mozart Orchestra Concert). The Vienna Mozart Orchestra and internationally celebrated opera singers and famed soloists performed works by Wolfgang Amadeus Mozart. We journeyed back to the 18th century. I was so spellbound! I wanted to get up and dance to the music of Mozart. The concert was phenomenal and breathtaking! The amazing first-class musicians, who were all dressed in magnificent historical costumes and nice wigs, presented a memorable and special night in Vienna's biggest and most eminent concert hall. We, the audience, enjoyed a concert of the baroque era, movements from symphonies, and solo concertos, as well as gorgeous operatic overtures, show-stopping arias, and duets from illustrious works, such as "The Magic Flute," "Cosi Fan Tutte," "The Marriage of Figaro," etc. The classical concert was enchanting. The arias were ethereal. Indeed, it was a spectacular performance! I love the classics. It was my cup of tea.

William and Susana, my children, played the classics in many piano recitals. They had piano lessons for several years.

Being there, in that magnificent concert hall, was a loving gift from the Lord God! I prayed, paused, reflected, and thanked God for His unfathomable love and blessing.

Great maestros such as Mozart, Beethoven, Brahms, Strauss, Chopin, Haydn, Shubert, et al are some of the musical luminaries who have resided in Vienna, this dazzling, and great city, and made Vienna their home. Mozart's pictures and posters are all over Vienna. He is the most prominent and dominant figure in the country of Austria.

Belvedere Palace, Vienna, Austria - We took the tour by using an audio CD guide that narrated the history of the palace. Belvedere means "beautiful view."

Prince Eugene of Savoy owned this palace. He was a military commander.

The Belvedere is magnificent and humongous. There is a formal French garden with fountains, statues, and cascades in the front and back of the palace. The Belvedere is a masterpiece of Baroque architecture. Exhibits here are paintings by renowned artists. There are religious paintings like the resurrection and the life of Jesus depicted in art, the coronation of the Blessed Mother, Mary, paintings depicting Roman life, portraits and landscapes.

One of the display rooms contains the resplendent bronze sculptures of the four Gospel writers: Saint Matthew, Saint Mark, Saint John, and Saint Luke. The lower palace is a museum that contains large collections of modern works of art, such as abstract paintings. Modern art seems fascinating as well, but I prefer the masterpieces by Rembrandt, Michelangelo, Leonardo da Vinci, El Greco, Rubens, Tintoretto, Velasquez, Zurbaran, Goya, et al.

"The Kiss," a painting by Gustav Klimt, a prominent Austrian symbolist painter, is extraordinary and popular.

More areas we covered and visited in Austria:

The Vienna Parliament Building – The architecture is strikingly beautiful. The Pallas Athena Statue fountain in front of the entrance is a famous landmark.

Vienna State Opera House – Another spectacular building for the performing arts – opera, ballet, concert, etc. It is the home of great opera tenors, sopranos, baritone, etc. – stage actors/actresses who perform during opera season.

The Weiner Rathaus – It is the City Hall of Vienna. A neo-gothic-style building.

Graben, one of the most famous streets in Vienna.

Albertina Museum houses masterpieces by Tintoretto, Picasso, et al.

Shopping Centers in downtown Vienna - They carry exquisite designer merchandise.

The Danube River - It is pristine, and it reminded me of the famous Vienna waltzes. I have a CD entitled "Blue Danube River" and another CD entitled "Vienna Woods." Now, when I play these CDs, I can picture the Danube River and Vienna Woods. How enchanting!

Raiffeisen Bank in Vienna – This is a good bank in Vienna for exchanging dollars to euros. The exchange is better in a bank rather than the hotel or any other outlet. The hotels charge a higher commission for money exchanges. Nearby is the Post where you can buy stamps and mail postcards.

Salzburg in Austria - The hotel where we stayed in Vienna offered trips or excursions. We booked for the trip to Salzburg. Salzburg is the birthplace of Mozart. Oh, my good heavens, the transportation to Salzburg was a big, beautiful Mercedes Sport Utility Vehicle (SUV).

Tom said, "Oh, we are traveling in style in a Mercedes SUV."

Indeed, the Mercedes SUV is stylish. A total of seven people booked this tour. On our way to Salzburg, Cordula, our driver and tour guide pointed at the Danube River, Benedictine Abbey, the Vienna Woods, and the Alps. Then, we stopped in the picturesque Lake District Salzkammergut (alpine scenery in the movie "The Sound of Music"). The alpine scenery is indeed breathtaking, as shown in the movie "The Sound of Music" – range of mountains and beautiful lake around. There are many boats, grand and beautiful homes, and gorgeous flower gardens. It is paradise! Cordula said this is a place for the affluent. Homes cost several million euros. Recently, a home was sold for 13 million euros. That is about $16, 510, 000.00 American dollars. This is indeed the playground of the rich.

Then, Cordula continued driving and took us to downtown Salzburg. It was fabulous! Cordula narrated Salzburg's history. We saw the following tourist spots on this guided tour:

Hohensalzburg – A medieval fortress

The home of Mozart - He was born at home.

The second home of Mozart where he grew up.

The Holy Trinity Church where Mozart was baptized.

The Mirabell Palace and Gardens in Salzburg, Austria – The architecture of the palace is high Baroque. It is stately. What a grandiose and fabulous place! The tour guide said this grand palace and the gardens were featured in the movie "The Sound of Music." Julie Andrews, who played Maria von Trapp, and the von Trapp (actors and actresses) children gathered around the splendid fountain in the gardens. I was so thrilled to seeing this place I had wished to see for a long time. I was very excited.

I started singing: "Doe - a deer, a female deer, Ray - a drop of golden sun, Me – a name I call myself, Far – a long, long way to run, Sew – a needle pulling thread, La – a note to follow So, Tea – a drink with jam and bread, that will bring us back to do, oh, oh, oh."

I was very happy seeing this fabulous place, and I marveled at everything. I put a smile on the faces of my fellow tourists when I was singing.

Beautiful and amazing statues abound in the spectacular, lavish, well-tended, and gorgeous flower gardens. The gardens are breathtaking!

In the awesome Marble Hall of the Mirabell Palace, exciting and blissful concerts are held. Tourists can attend an evening of culture and charm and see a nice concert and revel to the enticing music and stunning melodies.

Leopold Mozart, (the father of Wolfgang Amadeus Mozart), Wolfgang, and his sister Nannerl performed music at Mirabell Palace - glorious days for the Wolfgang musical family.

Saint Peter's Church – I prayed, paused, and reflected in the church. It is celestial.

Saint Peter's Churchyard and Cemetery – It is the oldest Christian grave-yard in Salzburg.

Downtown Salzburg – luxurious hotels, stores, souvenir shops, skyscrapers, etc. are plentiful.

Many musicians lined the bridge in Salzburg and played their instruments and people gave them money. Tom was missing his guitar. He gave a musician some euros and asked him if he could play his guitar. The musician was kind, and lent Tom his guitar. Tom played "Rhinestone Cowboy," "House of the Rising Sun," and other songs, and he could entertain the tourists walking by.

The Salzburg Outdoor Theatre - The No. 1 attraction in Salzburg is the music festival. The stage is huge and elaborate. Many people come to attend this spectacular event.

Chain Bridge – Tourists (couples) write their names in a padlock, pledge undying love, hook the padlock on the fence of the bridge, lock it, and leave it there. There are plenty of padlocks on this bridge.

We didn't bring an extra padlock, so we did not get to pledge everlasting love, eh.

I love speaking in foreign languages. The members of the hotel staff liked it. Ich liebe Wien (German for "I love Vienna"). I really love Vienna. I enjoyed this country so much. Mit liebe aus Wien (German for: "With love from Vienna").

At the Saint Stephen's Cathedral in Vienna, Austria

At the Musikverein Golden Hall in Vienna, Austria

Hungary

A young man, the tour guide drove a Sport Utility Vehicle (SUV) and drove us to Budapest, Hungary. According to the tour guide, the Royal Palace/Royal Castle in Budapest is the historical castle and palace complex of the Hungarian kings in Budapest. During the Austro-Hungarian Empire, the palace held extravagant ceremonies to symbolize peace between the dynasty and the nation. The palace is Gothic in style and later, Neo-Baroque style.

We arrived just on time for the "Changing of the Guards" in front of the palace. It is a tourist attraction. Young, handsome Hungarian men in blue uniforms were the center of attraction in this ceremony. Their performance was impressive and spectacular. The guards turned their rifles around, saluted, marched up and down the square, and pounded on their drums, etc. It was very colorful. I love the pageantry of the "Changing of the Guards" both in Budapest and London, England.

More important highlights we saw in Budapest:

The Trinity Square, the Matthias Church, Saint Peter and Saint Paul's Church, Hungarian State Opera House, Fisherman's Bastion, etc.

The Parliament in Budapest – It is one of the most marvelous buildings in Europe, an amazing work of Gothic architecture. The design is intricate and overwhelmingly amazing.

Hosok Tere (Heroes' Square) in Budapest in Hungary – This is a very remarkable square in the city. Tourists flock to Budapest to see this square. The Archangel Gabriel stands on top of the center pillar. He is holding the holy crown and the double cross of Christianity. On top of the colonnades, there are some effigies of freedom fighters, war heroes who fought for the country.

In Gellert Hill, an elevated hill overlooking the Danube River in Budapest, we, the tourists, enjoyed looking at the Danube River. According to the tour guide, the Danube River originates in Germany, flows to Hungary, Austria, Romania, Serbia, etc., then to the Mediterranean Sea. It was delightful seeing the beautiful and picturesque view of the Danube River. It was breathtaking to behold such beauty.

The statue of Andras Hadik, the Hussar of all hussars in the Castle Hill is just a stone's throw away from the Matthias Church in Budapest. I think this man symbolizes the best in military virtues - gallant, urbane, patriotic, dependable, and charming.

Austria and Hungary were strong Catholic countries and were parts of the Holy Roman Empire.

Hungary did not adapt the euros. I had to exchange euros to forints (Hungarian money) before I was able to pay for the entrance fee to enter the Matthias Church. I was just glad there was a booth nearby that took care of money exchanges.

Czech Republic

Johannes, who drove us in a comfortable SUV to Prague in the Czech Republic, was an outstanding tour guide. He was very knowledgeable. I have learned a lot about Prague, the capital of the Czech Republic. This city is also known as the "City of a Hundred Spires."

The tourist spots here are the following:

The Gothic Powder Tower, the gate or entrance to the city, an important landmark, the Charles Bridge, the Saint Vitus Cathedral, the Saint Nicholas Church, the Saint Michael Church, the Old Town Square, the medieval Astronomical Clock, charming baroque buildings and sublime Gothic churches are remarkable.

Prague Castle/Hradschin (Royal Palace) – According to Johannes, the tour guide, if the president is here, the flag is flown. It is magnificent and enormous. The architecture design is Baroque. The castle complex is one of the most significant landmarks in Prague.

There is a little Venice that is a canal smaller that the Grand Canal in Venice.

The Novena to the Divine Infant of Prague was originated in Prague. I pray this Novena all the time – continued health, healing of sickness, job promotion, safe travel, safe from harm, and to remain righteous always, etc.

The Charles Bridge is a famous bridge in the world. It is lined with several statues of Catholic Saints and one of them is Saint John of Nepomuk. There are plenty of padlocks on the railing of the Charles Bridge. Young lovers write their names on the padlock and pledge undying love for each other, then hook the padlock on the railing of the bridge and lock it.

Beethoven's Homes - Johannes, the tour guide showed us the two homes of Ludwig van Beethoven in Prague. Beethoven's symphonies and several of his compositions were performed in the Prague Concert Halls. I love the Symphony No. 5. It is powerful. I think it is thunderous. It is one of Beethoven's greatest musical works and also one of the most famous compositions in classical music. It is often used for commercials.

Switzerland

The one hour and ten-minute flight from Vienna, Austria to Geneva, Switzerland was smooth. I got to see the aerial view of Switzerland before the Austrian Airline landed. It was breathtaking! The country is surrounded by a range of mountains, and I saw a big, beautiful lake, and many skyscrapers.

Geneva, this charming cosmopolitan city is the center of the world's peacemaking organizations and the seat of the League of Nations.

On our second day sightseeing in Geneva, we purchased tickets for a bus tour. The driver of the beautiful, luxury coach (bus) took us on a tour to see this metropolis. The tour provided us with information on the top places of interest to see in Geneva. The tour guide talked about the following tourist attractions and pointed at them where they are located:

International Districts at Gare Cornavin, Palais de Nations Unies (Palace of United Nations), World Health Organization (WHO), World Trade Organization (WTO), International Health Organization (IHO), United Nation International Children's Emergency Fund (UNICEF – The Headquarters is in New York, the Regional Office for Europe is in Geneva), Copyright Protection building, Red Cross, etc. The nice tour continued to the shores of Lac Leman along Geneva's right bank with stunning view of the Alps, the tall Jet d'Eau, the astonishing Botanical Garden, etc. Then, the bus proceeded along Geneva's lovely promenades and to the beautiful Geneva's opulent shopping areas.

After the bus tour, we boarded a Choo-Choo train. This train took us to Geneva's Old Town, a Gothic labyrinth of cobblestone streets, Cathedral de Saint Pierre, and the Town Hall, incredible History and Art Museums, splendid antique boutique stores, etc. The tour continued along the old walls of the city to the theater areas. The Opera House is stylish. The tour concluded in fabulous Bastions Park where the enthusiastic tourists can see the historical Reformation Wall. The wall contains the sculptures of the founding fathers.

Palais de Nations - United Nations (UN – Nations Unies) Tour – Geneva. We got in queue for the security check. Touring the European Headquarters of the UN requires a thorough security check like we were boarding an aircraft. The security personnel asked what I had in the pockets of my light jacket.

I told him a small purse, credit cards, Kleenex, cash, dollars, and euros, etc. He told me not to remove my jacket since I didn't have a Swiss knife. Then, we proceeded to an office where an employee of the UN asked for my identification (ID). He took my photograph and issued me a badge for two (for me and my spouse). We got in another tour queue to pay for the tour.

The United Nations Office in Geneva is the most important UN Center after New York headquarters. The UN tour guide took us on a guided tour and showed us the UN building and annex. The comprehensive tour began on the second floor. The tour guide told us the history of the founding of the League of Nations, then the UN. There was a board that listed the principal organs of the UN – Secretariat, General Assembly, International Court of Justice, Security Council, Economic and Social Council, Trusteeship Council, and Repertory of Practice of UN Organs. He explained the functions of the principal organs – administering peace keeping operations, maintenance of international peace and security, surveying economic and social needs, human rights, etc.

There are 193 countries who are members of the UN (The Vatican is not a member). There are 193 flags, including the United States flag, flown nicely in front of the UN building. The tour guide said there are over 900 conferences held every year. There are thirty-four conference rooms. Through a glass window, we looked at the conference going on one floor below us. Spain donated a conference room. Some parts of the ceiling in the donated conference room were painted in red.

I felt so good sitting in the General Assembly Room. I could not believe I was there. I remember learning about Carlos P. Romulo in History class. He was a Filipino and the first Asian to serve as president of the UN General Assembly (1949). I was proud of him, although I never knew him. This General Assembly Conference Room is no longer used today. The General Assembly is now in New York (NY).

The interior decoration of the UN includes several remarkable works of art. Some were donated by several countries – a curved Buddha from Thailand, a painting of Beijing's Tiananmen Square from China, a painting from Bahrain, another painting from Kuwait, black and gray sharp nails perched on a big board from Germany, a model boat, a porcelain base, etc.

We walked to the annex building, and there were more donations from other countries. The elegant, wooden, curved doors of several rooms were donated by France.

The statue of Woodrow Wilson is in the flower garden. The League of Nations was very important to this American president.

It was a fascinating and an educational tour. I loved and enjoyed the UN tour so much. It was the realization of a life-long dream to see the UN headquarters in Geneva, Switzerland. I wanted to see the Palais de Nations - United Nations (UN – Nations Unies) for quite some time.

There is a "Broken Chair" across the street from the United Nations building compound. It is a reminder of the landmine victims.

There are several little fountains near the "Broken Chair." Kids play and get themselves wet.

The following are more tourist attractions we visited in Geneva:

Musee d'Art et d'Histoire – Museum of Art and History – We toured this Museum of Art and History. The museum houses enormous collections of old and new art and many more. It is Geneva's largest art museum. On the first floor is an Armory – guns, armors, shields, arsenal, etc. I read that the Duke of Savoy attempted to seize Geneva, but failed.

Across from the Armory is an Egyptian Museum - collections of Egyptian art, mummies, etc. On the second floor are dazzling paintings by well-known artists. Paintings of the "Annunciation," the "Visitation," the "Nativity," the "Presentation of Jesus Christ in the Temple," the "Crucifixion," the "Coronation of the Blessed Virgin Mary," miracles, saints, martyred saints, portraits of royal families, aristocrats, famous figures, and many more. Taking a museum tour whether is it given by a tour guide, or listening to an audio CD guide, or reading a pamphlet guide, or reading the description on the walls is always fascinating. It is great and priceless to acquire valuable knowledge, learn the history of several countries, and the many collection of arts found in museums.

Le Jet d'Eau – This fountain is Geneva's most famous landmark. It is in the middle of Lake Geneva. It is one of the world's tallest water fountains. It is large. It stands majestically in the lake. It provides a constant landmark when exploring the city. I watched this towering fountain shoots 500 liters of water high up into the air. It is amazing how this tall fountain shoots water into the air.

Lac Leman – Lake Geneva - We took a cruise on this beautiful lake. It is one of the largest lakes in Western Europe. I enjoyed the boat ride.

Flower Clock in Geneva - It is a well renowned Swiss clock. The clock is on the ground surrounded by flowers. The twelve numbers are written on the grass, and the dials (time, minutes, and seconds) on the center of the clock show the accurate time of the day. It is fantastic and incredible.

We went shopping in Rue de Rive and Rue du Rhone. I just gaped at the fashions and jewelry lining Geneva's most extravagant streets. Both Austria and Switzerland have first-class stores that house the creations of big name designers such as Christian Dior, Versace, Pierre Cardin, Louis Vuitton, etc. The fashion is trendy. After walking, one can just rest at one of the cafés at Place du Molard and Place de la Fusterie and watch the world go by. I love relaxing and watching the world go by after walking and walking long hours on tours.

Plainpalais Flea Market – We mingled with the locals at Geneva's largest outdoor flea market.

National Monument – A monument of two women, the union of Geneva with Switzerland

La Cathedrale Saint-Pierre – This is a Protestant church. It is grand. Romanesque columns are built in the façade of the cathedral. There is a museum nearby that contains the history of the Reformation.

Patek Philippe Museum – A fascinating museum of Swiss watchmaking.

Red Cross – A few meters away from the UN is the Red Cross Building. This gigantic building sits on top of a hill with the Red Cross logo above the tall building. The Swiss businessman, Henry Dunant, founded the Red Cross in 1859. The Red Cross is a dominant feature in Switzerland. There is a Red Cross logo just about everywhere - on the streets, in the shopping centers, on buses, on t-shirts, on buildings, in restaurants, etc.

Switzerland makes the best chocolate candies and cheeses in the world. I bought several Swiss chocolate candies and savored the scrumptious candies. Each candy I had melted in my mouth.

We visited the Hard Rock Café. It is very trendy. If you get tired of European food, and you are craving for American food, this is the best place to go.

Dinner at La Boucherie in Geneve, (Geneva) Switzerland

The La Boucherie, a four-and-a-half-star restaurant is a walking distance to our hotel. This was one of the restaurants we had dinner in Geneva. One night at dinner, Tom ordered a steak de boeuf with French rolls, vegetables, and French fries. The gorgeous steak was tender and cooked perfectly. I ordered a palatable chicken with French rolls, vegetables, baked potatoes, and dessert. The French sauce was superb. The appetizing food was delightful. For a souvenir, we got a beef bone that had the name of the restaurant, *La Boucherie.*

Nyon - The driver of the beautiful, luxury coach (bus) took us on an excursion to Nyon. The tour guide told us the history of Nyon. The Romans settled in Nyon. When we disembarked from the bus, we saw a beautiful fountain, the old town, museum buildings, Roman monuments, marina, and promenades by the lake. The tour guide took us to a building with many steps to climb. When we got on top of the building, the view took my breath away. We could see the beautiful Swiss Alps from a distance, the marina, a big ship, the harbor, the long and wide lake, etc. It was exciting. It was a paradise for people who love the countryside and water sport. Prolific and lush looking vineyards are also found in the little spick-and-span town of Nyon. We returned to Geneva by boarding a big ship. It was an hour ride. The scene along the way is eye-catching.

Vevey, Ouchy, Chillon, Lausanne and Montreux in Switzerland - The driver of the beautiful luxury coach (bus) took us on an excursion to the following places in Switzerland:

Ouchy – In Ouchy, the tour guide showed us the building where the Olympic Committee is planning the Olympic Games, the symbol of the Olympic Games, and some statues relating to the Olympics.

Vevey - It is known as one of the pearls of the Swiss Riviera. We strolled along the streets while waiting for a boat cruise to Chillon. In Vevey near the lake, you could see the amazing Alps. Europeans love to ski in the Alps. The statue of Charlie Chaplain is in the center of the town square. He lived in Vevey.

After waiting, we boarded a steamer boat to Chillon, another town. What an enchanting boat ride seeing the scenic landscapes all around along the ride. There were several other boats cruising on the pristine lake.

When you eat Nestle chocolate candies, think of Vevey. This is the town where the Nestle Company makes Nestle candies for export.

In Chillon, we visited the Chateau de Chillon (Chillon Castle). We toured the castle by using an audio CD guide. It is an extraordinary castle, medieval fortress, and one of the most famous monuments. It was owned by the Savoys. It is now a museum. The paintings of Jesus Christ and Saint John the Baptist adorn the big spacious room. Old utensils, tables, chairs, lots of pictures, artifacts, etc. are displayed in this museum.

Montreux is a splendid place to visit in Switzerland. Strolling around the Montreux streets was fun. It is a spectacular village by the lake. Exquisite flower gardens, luxury and first class hotels, skyscrapers, and expensive trendy and souvenir shops abound in this area. It is a fabulous sight to behold. It is paradise. Boats are available for cruising on the lake.

Lausanne in Switzerland is absolutely an enchanting place. It is trendy, elegant, and paradise. So many fun things one can avail in Lausanne. It is the playground for the sophisticated, the suave, the affluent, the crème de la crème.

The verdant vineyards in Lausanne and Montreux, the wine cities of Switzerland are spectacular. Grape plants are planted on terraces. It is a beautiful and an incredible sight to behold.

Saint Francis Church - It is the oldest church in Lausanne. It was a former Roman Catholic Church. It is now a Protestant church.

There are four national languages spoken in Switzerland. They are French, Italian, German, and Romansh.

Bonne nuit (Good night). Bonne nuit is pronounced as Bohn nwee.

A tout a l'heure. - See you later. A tout a l'huere is pronounced as Ah toot ah luhr. De Geneve avec amour (From Geneva with love). Au Revoir (Goodbye). It was time to catch a flight to another country.

In Geneva, Switzerland

A picture of the author by the lake in Geneva, Switzerland

At the Basilica of Our Lady of Geneva in Geneva, Switzerland

The author touring the United Nations compound in Geneva, Switzerland

Holland/Netherlands

Goedendag (Good day). The Netherlands is a monarchy. King Willem-Alexander is the King of the Netherlands. According to the tour guide, Queen Maxima, the Queen consort, is a commoner, but she won the hearts of the Dutch people. She is a much-loved queen. Queen Beatrix, the Queen Mother, abdicated in April 2013.

King Willem, the successor of Queen Beatrix, became the King of the Netherlands in April 2013. The tour guide said the king does not have any political power, just a figurehead.

In the Netherlands, we visited the following tourists' spots:

Amsterdam, Hague, Delft, Leiden, and Madurodam

Amsterdam - It is the capital of the Netherlands. Amsterdam gets its name from a dam in the river Amstel. The river Amstel runs through Amsterdam. The illustrious Dutch engineers built a dam in this river. A dam and the river Amstel blended together created the word Amsterdam, hence the existence of the City of Amsterdam. The Dutch engineers are well-known for building canals and dams to control the flood. Flood control is of foremost importance for the survival of the people in the Netherlands.

We purchased two tickets for the Hop-On Hop Off tour bus and toured the city. The tour highlighted the places of interest to explore in the city.

Church of Our Lady, Amsterdam - It is a magnificent Gothic cathedral. We attended Holy Mass in Latin twice.

The Basilica of Saint Nicholas, Amsterdam - It is the main Roman Catholic Church in Amsterdam. It is in the Old Centre district of Amsterdam. The church is dedicated to Saint Nicholas, who is the patron saint of Amsterdam. He is also the patron saint of sailors.

Dam Square – This is a principal location from which to explore Amsterdam. It is one of the centers of activities in downtown Amsterdam. When I was on Dam Square, I knew where we were at. Tom and I posed for a picture with a Dutchman and a Dutchwoman in typical Dutch costumes on Dam Square.

The Royal Palace – We toured the Royal Palace. The palace is filled with affluence. There are many fine, religious Christian paintings, life-size portraits of several kings, queens, princes, and princesses. Frescoes, sculptures, huge elegant chandeliers, beautiful furniture, collection of silverwares, porcelains, and many more are plentiful in this palace.

It was built in the 17th century as a town hall in the period of great prosperity in Amsterdam. During this Golden Age, Amsterdam thrived in the science, art, and trade.

The Canal Cruise - We boarded a boat on a cruise in the canals of Amsterdam. The boat sailed on the four major canals and took us on a sight-seeing tour by boat – Rembrandt's Square, Rijks Museum, Waterlooplein, Leidsestraat, Heren/Lelie, Golden Bend, Hermitage, Central Station East, Dutch houses, stores, and buildings, Rembrandt's House, Anne Frank's House, bridges, cafés (Hard Rock Café), restaurants, famous buildings, hotels, etc.

Anne Frank House's Museum, Amsterdam - We waited more than two hours in queue to see the house. It is unique. It is the hiding place where Anne Frank and her family and some other people hid from the Nazis during the war. Anne wrote her diary while in hiding.

We saw the living quarters upstairs where they hid - the living room, the dining room, the kitchen, the bedrooms, the attic, etc. After two years of hiding, they were betrayed and discovered by the Nazis. The betrayer was never found. No one knew who betrayed them. There were investigations to find out who was the culprit, but to no avail. All people in the secret annex were sent to concentration camps. Everyone died except Otto Frank, the father of Anne Frank. They almost made it. In a few months, the war would have come to an end.

In her diary, she wished that, "one day the terrible war will be over, and that time will come when they'll be people again and not just Jews!"

The evil of prejudice!

Central Station East – It is Amsterdam's main train station. It is the heart of the city – the biggest public transport that serves the city, its inhabitants, and visitors or tourists.

Rijksmuseum in Amsterdam - It is the largest museum in the Netherlands with more than two million visitors in 2015. Its exhibition called "The Masterpieces" displays the most famous pieces of Dutch art from the 17th century. There are plenty of paintings by Rembrandt van Rijn displayed in this museum. "The Night Watch" is one of the most popular.

I stood in awe when I looked at this life-size painting. The people in the painting looked like they were alive. "Jeremiah's Lamenting the Destruction of Jerusalem," also by Rembrandt, is another eye-catching work of art. (Rembrandt was born in Leiden in the Netherlands. We visited his place of birth). More artists whose works are on display at this museum are Johannes Vermeer,

Frans Hals, Ferdinand Bol, Jan Brueghel, William Claez, et al. "The Rest on the Flight into Egypt" by Jan Brueghel is one of my favorite paintings. One can see Joseph and Mary taking the infant Jesus to Egypt to escape the wrath of Herod. More to see are collections of sculptures, fine Christian paintings, treasury coins, Dutch art and history, Dutch dolls, Dutch dollhouses, artifacts, Oriental collections, traditional Delftware, etc. (My mom also toured this place with her cousin Auntie Senyang, and my cousin Ruding).

Vincent Van Gogh Museum, Amsterdam - This modern museum houses some 200 paintings and 550 sketches of Vincent Van Gogh. This is the largest in the world collection. On display are also hundreds of letters by Van Gogh, and some selected works by his friends and contemporaries.

Madame Tussauds Wax Museum, Amsterdam - Madame Tussauds Wax Museum is a very popular tourist attraction located on Dam Square in Amsterdam. I posed for a picture with the wax figures of King Willem-Alexander, Queen Maxima, and the Queen Mother. I was rubbing elbows with royalty (just kidding). I also posed for a picture with the wax figures of Pope John Paull II, Elvis Presley, James Bond (Pierce Brosnan), et al. Presidents John Kennedy and George Bush, Prime Minister Tony Blair, and several other world leaders, and American movie actors/actresses/singers also have wax figures in the Madame Tussauds Wax Museum.

At the Madame Tussauds Museum, I sang karaoke. I belted the song "My Way," a song popularized by Frank Sinatra. Several tourists stopped and watched my singing.

At the end of the song, one of the onlookers asked me, "Are you a singer?"

I replied, "No, I only sing during karaoke nights at the Karaoke Club in the U.S.A., mostly on Friday nights."

She thought I was a singer. She and some other tourists said that my singing was good. They were kind. Tom also belted a song, a Country Western song. We had a lot of fun at this museum.

Het Scheepvaart Museum, Amsterdam - The National Maritime Museum – It is captivating. There is a replica of a 17th century sail ship at its quay. We toured the ship. After touring the ship, we toured the whole museum. It contains a rich collection of maritime artifacts, fine paintings, mostly paintings of ships, especially warships, old maps, and remarkable ship models. These colorful displays will make one understand the history of the Netherlands and the Dutch people. I read a sentence on display that says that the Netherlands is a small nation, but centuries ago, it was one of the world's greatest powers.

This is the place where I read the popular statement or saying: "God created the world. The Dutch created Holland."

Magna Plaza, Amsterdam – We went shopping for souvenirs at Magna Plaza. It is a gigantic shopping mall in downtown Amsterdam in the Netherlands. The architectural styles of this monumental building are Neo-Gothic and Neo-Renaissance. It is one of the Top 100 Dutch heritage sites. The department stores carry enormous expensive merchandise in this mall – designer clothes, handbags, purses, cosmetics, shoes, sunglasses, unique and awesome products, and just about everything - you name it, in this humongous mall. The duplicates (copies, not original) of all the works of Rembrandt van Rijn, one of the greatest painters in European art and the most remarkable in Dutch history during the Dutch Golden Age are found in this mall.

The Music Lover - My hubby loves music. He played guitar in one of the music stores in Amsterdam. Wherever we were in Europe, we always had to look for a music store for Tom.

Delft, Holland - The driver of the beautiful luxury coach (bus) took us on an excursion to Delft. It was popularly known for its historic town center with fascinating canals. We visited a Delft Blue pottery factory, and saw the making of beautiful and exquisite Delft Blue pottery products known as Delftware.

The prolific painter, Johannes Vermeer, hails from Delft.

Earlier in the day, we visited a diamond factory and diamond cutting was demonstrated. It was amazing. Amsterdam is world-renowned for their diamonds. They export diamonds around the world.

At the diamond factory, the tour guide took us to a room. The room was locked. We were told we could not get out of the room until the display of diamonds was over. The lady employee showed the tourists various kinds of exceptional diamond jewelries – rings, earrings, bracelets, necklaces, and brooches. She placed a diamond ring on my finger. It was so tempting to buy that diamond. I asked how much is it in American dollars? She said the price was over $46,000.00. I did not buy it. It was not practical to spend that kind of money for a piece rock.

Delft Historic Town Center - It is wonderful to gaze at the remarkable architecture of the buildings in this medieval town. The Nieuwe Kerk is a beautiful and impressive building that houses the tombs of the royal family of the House of Orange.

Madurodam in Holland - The driver of the beautiful deluxe coach (bus) took us on an excursion to Madurodam. This park is in Hague, Holland. It is amazing. It is a must-see for tourists. It contains replicas of the famous landmarks in Amsterdam and Holland and historical places, etc. Tom took more than a hundred pictures of this park. Children love this miniature park. They enjoy the many things the park has to offer.

The tour guide said Madurodam was named after George Maduro, a Jewish law student from Curacao. He strongly fought the Nazi forces. He was a member of the Dutch resistance fighters. He died at Dachau concentration camp.

Hague in the Netherlands - The Seat of the International Court of Justice of the United Nations (UN) is at the Peace Palace in Hague in the Netherlands. The role of the Court is to settle legal disputes in accordance with international laws.

In Hague, there are many embassies of several countries from around the world. This is the place where you will find many diplomats from many nations including members of the U.S. Diplomatic Corps – ambassador, charge d' affaires, attache, envoy, consul, et al.

I took a picture of the home of the U.S. ambassador. An American flag flies gloriously in front of the building. Whenever I saw the U.S. flag in the countries we visited, I felt a sense of pride being an American citizen!

Belgium
In Belgium, we visited Flanders, Antwerp, and Brussels.

Beautiful Antwerp in Belgium at the Market Square. This place is breathtaking! It is spectacular! The tour guide told us the history of Antwerp. Here is the story of the statue of Silvius Brabo at the Market Square according to the tour guide. The legend says there was a mean and terrible giant who controlled the river traffic, demanding exorbitant tolls. Those who refused to pay got their hand cut off. One day, a young and valiant Roman soldier named Silvius Brabo managed to kill the giant. He cut the giant's hand and threw it in the Scheldt River. The statue in the Square shows Silvius Brabo throwing the hand of the giant.

Antwerp is a port city on the River Scheldt in Belgium. It is the world's principal center for cutting, polishing, and trading precious diamonds. Antwerp comes from the Dutch "hand werpen" meaning "hand thrown."

The Cathedral of our Lady in Antwerp in Belgium is another absolutely divine place of worship in Europe. It took my breath away when Tom and I toured this church.

Brussels in Belgium - The tour guide narrated the history of Brussels. I stood in awe breathless looking and enjoying Brussels. The Town Hall is a Gothic building from the Middle Ages.

The other historical buildings are all splendid.

The Manneken Pis, Brussels, Belgium - The tour guide told us the story of the Manneken Pis. It is world famous. Every year, there is a holiday in Brussels celebrating the Manneken Pis. The legend says that a very wealthy merchant came to visit the city. Suddenly, he could not find his son. He got scared, so he asked everybody to help him find the boy. Everybody went out to look for the boy. They found him. He was peeing. The merchant had someone built a statue of the boy peeing as a gesture of thanks to the people who helped him find his son.

When we were in Brussels in Belgium, I remember Father Robert E. (He was a Belgian priest with the Marian Order), my favorite priest in Catholic School who inspired me in the path of holiness. I wanted to look for him, but I had a feeling he had already gone to Heaven. He was in my mind all the time when I was in Belgium. He was one of the priests who shaped my upbringing and instilled in me a deep Catholic faith.

Tot ziens (Goodbye in Dutch). It is time to fly to Berlin, Germany.

Tom playing guitar at the Madame Tussauds Wax Museum in Amsterdam, Holland

*At the Madame Tussauds Wax Museum in Amsterdam, Holland with the wax fig-
ure of Pope John Paull II, now Saint John Paull II, the Great*

Tom playing guitar at a music store in Amsterdam, Holland.

Ofelia relaxing after a tour of the Rijksmuseum in Amsterdam, Holland.

Ofelia posed for a picture with the wax figure of Elvis Presley at the Madame Tussauds Wax Museum in Amsterdam, Holland.

In Brussels in Belgium

At the Market Square in Antwerp, Belgium

Berlin in Germany

Guten morgen/Guten tag/Guten abend (Good morning/Good afternoon/ Good evening).

We signed up for a private tour of Berlin. We toured with six people. The tour guide driving his SUV took us to the places of interests. He showed the highlights of Berlin. We visited the places on our own after the orientation tour.

The following are the tourists' attractions we visited in Berlin:

The Brandenburger Tor (Brandenburg Gate) - It is one of the well-known and important landmarks of Berlin. In this Square, President Ronald Reagan delivered his famous speech.

He said, "Mr. Gorbachev, tear down that wall!"

Lo and behold! The people of Berlin tore down the wall uniting East and West Berlin. I had goose bumps when I saw the remnants of the wall. I remember reading about the watch tower and the daring escapes of some of the East Berliners, etc. Some of them made it to West Berlin; some of them perished and died.

I read on a bulletin board the German government invited some talented people to show their talents on some of the remnants of the Berlin wall. The remnants have paintings of the people who were invited to showcase their talents.

An American lady from the U.S.A. had a painting on one of the remnants of the wall. It is a beautiful painting, and New York was inscribed on the remnant.

The U.S. Embassy, the British Embassy, the Russian Embassy, etc. are near Brandenburger Tor.

The Berlin Cathedral - Berliner Dom - The main altar of the Berliner Dom is impressively beautiful and majestic. The architecture is resplendent and the Romanesque columns are so awesome. In the interior of the church are amazing frescoes, exquisite religious and Christian paintings, holy sculptures, golden candelabras, etc. The rich gold color decorations on the walls and the altar are dazzling.

It is, indeed, a marvelous sight to behold. I stood there looking joyfully at the main altar not wanting to blink. I was so spellbound! The scene took my breath away! How grand are these architectural designs and what amazing geniuses they have in their historical past. I was so amazed, excited, and I had this indescribable feeling of euphoria.

The basement is a cemetery. The tombs of kings and queens, princes, princesses, members of the royal family, and aristocratic families were buried in this church.

Charlottenburg Palace or Schloss Charlottenburg - It is the oldest and largest palace in Berlin. What a splendor! Internal decorations are in the baroque and rococo styles. The grand rooms are elegant. The Golden Gallery is marvelous and has a large collection of fine paintings. The Porcelain Museum contains an amazing array of Chinese and Japanese porcelain.

We took a stroll in the baroque style gardens. They are fabulous and are a popular attraction.

Reichstag - It is another historic landmark in Germany. I would describe it as grandiose. Don't miss it, if you would visit Berlin.

Holocaust Memorial - This is a memorial to the Jewish victims of the Holocaust. It is a poignant reminder of the persecution the Jewish people had suffered.

Alexander Platz - We visited Alexander Platz. It is in East Berlin, and it is one of the famous squares. There is a huge shopping center in the square. I browsed at the merchandise. Then, we relaxed and listened to the playing and singing of street musicians. Street musicians are a gem. We gave them some euros and chatted with them. They invited us to visit Poland. They are from Poland. The East Side Gallery is in Alexander Platz. This is another museum to explore.

The Tiergarten - The Tiergarten is a big, popular park in Berlin. It is notable for its urban gardens. Tom and I sat here enjoying the pretty flowers in the well cultivated and lavish garden. We relaxed, stayed calm, and just watched the world go by.

On the side of the walkway are pictures of prominent men and women who had distinguished themselves in their chosen profession. Marlene Dietrich, German-American actress and singer was one of them.

Deutsches Historisches Museum – German Historical Museum - We toured the museum. There are two buildings that house the exhibits in the museum. The architectural designs of the buildings are fantastic. The museum presents German history, ancient Germany, unification of Germany, etc. There are exhibitions related to the Nazi period. This is one of the best museums in the world. The museum contains many astonishing collections – historical documents, maps, history of monarchies, religious icons, fine paintings and Christian paintings, sculptures, applied arts, weapons, harnesses, military devices, medals, uniforms, flags, treasury, etc.

There are more than 8,000 historical things articles/devices relating to politics, social, and economic advancements, etc.

Checkpoint Charlie - Charlie was the name given by the Western Allies to the Berlin Wall crossing point between East Berlin and West Berlin.

Two young men in military uniform standing at the checkpoint looked sharp. The U.S. flag is displayed.

Nearby is the Mauermuseum, a museum that tells the history of the Berlin Wall – the daring escapes of some East Berliners, the balloon escape, the East German tower, etc.

Gendarmenmarkt in Berlin in Germany - This is a famous and popular square in Berlin. It is the French section in Berlin. It is the site of the Konzerthaus (Concert Hall). The French and German Cathedrals are nearby. I took several pictures of the statue standing in the square. He is Friedrich Schiller, a great German poet, philosopher, and historian. The legendary Maestro Herbert von Karajan, a world-renowned conductor and a prominent figure in European classical music had conducted several concerts and symphony performances by the stellar Berliner Phiharmoniker Orchestra in elegant and spectacular Concert Halls in Berlin.

I have several CD recordings by the legendary Berliner Phiharmoniker Orchestra conducted by Herbert von Karajan.

The Victory Column in Berlin in Germany - It is a significant tourist attraction in Berlin City. It is a monument celebrating the Prussian victory in the Danish-Prussian War. Goldelse is the nickname the Berliners have affectionately given the statue. It is tall and stands majestically.

Kingdoms kept fighting one another since time immemorial! Every time we toured a historical museum in each country we visited, there was always a history about war – who they fought, who they defeated, who died, who the heroes were, etc. People fought one another since time immemorial. Even today, there is still fighting! Aggression is one of the leading causes of war!

Friedrichstrasse Street in Berlin in Germany - On this street, you will find beautiful and trendy merchandise in big and fantastic department stores. It was fun to shop and marvel at the awesome and different kinds of things in various stores.

Kaufhaus des Westens (KaDeWe) - KaDeWe is a large department store in Berlin. The tour guide dropped us off from his SUV and told us to have lunch on the second floor. We took the elevator ride to the second floor. I could not believe what I saw. So much food, just about anything - canned goods, dried goods, colorful food, gourmet food, etc. were available. Bar restaurants were abundant. It was amazing. We had a difficult time choosing where to eat. We ended up having lunch in a regular restaurant outside of this building. We chose the one that served regular meals. I ordered the most superb German food on the menu. Thank God for the blessing. I prayed before meal. I paused and reflected on God's goodness to us.

Unter den Linden - We took a stroll in Unter den Linden, a boulevard in the Mitte district of Berlin. Lush Linden trees with luxuriant foliage lined both sides of the walkway. It is wonderful to relax and let the gentle zephyr brush the cheeks, and just enjoy God's creations, the trees and nature.

Museum Island - Berlin's Museum Island is extraordinary. It contains five museums world famous. It is in the River Spree.

The Fuhrerbunker - The tour guide took us in front of a building in Berlin, stopped his SUV and pointed at the building.

He said, "That is the building where Hitler died. There is an underground bunker in that building where Hitler hid. He shot himself. If someone is telling you that Hitler is still alive, and he is impersonating Elvis Presley, don't believe that person. Hitler is dead, and he died in the underground bunker in that building."

Bis spater (See you later). Auf Wiedersehen (Goodbye). It is time to fly to Ireland.

The Brandenburg Gate in Berlin, Germany

Ireland

Ireland is an enchanting and charming island country in the North Atlantic. Majority of the people are Roman Catholics.

On our second day in Ireland, we purchased tickets and boarded the Hop-On Hop-Off tour bus for a two-day tour. We toured by bus and the orientation tour mentioned the highlights to see in Dublin. We toured Dublin on this bus twice. After the bus tour, we visited several places on our own.

In Dublin, the capital and largest city of Ireland, we toured the following most-visited tourist attractions:

Saint Patrick's Cathedral - It is one of the largest cathedrals in the heart of the City of Dublin. It is a pilgrimage site. We toured the cathedral. It is celestial. The interior - the sculptures, the Christian paintings, the stained-glass windows, and many more make one stand in awe at this splendid cathedral.

Christ Church Cathedral - The medieval Christ Church Cathedral in Dublin is also known as the Cathedral of the Holy Trinity. It is marvelous. This cathedral also serves as a place for concerts. The choir of the Church Christ Cathedral in Dublin is one of the best choirs in Dublin.

Saint Mary's Pro-Cathedral - Dublin, Ireland - It is a Roman Catholic Cathedral, and it is absolutely divine! There are plenty of amazing religious and Christian holy statues. We attended Holy Mass. It was wonderful.

Dublin Castle - According to the tour guide, a man with a beautiful accent, Dublin Castle in Dublin in Ireland is an important place in the history of Ireland. The castle is marked by exceptional elegance, splendor, and charm. It was built for King John of England as a protection fortress against invaders.

Today, the castle is used for governmental purposes, like ceremonial purposes, such as the inauguration of the Irish President. It is also used for hosting conferences like those of the European Council.

From the tour guide, we learned the history of the Dublin Castle. Notable parts of the Dublin Castle are the State Apartments, Chester Beatty Library, beautifully decorated private quarters and entertaining halls of the State Apartments, home to several members of royalty and British leaders. There is a collection of priceless artifacts in this castle. In the Dublin Gardens, there was once a black pool, dubh linn, from which the city Dublin got its name.

After the guided tour, we toured the castle by ourselves. There is an area in the Dublin castle that tells the history of the Easter Rising of 1916. It is on the wall.

I read James Connolly played a major role in the Easter Rising of 1916. He was wounded badly during the fighting. He was arrested later when the rebels surrendered. He was charged with treason, sentenced to death, and shot by firing squad.

The Irish people's rising against British rule paved the way for the independence of the Republic of Ireland.

Trinity College - This college is in the heart of Dublin, Ireland's capital. We took the guided tour. According to the tour guide, this college was founded in 1592 by Queen Elizabeth I on the grounds of an Augustinian priory.

It was originally a college only for men. It was opened to women years later with much opposition. It is filled with much history. Trinity College is best known for the Book of Kells housed in the "Long Room" in the Trinity College Library on campus and is one of the leading visitors' attractions. The Book of Kells consists of the four gospels (Saint Matthew, Saint Mark, Saint John, and Saint Luke) written in Latin. There are so many beautiful and astonishing sketches and symbols in the Book of Kells. The pages of the Book of Kells are turned once a year. If you happen to be there when the pages are turned, you have to come back on another day as the library is closed to the public on this day.

Temple Bar - We checked this bar. It was crowded. We could hardly find a seat. We browsed around. Then, we listened to a young man belting a song.

I had my picture taken with two young men who were so friendly and posed for a picture with me.

We left the bar and stepped outside. This is the Bohemian section in Dublin, Ireland. Like-minded people - artists, painters, musicians, poets, literary pursuers, writers, adventurers, wanderers, etc. congregate here. In the open air, there were street musicians and artists playing music. I danced and danced alone by myself while those musicians were playing music. People on the streets were clapping their hands and smiling at me while I danced.

They were pointing at me, and I guessed they were telling one another, "Look, look at her. She is dancing by herself."

I was enjoying myself that I have realized my dream to visit Ireland. I was smiling from ear-to-ear. Oh, well, I thought I was a gypsy! (I am laughing loudly). Has anybody seen the opera Carmen? The leading character is a gypsy. So, I danced and danced like a gypsy. I was having the great time of my life. I am at my happiest moment when I am in Europe! After all, I am Eurasian (European and Asian). My grandfather, Agustin Aguinaldo, was part Spanish.

We truly enjoyed the street musicians. They are a jewel. We have always stopped, listened, and watched their performance. I put some euros in the open container for the musicians.

O'Connell Street - Fely, the happy tourist, took a break from touring, sat down for a while, and watched the world go by on O'Connell Street. It is the busiest street in Dublin, followed by Abbey Street.

Daniel O'Connell Memorial Monument – Dublin. The O'Connell Memorial Monument, the memorial statue to Daniel O'Connell stands tall to the entrance of the street that was named after this great man.

Daniel O'Connell was an Irish man, a barrister, and a political activist. He was a staunch liberator. He campaigned vigorously for Catholic Liberation. He wanted Catholics to have the right to be able to sit in the Westminster Parliament. His campaign for Catholic Emancipation had succeeded! Catholic Emancipation was achieved! I would say this great man was the "cream of the crop" during his time.

Daniel O'Connell became the first Roman Catholic – Lord Mayor of the city of Dublin. I am so proud of him, a fellow Catholic.

Another memorial statue of Daniel O'Connell is in the Dublin City Hall. I took pictures of both statues.

National Gallery of Ireland (Dublin) - This museum houses European art, as well as national collection of Irish art. The gallery has an extensive Irish painting as well as Italian Baroque, and Dutch masters painting.

An exquisite collection of world renowned masterpieces abounded in the gallery. World-renowned artists on display include Da Vinci, Rembrandt, Vermeer, Monet, Renoir, Caravaggio, et al. The life-size painting of Caravaggio's "Taking of Christ" is sublime and amazing.

The many captivating Christian works of art took my breath away! I was spellbound enjoying the masterpieces. Wide variety of superb bronze sculptures on display were delightful for the tourists' eyes to behold. An ethereal experience!

We watched a movie that was presented by the museum employee. The movie explained how several of the paintings on display were created by the artists, and what they represent. It was fascinating.

National Wax Museum - This museum took us on an adventure through Irish cultural heritage.

It is an entertaining family and visitors' attraction. Also on exhibits are life-size wax figures of popular and eminent men and women who had distinguished themselves in what made them famous. Some of the characters in movies also have wax figures in this museum, such as Superman (Christopher Reeve), ET, Gollum (Lord of the Rings), Crocodile Dundee, Teenage Mutant Ninja Turtles, etc.

More wax figures on display are Irish figures of historical significance, such as Michael Collins (Easter Rising – group of Irish nationalists), famous world leaders, World War II leaders, et al. And, oh, the Chamber of Horrors scared me. Frankenstein and Dracula looked harshly at me and I thought they will grab me!

The General Post Office - The General Post Office on O'Connell Street is the headquarters of the Irish Post Office, An Post. We toured the post office. There is a large collection of stamps displayed on several boards. There are so many fantastic collections of stamps year after year. Exhibits also include postal and telecommunication devices. An audio CD is provided for the tour. The CD narrates the pictures on display.

Molly Malone Sculpture - Molly sells fish during the day. At night, she also works doing the oldest profession in the world since time immemorial. Just guess what that is. I won't tell you.

Phoenix Park - It is a big urban park in Dublin, Ireland. The U.S. ambassador has a residence in this park. We took the bus tour to see the park twice.

Many people visit this park. They explore the park, walk, run, sightsee, have a picnic, a party, gather with friends and kids, or just relax in the 1,750 acres of vast land. It is a popular area to visit.

On excursions, we visited the following tourist destinations in Ireland: Wicklow, Dun Laoghaire, Bray, Laragh, and Glendalough

Wicklow, Ireland - The Powerscourt House in Wicklow - We had an excursion to Wicklow. This is another picturesque place to visit in Ireland. The tour guide narrated the history of Powerscourt House. Once upon a time this was once a thirteenth century medieval castle that was owned by the Le Power Family from which Powerscourt got its name.

Fabulous flower gardens – The lavish gardens are filled with delightful and amazing sculptures of gods and mythical creatures. The spectacular Italian Gardens with many stunning and exquisite flowers, the Walled Garden, the dazzling Japanese Garden, the fragrant Rose Garden, and many more abound in the compound of the castle. The central fountain surrounded by individual garden is remarkably enjoyable. The panoramic view of the forty-seven acres of lush land in this area is captivating and exciting.

Glendalough in Ireland - We visited Glendalough. The tour guide told us the history of the town. It is a glacial valley. We visited the ruins of Saint Kevin's Abbey and an old cemetery. Saint Kevin, a hermit priest founded this monastic Abbey. The natural scene is spectacular. This valley is surrounded with trees, flowering plants, lakes, and meadows.

Dun Laoghaire – Ireland -We visited Dun Laoghaire. It is a seaside town in the County of Dublin. It is a charming town. In the harbor are big ships, big boats, and small boats, etc. I had a picture taken with the sea on the background.

The Coastal Tour – It is wonderful, and the scenery is fabulous.

Note: According to the taxi driver who drove us from Dublin Airport to the Sheldon Park Hotel in Dublin, Americans are very much loved in Ireland. When we went on a coastal tour, the tour guide said the same thing. From my own observation, yes, indeed, the American people are much loved in Ireland. I enjoyed our stay very much!

So long folks. It is time to fly to Scotland.

Scotland

Edinburgh is the capital city of Scotland. Discover the epic splendor of this magical, enchanting, and breathtaking European city. Revel in its enigmatic centuries of history, culture, arts, traditions, and pageantries, etc.

In Edinburgh, we visited the following fascinating places of interest:

Edinburgh's Castle - The first place we visited in Scotland is the Edinburgh Castle. We toured the castle and the buildings in the compound. It is a magical place. It is one of Edinburgh's must-see top visitors' attractions with centuries of history. Some of the highlights of the castle are the following:

There are some performers in regal costumes who bring Scottish historical past to life. I am mystified by their legendary performances.

King's Lodging – In this room, Mary, Queen of Scots gave birth to the future King James VI of Scotland. Later, he became King James I of England after the death of Queen Elizabeth I.

Crown Jewels Exhibition Room - The Honors of Scotland – including crown, scepter, sword, and other emblems, and symbols of Scottish royalty are displayed. During the time Oliver Cromwell seized Scotland, the crown, scepter, and the sword were hidden. They were found a hundred years later. Visitors can see the oldest regalia in the continent of Europe. The crown jewels are eye-catching and resplendent.

The Regimental Museum - This is an incredible museum. On exhibits are more Scottish regalia and other ornaments. Medals of military men abound in the Regimental Museum. Portrait paintings of some members of the royal family are also displayed.

In the defense area of the castle compound, we looked at the Argyll Battery (six gun battery). They look amazing and powerful. In this area, you can look down onto Princes Street, and see the winding medieval lanes, cobbled streets, etc. Princes Street is one of the nicest areas to shop, eat, and see more of great tourist attractions in Edinburgh. From here, one can also see panoramic views. It **is** breathtaking to behold!

The One O'clock Gun – This is a widely known time signal. It is fired every day at 1300 hours except on some designated days. It has been fired just about every day at 1:00 P.M. since 1861.

Great Hall - Built for business of state. Oliver Cromwell used it as a garrison for his army. Now, today, arms and armor and a "key" to the Castle are displayed. The hall is grand, and it is impressive.

The Scottish National War Memorial – It is a shrine honoring those who died during the war, from World War I and onwards. There are many names of those who died during several of the wars they fought.

The Royal Scots Dragoon Guard Statue – He is wearing a colorful Scottish costume – a kilt.

Saint Margaret's Chapel – This chapel is several centuries old. It is the oldest building in the compound.

The statue of Robert the Bruce, one of the kings of Scotland looked great.

Governor House in the Castle's compound - Tom and I posed for a picture in front of the nice house.

Prison building – It looked dark and gloomy.

The Royal Edinburgh Military Tattoo is held from 2 to 25 August (the dates could change) just in the front of the Castle entrance. This is a spectacular and phenomenal show. I enjoyed this place so much. It is amazing and awesome for a history and a museum buff like me.

Hop-On Hoff-Off Tour Bus - The next day we purchased two tickets to get on the Hop-On Hoff-Off tour bus for two days. The bus brought us to the most popular destinations and important places in Edinburgh. We also learned more of the history of Scotland and Edinburgh. We toured Edinburgh twice on this bus.

More tourists' destinations we have visited in Edinburgh are the following:

The Palace of Holyroodhouse - The Palace of Holyroodhouse in Edinburgh is a magnificent Baroque Palace. It is located at the end of the Royal Mile. It offers an experience very rich in history. It is the official residence of Queen Elizabeth II in Scotland. Mary, Queen of Scots (she was the last Catholic monarch of Scotland) and her second husband, Henry Stuart, Lord Darnley, lived here. Visitors can see the following: grand and lavishly decorated rooms, extravagant furnishings, some impressive works of art, splendid portraits in the portrait hall, Mary, Queen of Scots' bedchamber, Lord Darnley's bedchamber, etc.

"Rood" is an old word for a Christian Cross – the Cross which Jesus Christ was crucified upon. Holyrood means "Holy Cross."

Palace of Holyroodhouse means Palace of the Holy Cross House.

The Augustinian Abbey Ruins - Tom took several pictures of the fantastic and majestic abbey ruins. You will see the abbey ruins when the tour is about to conclude.

The exit leads to the gorgeous flower gardens and amazing grounds of the palace. Currently, this palace is the setting for state occasions and official entertaining.

The Royal Mile - The souvenir stores in the Royal Mile in Edinburgh provide a wonderful shopping experience. The stores offer exuberant choice of awesome souvenirs. Tom bought a bagpipe and a kilt. He would like to play his bagpipe wearing a kilt. I bought a shirt and a purse bearing the country's name "SCOTLAND." I enjoyed shopping in the Royal Mile. It was wonderful just to stroll and shop for souvenirs. It was extremely fun.

Beautiful and impressive buildings with stunning architecture in the Royal Mile are astounding.

Sir Walter Scott - There are several statues of prominent men in downtown Edinburgh. One of them is Sir Walter Scott, famous Scottish poet and writer. He wrote the following books: *Ivanhoe*, *The Talisman*, *Waverly*, etc.

The Statue of the Duke of Wellington - The statue of the Duke of Wellington was in walking distance from our hotel. I looked at this grand statue meticulously and pondered about the life of this distinguished man. Together with the Allied Army, Wellington and his men defeated Napoleon Bonaparte at the Battle of Waterloo. He was one of the greatest military commanders of all time.

The National Gallery in Edinburgh - The National Gallery in Edinburgh is the national art gallery of Scotland. The exhibitions are stunning. The gallery displays the incredible and great masterpieces of prolific artists and painters such as Anthony Van Dyck, El Greco, Francisco de Goya, Tintoretto, Leonardo da Vinci, Raphael, Sandro Boticelli, Gian Lorenzo Bernini, Rembrandt Van Rijn, Paul Cezanne, et al. I particularly loved the life-size painting of "Jesus Taken Down the Cross" by Tintoretto. This is the ultimate manifestation of Christ's everlasting love - dying on the Cross for the salvation of mankind. "The Virgin Adoring the Sleeping Christ Child" by Boticelli, "Christ Blessing (The Saviour)" by El Greco, and "Christ in the House of Martha and Mary" by Johannes Vermeer are enthralling. There is an exuberant display of more Christian works of art in this gallery – spreading Christianity through works of art. The Portrait Gallery is enchanting and captivating as well. Sculptures abound in the gallery.

The Royal Yacht Britannia - The Royal Yacht Britannia in Edinburgh, Scotland - It was the former Royal Yacht of Her Majesty Queen Elizabeth II. It was her floating royal residence away from home. The yacht is immense. We purchased the entrance fees, and using an audio CD guide provided with the entrance fees, we toured the resplendent ship. There are numerous of incredible memorabilia. I am listing some of the following items we saw on the ship:

- Binnacle on the Veranda
- Admiral's Cabin and Quarters
- Chief Petty Officers' Mess
- Engine Room
- Sweet Shop
- Tea Room
- Royal Bedrooms
- Sun Lounge - It was the Queen's favorite.
- Dispensary – Medical staff, doctors, medicines, etc. were available for the royal family and the crew.
- Elegant Drawing Room - This was the room for the members of the royal family for relaxing, chatting, playing the piano, playing cards, etc.
- State Dining Room – This is a grand and luxurious room – There are stunning silverwares, fabulous crystal drinking glasses, exquisite plates, fancy long dining table cloth, dazzling chandeliers, etc. The world's most influential and prominent people such as Winston

Churchill, Boris Yeltsin, Rajiv Gandhi, President Ronald Reagan, President William Clinton, Nelson Mandela, et al had dinner in this affluent room with Queen Elizabeth II, royal family members, and prominent British government officials. The audio guide said setting the large dining table was meticulous. The placements of the silverwares, plates, crystal drinking and glasses, etc. are measured!

I enjoyed this incredible tour so much. It was indeed a fascinating and an enjoyable tour.

After touring the Royal Yacht Britannia, I posed for a picture in the Exhibition Hall. Then, we visited the souvenir store. I bought a dazzling tiara (fake stones, not precious) with glitters fit for a queen. I wore it once in our hotel suite at the Holiday Inn Hotel, and had a picture taken.

I told Tom, "This is Her Majesty, Queen Ofelia." I was pretending for fun only. I thought I would wear it to church may be occasionally, but I haven't had the courage to wear it yet. It is on display on the book case in the living room of our home.

The Hard Rock Café in Edinburgh in Scotland - It is always good to visit any Hard Rock Café in Europe and buy a Hard Rock Café shirt or some souvenirs. Tom likes buying miniature guitars at Hard Rock Cafe. Also, every Hard Rock Café is unique and one is not the same as any other. The pictures of rock stars and other decorations are different.

The Holiday Inn Hotel - We stayed at the Holiday Inn Hotel on the fifth floor during our trip to Edinburgh. If you would travel to Edinburgh, I recommend this hotel. It is centrally located, and it is in the heart of the city. Breakfast is provided with the cost of the room. The breakfast is brunch. Food is superb and plentiful. The members of the staff of this hotel are courteous and friendly.

We signed up for an excursion and visited more places in Scotland frequented by tourists.

The driver of the beautiful luxury coach (bus) took us on an excursion to Costorffin, Glasgow, Aberfoyle, Loch Lomond, Trossachs, and Sitrling.

Glasgow, Scotland - Glasgow means "green hollow"– It is a big city in Scotland, and it is a major port. It is known widely for its architecture – the Victorian and art nouveau. Regarding culture – the opera, ballet, and theatre performances are held in Glasgow theatres. The performing art is my cup of tea. I love the performing arts.

Aberfoyle - It is a lovely holiday village in Scotland. The Scottish Centre tells the story of how wool is made from the sheep to the shop. We visited a store that sells plenty of ravishing coats made of wool. The main street is attractive and it is lined with cafes, shops, and restaurants. There were so many sheep in the sheep farm, and it was interesting observing them.

Loch Lomond and Trossachs National Park - We purchased tickets and boarded a big boat in Loch Lomond. It is a fresh water Scottish loch or lake in Scotland. During the one-hour cruise, we relaxed and enjoyed the scenery. The panoramic view was refreshing and fabulous. We saw mountains in the distance, lush trees, vegetation, rugged hills, many kayaks, canoes, every kind of watercraft, jet-ski, big, private boats, elegant castles in the distance, and of course the sparkling freshwater loch, etc.

While we were sitting comfortably on the boat, Tom suddenly startled me and said, "I saw a Loch Ness monster emerging in the water, and it is going to grab you and sink the boat."

I said, "Where?"

There was none! He was just kidding me. He likes to kid. He likes to scare me, but sometimes he makes me laugh.

What a unique and tranquil adventure it was. A 360-degree of breathtaking beauty!

The Visit to Stirling Castle - We toured the Stirling Castle. It was a guided tour. The tour guide, a man with a beautiful Scottish accent conducted the tour. He narrated the history of Stirling Castle. This was a very valuable castle for successful military strategy in Scotland. This castle has been fought over in several bloody battles. The castle was lost to the British. It was regained and lost again, was regained again, etc. The castle had changed ownership so many times.

The tour guide also said little infant Mary, Queen of Scots and her mother were moved to Stirling Castle for their safety. King Henry the VIII wished to have infant Mary as a future bride for his infant son. They did not want the wish of the King, so Mary was hidden in the Stirling Castle.

The life-size statue of Robert the Bruce, one of the kings of Scotland, is on the lawn of the Stirling Castle in Scotland. There are several old buildings in the compound of Stirling Castle.

England

I love England. I love English literature. English is my favorite subject. London, the capital of England and the United Kingdom, is a remarkable and fantastic city with incredible history dating back to Roman periods. Tourists have many reasons to visit London, one of the most populous cities in England, and explore its history, culture, arts, traditions, pageantries, and sightseeing attractions frequented by tourists.

The Double-Decker Tour Bus - My momma and I hopped on this open-top double-decker hop-on hop-off tour bus on a sightseeing tour of the resplendent and astonishing city of London, and discovered London's top tourist attractions.

We visited the following places of interest highlighted on the tour, the must-see sites to visit:

Buckingham Palace - It is the official residence of Her Majesty, Queen Elizabeth II, and her husband, Prince Philip, the Duke of Edinburgh, the prince consort in the city of London. It is here where most state occasions are held. In this palace, Queen Elizabeth II and her spouse receive and entertain guests, such as heads of state, presidents, prime ministers, monarchs, dignitaries, etc. from all over the world. Buckingham Palace is grand and impressively beautiful. Mom and I toured the areas open to the public.

We explored the grand staircase, the elegant State Rooms, and the beautiful Throne Room. There are nineteen State Rooms. They are extremely awesome and elaborately decorated. Investitures and ceremonial receptions are regularly held in the Ballroom.

The fine art exhibits are exquisite works by Rembrandt, Rubens, Vermeer, Canaletto and Claude, Poussin, Van Dyck, et al. The paintings in the State Room also include exquisite portraits of the members of the royal family from the past and present. Glittering and huge candelabras, ornamental vases, marble columns, fine English and French furniture, sculptures, porcelain effigy, precious antiques, etc. decorate the State Rooms.

The portrait of Queen Elizabeth II is beautiful. She is regal in her queen outfit with a sparkling crown on her head. She is a much beloved queen. I am a fan of royalty. I love English regalia, and English royalty. There is a collection of Sevres porcelain. They are fabulous.

While we were in queue waiting to tour the palace, a young Japanese woman was offering $500 to anyone who would give up their line and take their place. She said she is leaving the next day, and that day is the only chance she had to see the palace. No way would Mom and I give up our line for $500. Seeing Buckingham Palace was priceless!

Ofelia in front of the Edinburgh's Castle in Edinburgh, Scotland

Tight security was observed before touring the palace. We were inspected thoroughly like we were boarding an aircraft. It took a total of almost three hours standing in queue to enter the palace.

Additional highlight of this Buckingham tour is the Special Exhibition. Separate tours are available for the gardens. Then, you can visit the garden café and garden shop.

The Changing of the Guards – Buckingham Palace. In front of Buckingham Palace, we watched the "Changing of the Guards." It is one of the most beautiful ceremonies I have ever seen. The guards in their colorful uniforms marching and playing musical instruments were awesome to behold. What a sight! I love the spectacle, the elaborate display, the magnificence and the grandeur of the "Changing of the Guards" ceremony and other English ceremonial traditions.

The beauty and the pageantry of England with all its splendor and glory – just awesome!

In London, we toured more places, and enjoyed the following tourists' spots frequented by tourists.

Westminster Cathedral – The Westminster Cathedral in London is a Roman Catholic cathedral. It is also known as the "Cathedral of the Precious Blood of our Lord, Jesus Christ." It is a magnificent church. Mom and I toured the cathedral. Above the entrance door of the church, there is an arch. In the middle of the arch is the image of Jesus Christ.

Above the arch are the words:

Domine Jesu Rex Et Redemptor (O Jesus, King and Redeemer).

Per Sanguiem Tuum Salve Nos (Protect Us by Thy Blood).

The interior is celestial, awe-inspiring, and breathtaking. The big Crucifix is hung high above the main alter. It is glorious to see the well decorated ceiling with heavenly angels, the Christian sculptures and objects, the beautiful arches on both sides of the church, the mystifying mosaics, etc. The visit to this cathedral is divine. There is a sculpture of Saint Peter in this Basilica. It is almost like the sculpture at Saint Peter's Basilica in Rome.

Mom and I enjoyed touring the Westminster Cathedral in London.

Saint Paul's Cathedral, London – We visited Saint Paul's Cathedral in London. It is an Anglican cathedral. The dome of this cathedral is world-renowned. It is one of London's skyscrapers. The interior is celestial and astounding. Looking at the main altar and rich work that's abound in the cathedral, gives one a divine feeling. The wedding of Prince Charles, Prince of Wales, and Lady Diana Spencer took place in this cathedral.

Trafalgar Square – It is a public square in the city of Westminster, London. It is a historical landmark. It is crowded. It is the busiest and it is a charming part of London. There are many, many pigeons. The Nelson's Column (Admiral Lord Nelson) stands majestically in Trafalgar Square.

Admiral Horatio Nelson was the most famous admiral of the Napoleonic Wars and the greatest sea warrior in the history of the British.

Westminster Abbey – The architectural design is Gothic. It was formerly a Roman Catholic Benedictine Abbey before the English Reformation. It is a place of coronation where English kings and queens were crowned. Queen Elizabeth II was crowned in Westminster Abbey in June 1953. It is also a burial site of English and British monarchs, statesmen, poets, priests, soldiers, heroes, etc. as well. There are plenty of beautiful tombs.

Pageant of British history comes alive in seeing this Abbey. It is an essential part of the tour, if you visit the beautiful city of London.

Mom and I attended a concert at Westminster Abbey. It was performed by a group of young school children. It was lovely.

Saint Martin-in-the-Fields – It is an English Anglican church near Trafalgar Square. The architecture is beautiful. The interior is ethereal.

National Gallery – It is in Trafalgar Square and an art museum. We toured the National Gallery. It is spectacular. There are more than 2,300 paintings from the 13th century to 1900. It is mystifying looking closely at some of the great paintings of all times especially the Christian paintings. I will mention some of them:

"The Virgin and Child" by Leonardo da Vinci, "Mond Crucifixion" by Raphael, "The Entombment" by Michelangelo, "Agony in the Garden" by Giovanni Bellini, "Mars and Venus" by Sandro Botticelli, "Samson and Delilah" by Peter Paul Rubens, "Bacchus and Ariadne" by Titian, "Belshazzar's Feast" by Rembrandt, "Music in the Tuileries" by Edouard Manet, etc.

10 Downing Street – It is the headquarters of Her Majesty's government and the official residence of the Prime Minister of England. We took a stroll in the area. It is a nice place to live in London.

Palace of Westminster is also known as the Houses of Parliament. This is where the members of the House of Lords and the House of Commons of the

United Kingdom work. It is a grand, magnificent building whose architectural style is Gothic, and it is one of the most noticeable in the world.

Sir Winston Churchill, Parliament Square - The statue of Sir Winston Churchill is in Parliament Square. I looked at this statue closely and admire it. Sir Winston Churchill is one of my favorite statesmen. I love his famous words, "We make a living by what we get, but we make a life by what we give." I live by them.

The Clock Tower – It stands majestically at the north end of the Houses of Parliament. "Big-Ben" is the nickname for the great bell of the clock. It is beautiful, and I was told this clock is the most accurate clock in the world.

Kensington Palace is the official residence of some members of the royal family. It is awesome. The state rooms are open to the public. We toured the palace. The artworks collection in the King's Gallery is awesome. The palace gardens are gorgeous.

The Tower of London - Crown Jewels - Momma and I visited the Tower of London. It is world-renowned, and it is one of the most visited places in London. The Crown Jewels are stunning and awesome. Wow! There are many huge sparkling diamonds, fine rubies, pearls, emeralds, and other precious gems. I stood in awe in seeing such beauty and affluence. In addition to the Crown Jewels, there are other collections of objects such as sabers, armors, shields, replicas of knights, etc.

I have my picture taken with a Yeoman Warder (Beefeater). I love his colorful uniform. It is regal. The Yeomen Warders of Her Majesty's Royal Palace and Fortress, Tower of London, popularly known as the "Beefeaters," are ceremonial guardians of the Tower of London.

The following are some of the highlights or major attractions in the Tower of London. We saw:

White Tower, The Bloody Tower, The Medieval Palace, The Tower Torture, and the Fortress.

Tower Bridge - It is an iconic symbol of London. It is a must-see landmark. This is a bascule and suspension bridge. I stared at it, and saw how marvelous it is.

Piccadilly Circus and Leicester Squares are two busy squares in the heart of London. The fountain in Leicester Square is lovely.

Leicester Square – There is a statue of Charlie Chaplain in this square. He was an actor, comedian, and filmmaker.

Covent Garden Plaza – Remember the movie "My Fair Lady"? The movie actress, Audrey Hepburn, who played Eliza Doolittle, peddled her flowers in Covent Garden. Shopping, bars, restaurants, history, theatres, markets, culture – you name it, Covent Garden has just about everything.

The Movenpick Restaurant in London - The Movenpick Restaurant is a Swiss restaurant. You choose your food, and the chef will cook the meal for you – food to die for! This is our favorite restaurant in London. Momma and I dined here often. This restaurant offers the best ice cream in the world. We had superb ice cream. I have never seen such giant cheese in my whole life till I saw some in this restaurant. Yummy!

At the James Park - My momma and I enjoyed relaxing at the James Park in England. Some English people we met in London told us Queen Elizabeth II visits the park every now and then. She mingles with the common people. Mom and I sat there hoping the Queen will arrive and be able to chat with her. She did not visit that day. We were not lucky to have seen her. That would have been a wonderful experience of a life time. It would have been so fantastic, if my momma and I were able to meet her.

The Brompton Arcade in the Knightsbridge in London - It is one of the most exclusive and expensive shopping centres (that it is how centres is spelled in England) at the heart of London. It is close to Harrods and Harvey Nichols. Brompton Arcade is an attraction for the affluent people. Interesting boutiques, bars, restaurants, chains of stores, and cafés abound in the Arcade.

London shopping - My momma and enjoyed window shopping in London. It was delightful to see many beautiful and luxurious merchandise sold in several stores in London. I bought a purse at Harrods, music of the musicals we have attended, *Les Miserables* cups, and some pictures of the interesting places in the city of London. It was just one of the fun things Mom and I did in London besides touring and touring historical and tourist's places. I am remembering wonderful memories bonding with my mother.

River Thames – It is the longest river in England. It is fun to take a boat cruise and see the major attractions around London on a boat.

Planet Hollywood – It is a restaurant that makes you feel like you are a Hollywood celebrity. The food is delicious. Mom ordered a pizza. I ordered a grilled chicken with all the trimmings.

Hard Rock Café – The theme is Rock N Roll. Pictures of some famous rock stars, movie stars, singers, Hollywood stuff, and rock memorabilia are on display in the restaurant. Momma and I had lunch at the Hard Rock Café in London. We had American classics and hamburgers. The burger was juicy and delicious. Mom and I enjoyed the Hard Rock Café in London, and the typical scrumptious American food we savored. My nephew Emmanuel gave me a Hard Rock Café shirt he bought in London when he went overseas. The shirt is too big for me. I could not wear it, but I kept it in my closet for remembrance.

Hyde Park – It is one of the largest parks in London. It is also a concert venue. At the Speaker's Corner, you can stand there, and deliver a speech stating your cause. I would like to return to London and deliver a speech at the Speaker's Corner to encourage and invite people to feed the poor. It is good to have a passion in feeding the poor.

Live Theatre Shows - We attended the following live theatre shows in London:

Les Miserables – We attended the performance of *Les Miserables* at the Palace Theatre. This enormous theatre in London's West End is beautiful and daunting. The performances of the cast were phenomenal. I got sentimental. I cried watching this London musical. It was the first time I have seen it. As the years went by, I attended this show six times. This musical is a hit. My favorite songs in this musical are "On My Own," the song sung by Eponine (one of the characters of the show) and "Bring Him Home," the song sung by Jean Valjean (the leading character). I enjoyed this delightful show so much.

The Phantom of the Opera – We attended the performance of *The Phantom of the Opera* at the Her Majesty's Theatre. This theatre in London's West End Theatre District is magnificent. I stood in awe, wondering how fantastic the theatre is. The extravagant production of this live theatre show is spectacular. It is world-class. The captivating score of this hit musical was composed by Andrew Lloyd Webber, one of my favorite contemporary composers. The rapturous music will send you into bliss. See the show, and watch for that immense chandelier! It was a thrill. With great delight, we enjoyed the show so much. I think everyone was ecstatic. My favorite song in this musical is "All I Ask of You." It is the duet of Christine and Raoul, the leading characters.

Sunset Boulevard – This live theatre show about an aging movie star and her young lover was performed at the Adelphi Theatre in London's West End Theatre District. This is another resplendent theatre. The enchanting score was composed by Andrew Lloyd Webber. The melodies are gorgeous. The performances of the stars were legendary. I love the song "With One Look." It is a solo number by the leading character named Norma Desmond. This is another fun and enjoyable musical. Mom and I truly enjoyed this sophisticated and enthralling musical.

Starlight Express - The Apollo Victoria Theatre in London, England is where the *Starlight Express* was performed. This live show is a rock musical, and the lovely score was composed by Andrew Lloyd Webber. The cute story is about a young kid's dream in which his toy train set comes to life. The actors wore roller-skates during the performance.

Cats – We attended the performance of *Cats*. This legendary and magical musical is a nice treat. The cats are personified. You will meet the cats named Grizabella, Old Deuteronomy, Victoria, Jennyanydots, Rum Tum Tugger, Bustopher Jones, Macavity, et al. The timeless music, the beautifully choreographed dancing and the overall performances were phenomenal. Who can forget the song "Memory?" Andrew Lloyd Webber composed the wonderful score.

Stratford-Upon-Avon - One of my favorite points of interest in England is Stratford-upon-Avon. It is a medieval town in Warwickshire in England. Mom and I took a taxi to see Stratford-upon-Avon. I was wondering if it may not be the right thing to do as the place was far away from where we were. I thought it was too expensive to hire a taxi driver.

Momma said, "Don't worry; don't miss the place you would like to see. Go for it. You will regret it, if you don't go."

So, with that encouragement, I heeded her encouragement. We hired a taxi driver named Charles. Charles was so kind. He drove us to everywhere we wanted to go.

The following are the points of interest we visited in Stratford-upon-Avon:

Shakespeare's Birthplace – It is a modest home. It is quite a nice home. I took a picture of it. It is beautiful. This is the place where Shakespeare was born.

Church of the Holy Trinity – This is the church where Shakespeare was baptized. He was buried in this church.

Anne Hathaway's Cottage – This is the home of Anne Hathaway, the wife of William Shakespeare. Anne was eight years older than Shakespeare. She was twenty-six years old and William was eighteen years old when they got married. The home was cozy. The pieces of furniture and home decorations reveal a sort of a well to do family.

Mary Arden's Farm – Mary Arden is the Momma of William Shakespeare. This farmhouse was owned by Mary Arden. We toured the home, and the ceiling was low. I had to stoop. It was, however, a beautiful home.

Hall's Croft - John and Susanna Hall's residence. Susanna was the oldest daughter of William Shakespeare. It was a beautiful comfortable home.

The Shakespeare Monument - The monument shows Shakespeare seated at the peak overlooking statues of the characters of some of his plays. They are: Hamlet, Lady Macbeth, Falstaff, et al. The memorial is in the dazzling Bancroft Gardens.

Royal Shakespeare Theatre – In the theatre, the plays of Shakespeare are performed. It is a strikingly beautiful and impressive theatre.

There are also some sculptures of the characters of Shakespeare like Portia in the play *The Merchant of Venice*, Hamlet in the play *Hamlet*, et al in one of the buildings we visited.

The Trees - There is a garden that contains the trees mentioned in Shakespeare's plays.

Harvard House – It is the house of the mother of John Harvard. We looked at the furnishings, the home decors, the living and dining rooms, the utensils - plates, pots and pans, spoons in the kitchen, etc.

William Shakespeare is one of my favorite bards. I am happy I was able to see Stratford-upon-Avon. Charles, our taxi driver said to me, "I have never met someone who loves Shakespeare that much." I gave him a very good tip for driving us around. He took care of us very well, so he deserved it. He was happy and grateful. He had a big smile. I appreciated him very much.

Shakespeare's literary works are full of passion and extremely beautiful language. In Shakespeare's play when a man falls in love, he does not just say, "I love you," to the maiden. He would include exquisite language in wooing her. Shakespeare was born several centuries ago, yet his works are still very much in our midst today. His plays are studied in school, performed in theatres, and made into movies.

I have the movies (DVDs) of all his thirty-seven plays. I have the BBC productions. I enjoy watching them every now and then.

Shakespeare's Plays - My favorite play is *The Merchant of Venice*. If you have seen, or read, the play, you will remember the characters - Shylock, Portia, Bassanio, Antonio, Jessica, Gratiano, Nerissa, Duke of Venice, et al.

My other favorite plays are: *Two Gentlemen of Verona, The Tempest, The Merry Wives of Windsor, As You Like It, All's Well That Ends Well, Love's Labour's Lost, The Winter's Tale, Hamlet, Othello,* and *Julius Caesar.*

I love the English accent. It is lovely. I love London and Stratford-upon-Avon. London is one of my favorite cities in Europe. My favorite city is Vatican City, Rome is the second, and London is the third.

Dover – We boarded a tour bus that took us to Dover. Oh, the white cliffs of Dover are really white. The bus driver drove the bus and entered the big ship and parked the bus. We got out of the bus and sat down in a nice comfortable room. The ship sailed in the English Channel to Calais. This ship is like a big building. There are bars, restaurants, stores, etc. Mom and I had lunch, and it was superb. When the sailing was over, the bus driver took us on a tour to Paris. That was the first time we went to Paris. Years later, we returned again and again.

Cambridge in England is a city in Eastern England. It is the home of the University of Cambridge, a very prestigious University. Mom and I boarded a tour bus. The driver drove us to the tourists' attractions in Cambridge. The tour guide told us the names of the different universities and colleges we were seeing on the tour. He pointed at the Trinity College and said that Prince Charles attended Trinity College. After the tour, the tour guide dropped us off at the Kings College Chapel. It is a towering Gothic Chapel. We toured the interior of the chapel. It is breathtaking. It took my breath away. It is sublime! The main altar, the religious articles, the stained-glass windows are awe-inspiring.

In Stratford-upon-Avon in England

At the Westminster Cathedral in London, England

Momma Librada in London, England

The author attended the performance
of "Les Miserables" in London with her Momma Librada.

*Ofelia and her Momma attended the performance of "The Phantom of the Opera"
in London, England.*

Spain

In sunny Spain, we lived in Menorca, a little Balearic island in the Mediterranean Sea. It is known for its long beaches and turquoise color water bays. My son William and I watched the harbor from the balcony of our apartment every now and then. Ships come and go. Boat contests were held in the Mediterranean Sea.

Barcelona and Madrid - We visited Barcelona and Madrid. Madrid is the capital of Spain. We toured the following tourist attractions in Madrid:

Royal Palace – Madrid, Spain - This is a gigantic palace. The architectural style of the palace is Classicism and Baroque. We took the guided tour. A beautiful Spanish lady conducted the tour in English. She said state ceremonies and other state functions are held in the palace. The palace is the largest royal palace in Europe with 2,800 rooms. You can see such opulence in the palace. There is a collection of great historical and artistic importance. In the interior are awesome frescoes by distinguished men. Candelabras, porcelains, watches, silverware, furniture, and many Flemish tapestries are displayed. There is a Royal Armoury – weapons, armours, etc. are preserved. Art work by Caravaggio, Velasquez, Francisco Goya lavishly adorn the palace.

The Crown Jewels – Brilliant cut diamonds and other sparkling precious gems are locked in a glass case, but tourists can view them very well. I stood in awe trying not to blink, so I can admire and enjoy the beauty of the treasured stones.

Museo Nacional del Prado - The Prado Museum is the primary Spanish national art museum. It houses an exquisite collection of European art from the 12th century to the early 20th century. This is the first art museum I have seen in Europe. This museum started my passion and love for art museum as well as historical museum. Featured artists whose masterpieces are on exhibits in this museum are by famous painters/artists such as El Greco, Fra Angelico, Francisco de Goya, Diego Velasquez, Francisco Zurbaran, Raphael, Peter Paul Rubens, Rembrandt van Rijn, Antonello de Messina et al.

My favorites are: "The Annunciation" by Fra Angelico; "Agnus Dei (Lamb of God)" by Francisco Zurbaran, "Dead Christ Supported by an Angel" by Antonello de Messina, and "The Clothed Maja" by Francisco Goya. The portrait paintings of kings and other members of royalties looked so real as if they are alive, and they are talking to you.

Statues - In Central Madrid at the Plaza de Espana are the equestrian statues of Don Quijote (Quixote) de La Mancha and Sancho Panza, fictional characters in the novel *Don Quixote* written by Don Miguel de Cervantes Saavedra.

Buen Retiro Park - It is a public park and one of the largest parks in Madrid. The equestrian bronze statue of King Alfonso XII is in the middle of the park overlooking a lake. I saw swans in the lake. I sat down and enjoyed the nature in the park - blooming flowers, lush trees, and feeling the gentle zephyr brushed my cheeks. We are reminded of God's presence in the mystifying beauty of nature all around us. We must look and feel God is there.

Plaza Mayor, Madrid - We visited the Plaza Mayor. It is a grand monumental square in Madrid. At the center of the square is a bronze effigy of King Philip III. It was used for royal coronations, bull fights, and other celebrations before. Nowadays, it is used for public festivities. It is a crowded place. It is a popular tourist spot.

Hasta la vista. (See you later). Adios (Bye).

The Souvenirs

I think I over bought souvenirs, but when it comes to the Lord, it is priceless. I bought eighteen Rosaries and several Shepherd Cross, or Papal Cross in Vatican City, Rome, and Lourdes. Most of the Rosaries have the replica of the Shepherd Cross and the four major basilicas in Rome. The Rosaries in Lourdes have the crucifix and the replica of the Blessed Virgin Mary (Our Lady of Lourdes) and Saint Bernadette. They are all made in Italy. I am feeling holy praying the Rosary, taking turns using each Rosary. I rotate which Rosary to use on a given day. Whatever it takes to make you feel the nearness of the Lord and the Blessed Mother Mary, is all right.

I bought more souvenirs – two bracelets with Shepherd Cross (Papal Cross) and images of Papa Francesco and Saint Peter's Basilica, two bracelets with the image of Saint Bernadette praying to the Our Lady of Lourdes, a hat in Lourdes, a hat in Rome, three handbags, nine scarves, pins, refrigerator magnets, Eiffel Tower replica, banners with landmarks of Paris, Pisa, and Rome, a shirt with the landmarks of Italia, statue of Our Lady of Lourdes, containers for Lourdes water (I brought some water.), picture of Papa Francesco, a stained picture of the Notre Dame Cathedral to put on our window, and two raincoats in Paris, etc. I choose which beautiful Rosary to use when I pray the Rosary every day.

Tom bought several coins of the major basilicas and cathedrals. We had fun shopping, and I love the Rosaries and Christian objects.

Canada

The flight to Canada was smooth with no delays. We had a great time on a vacation. In Canada, we toured the following tourists' attractions:

Montreal in Canada - Montreal is known as the New France. It was founded by the French people on May 17, 1642. The inhabitants of Montreal are bilingual, speaking both French and English. The English also came to Montreal and settled here. I felt like I was in Paris again. I love the French language. It is fascinating. Montreal is the largest city in the Quebec province of Canada. Our priest friend told us the people in Montreal are friendly. How true! They are indeed friendly.

The InterContinental Hotel in Montreal - Jan B., our travel agent who had always helped us in planning our travel every year, reserved for us to stay at the InterContinental Hotel. The hotel is described as a luxury and elegant hotel. Indeed, it fits the description. The lobby is richly decorated with exquisite and sparkling grand chandeliers, nice sofas, tables, and more. The bars and the restaurants are beautiful. Our room was on the 25th floor in this high-rise hotel. One of our priest friends loves high-rise hotels.

The rooms in the hotel were very spacious. The rooms contained a big television, a large king-size bed, one wing chair, another chair, one round table, a square bigger table, nice lamps, a dresser with several drawers, a closet for clothes with white robes, a refrigerator filled with bottles of water for free, hairdryer, fragrant hand lotion, and other toiletries.

The breakfast was a brunch. There was abundant, superb food served for breakfast – various kinds of bread, desserts - croissants, cinnamon rolls, muffins, cakes, cheeses, boiled eggs, scrambled eggs, meats, French food entrees cooked every morning, fruits, marmalades, juices, chocolates, etc. We savored the delicious food. Thank God for the blessings. God is kind.

I read from a travel magazine the concierge in a hotel was very knowledgeable. The concierge knew everything about travel. Example: If a show was solidly booked, and a tourist wanted to see that show, the concierge would find a way to get the person into that show.

This statement is true. I met two concierges at the InterContinental Hotel in Montreal in Canada. They were Madame Chantal and Mr. Gerry L. Madame Chantal and Mr. Gerry L. were extra friendly and courteous. When my husband and I needed help with our travel needs, they provided us with the most stellar assistance a traveler could only dream. Their willingness to go the extra mile in serving us made them valuable members of the InterContinental Hotel in Montreal. They performed their job superbly in meeting the customers' needs. They were awesome, wonderful, and remarkable. A million thanks to Madame Chantal and Mr. Gerry L. Thanks to their supervisor, as well, for having employees like them.

The Elegant Dinner - Every day dinner was served in the Osco Restaurant, the restaurant in the InterContinental Hotel. It was elegant, warm, and nicely decorated with lovely, glittering chandeliers, and other fine decorations. On the dining tables were exquisite table cloths, stylish cloth napkins, a candle base, nice silverwares, and chic drinking glasses. The list on the menu offered a wide selection of entrees. One night for dinner, I ordered a menu of succulent large shrimp flambees with absinthe, confit fenne. The menu included salad greens, asparagus, and purple potatoes. The scrumptious, mouth-watering flavors of the Provencal dish with all the trimmings were enjoyable. The restaurant served the most superb French food. Adjacent to the Osco Restaurant was the lovely Sarah B. Bar, which provided alluring various kinds of wines.

Thank God for the blessing of a nice vacation and superb food. All these things are blessings from God. God is kind. I always pray before a meal and give thanks to the Lord God.

We also had dinner at an elegant and nice restaurant in Place Jacques-Cartier. The food was superb, as well. I am grateful to the Lord.

La Basilique Notre-Dame de Montreal - The first place we visited in Montreal was the La Basilique Notre-Dame de Montreal (The Notre-Dame Basilica of Montreal). La Basilique Notre-Dame de Montreal vous accueille! (The Notre-Dame Basilica of Montreal welcomes you!) We took the guided tour and visited the La Basilique Notre-Dame de Montreal.

The tour guide said, "How many of you have heard about Sainte-Chapelle?"

I raised my right hand and said, "We were in the Sainte-Chapelle in Paris last year, August 2015."

The tour guide said, "Wow." She began the tour and said, "The Notre Dame Cathedral in Montreal was patterned after the Sainte-Chapelle in Paris. The architectural design is Gothic. Gothic style architecture is the pointed arch. The style also shows like there are two hands clasped together in prayer. Do you see the Corinthian columns? They are beautiful. Look at the ceiling. The ceiling depicts Heaven. See the stars? They are made of real gold leaf. Can you imagine how much gold was used for the many stars you see in the ceiling? The basilica's architect was James O'Donnell." She continued the tour by talking about the organ – the much talk about organ, the sanctuary, the altar, the heavy bells, and the ornaments/objects, etc.

After the guided tour, Tom and I explored the cathedral by ourselves. On the main altar above the Tabernacle is a Crucifix. Above the Crucifix is the image of the Blessed Mother Mary being crowned by her son, Jesus. On the right side of the altar on the wall is the statue of Saint Peter holding two keys. On the left side of the altar on the wall is the statue of Saint Paul holding a book and a sword. On the right side of Saint Peter is the statue of Saint Mark. There is a statue of Abraham holding a knife on his right hand ready to strike his son Isaac to offer him as a sacrifice to the Lord. The boy, Isaac, is lying down on files of wood. This scene depicts God testing Abraham.

The paintings of the Stations of the Cross, and other exquisite Christian paintings are sublime. The life-size statue of the crucified Jesus on the side altar seems real as if He is talking to you. I could feel His excruciating pain and agony. Seeing some of the paintings of Jesus, and looking at His eyes, He seems alive, and He is looking after you and taking care of you.

I prayed in the divine and awe-inspiring Blessed Sacrament Chapel. I paused and reflected. I prayed profoundly for me, my family, relatives, classmates, students, friends, town mates, my former co-workers, supervisors, and directors.

We attended Holy Mass at La Basilique Notre-Dame on a Sunday. The Holy Mass was celebrated in French. The outstanding and beautiful liturgy, the cantor with an ethereal and powerful soprano voice who sang the songs during Mass enhanced the liturgy, the music from the amazing organ were completely angelic, uplifting, moving, and touching. I was ecstatic. My heart and mind filled with an indescribable euphoria.

In front of the Notre Dame Cathedral is a square. There are street musicians who play music. On the right-hand side, the band played classical music.

We sat down and relaxed. Then, we moved to the further left and listened to the music of two musicians. The solo performer played music using wooden instruments I had not seen in my life. I was not familiar with the music, but it was pleasant.

In one of the squares, is a monument of the effigies of two of the founders of France – Paul de Chomedey, Sieur de Maisonneuve, co-founder and governor of Montreal, and Jeanne Mance, co-founder, established the first hospital in Montreal.

The following day, we bought two tickets for the Hop-On Hop-Off bus tour for two days. The red bus was a double-decker bus similar to the Hop-On Hop-Off bus in London. The second was a deluxe motor coach. On the first day, we boarded the red bus. On the second day, we boarded the deluxe motor coach. We enjoyed a two-hour narrated tour on the first day, and another two-hour narrated tour on the second day.

We explored several places of interest on our own. The following are the tourists' attraction areas we have visited:

Chateau Ramezay - It is a museum and a historic site in Montreal. We paid for our entrance fees and took the self-guided tour. The chateau was built in the 18th century. It was a prestigious residential place, the home of Governor Claude de Ramezay. Reading the history, one can learn the history of Montreal, the inhabitants, settlers, soldiers, farmers, leaders, etc. Artifacts, pictures, objects, historical figures are some of the exhibits.

The French style colonial garden has abundant plants – trees, flowers, and vegetables. A gardener was planting when we toured the garden. I asked her what they do with the harvest. She said they give them to a place that feeds the poor. I told her I was happy to know they helped the poor.

Montreal Museum of Fine Arts - After purchasing our tickets, we toured the large art museum. We watched a movie onscreen, the re-enactment of the eruption of Mount Vesuvius. It was like being in Pompeii in Italy again. The exhibits include replicas of people who were affected by the catastrophic explosion.

More exhibitions we looked at and enjoyed were: Works of Toulouse-Lautrec, Chihuly's glass work, many fine landscape paintings, portraits and historical paintings, sculptures, etc. In this museum is a rich collection of 41,000 works. The museum was established 154 years ago.

Bank of Montreal - The museum displays money, coins, and the history of the founding of the Bank of Montreal. Queen Elizabeth II's picture is on the paper money. In the façade of the exterior of the bank is a small portico of Corinthian columns. The architecture is splendid. It looks like a building in Rome. The Corinthian columns in the interior of the bank made me feel like I was in Europe. I exchanged some U.S. dollars to Canadian dollars for taxi. The rate of exchange is the U.S. dollars are higher, unlike in Europe. In Europe, the rate of exchange is the U.S. dollars are lower than the euros. You lose quite a bit of dollars in Europe.

Sir George-Etienne-Cartier National Historic Site - It is the home in Montreal owned by Sir George-Etienne-Cartier, co-premier of the province of Canada. He was a lawyer. He and his wife had two beautiful daughters. You can read his legacy on the walls inside the museum. We saw the elegant home, the exhibits, the historical figures, the collection of fine things, such as china dinnerware, glasses, silverwares, etc. The living and the dining rooms of the home are resplendent. We learned more of the history of Montreal and the people who shaped Montreal, this lovely metropolis.

I had an accident descending the stairs after touring this museum. Tom told me to give him my purse so I could descend better. I got distracted. I should have stopped when I was talking to him, but I kept descending the stairs. I missed one step. I fell on my behind, right knee, and right arm. That startled me. I thought I would land in the hospital. Thank God I was fine. I bruised my knee and it was swollen. I put some ice in a towel and wrapped the bruised knee with it. The swelling subsided in a few days. I kept reminding myself to be careful and not land in the hospital.

The City Hall - We attended the guided tour of the City Hall in Montreal. The tour guide narrated the building of the City Hall. It was built between 1872 and 1878. It was rebuilt because a fire in 1922 destroyed the building. It is a big five-story splendid building and the seat of the local government in Montreal, Quebec, Canada. It is impressively beautiful.

Marche Bonsecours - It was the city hall until the new city hall was built. Now, it is a shopping place that provides trendy designer merchandises. We went shopping, and I bought a few items. Most of the products are made locally.

Old Montreal - We wandered around and walked leisurely in Old Montreal, a historical district. Visitors like the extraordinary energy of this vibrant area of the city. The visit includes a different and unique shopping experience. Many people live and work in Old Montreal. It is an excellent place to live and the neighborhood is good.

Saint-Paul Street - We took a stroll in the oldest street in Montreal. We visited some of the boutiques, art galleries, cafes, and restaurants. It was just fun seeing the art galleries. For an art enthusiast like me, art galleries suit me just fine.

Place Jacques-Cartier - This market place in Montreal is very busy and crowded. The towering Monument of Admiral Nelson in Place Jacques-Cartier reminded me of the Admiral's monument in Trafalgar Square in the centre of

London. Restaurants and stores are plentiful. We visited an Inuit Art Gallery dedicated to Inuit Art. The sculptures are amazing. They are, likewise, expensive. I marveled at how heavy stones were curved into a walking bear, caribou, kayak, flying eagle, duck, bird, sculptures of persons, etc. What great talents!

Pointe-A-Calliere - The one of its kind underground tour through archeological remains was fascinating. The tour guide described it as the very birthplace of Montreal. The tour started in a cemetery, and moved on to the different places in the underground including the sewer.

The tour guide said, "Yes, you will see the sewer."

We learned more of the history of Montreal, the inhabitants, settlers, business, trade, their way of life, etc. through the archaeological remains from every period in Montreal's past.

The tickets for the underground tour included the "Of Horses and Men," the Emile Hermes Collection, Paris. This museum houses the collection of Emile Hermes and the story of his life. This French gentleman and businessman had gathered an abundant collection of horse-related artworks including books, carriages, unique objects, replicas of horses, saddles, etc. I learned more about horses.

Notre-Dame-de-Bon-Secours Chapel/Marguerite-Bourgeoys Museum - The Notre-Dame-de-Bon-Secours Chapel is a church in the district of Old Montreal. It is the oldest church built in 1771. The main altar, the Blessed Sacrament Chapel, the statues of saints, the Stations of the Cross, and other religious objects are celestial. I lighted votive candles, and put some Canadian dollars in the box. I love lighting votive candles when I visit a church. The lighted votive candles are a symbol of prayers. I prayed, paused, and reflected in this chapel. I prayed for me, my family, relatives, classmates, students, friends, town mates, former co-workers, supervisors, and directors.

The Cruise in Montreal - Montreal is an island. We boarded a big beautiful boat and toured Montreal by boat. This is a relaxing tour on the Salt Lawrence Seaway. You take a tour sitting down on a boat. We sat on the open space, so we were able to see the tourist spots better narrated and mentioned by the English-speaking tour guide, a young maiden. We saw the Montreal port, the light house, the Jacques Cartier Bridge, Honore Mercier Bridge, the historical buildings, dazzling landscape, and much more. This is a wonderful tour if you wish to escape for a while from the stress and anxieties of touring and touring nonstop every day.

Saint Joseph's Oratory in Montreal - Many people come to Saint Joseph's Oratory on a pilgrimage. The church is a pilgrim site. It is an important sanctuary in the world dedicated to Saint Joseph. Saint Brother Andre Bessette founded the Oratory. He is known as the invisible host at the shrine. I read a pamphlet that said his intercession is powerful.

The Basilica is impressively beautiful. The architecture of the exterior is comparable with the Italian Renaissance. Five arches are on the main front of the basilica. The Corinthian columns are similar to some of the basilicas in Europe. The color of the big dome at the top of the basilica is green. At the peak of the dome is a cross. The tour guide said the dome is the highest structure in Montreal.

When we arrived, the guided tour had already started, but we managed to get in. A lady in the information desk called the tour guide, a young lady, and asked her where she was. After we were given direction, we found the tour guide, so we could take the guided tour together with the other tourists. The tour guide took us on a guided tour.

We saw the following:

- The Votive Chapel
- The Tomb of Brother Andre
- The Saint Joseph Oil
- The Crypt Church
- The Hall of the Renovation Project
- The Concourse, The Terrace, The Exhibition on Brother Andre, his life, his work
- The Main Portico, of the Basilica
- The Basilica and Saint Andre Bessette Chapel
- The Blessed Sacrament Chapel
- The Brother Andre's Room
- The Preserved Heart of Brother Andre - I asked the tour guide if that was really the heart of Brother Andre. She said it was. Then, she explained the process of preserving the heart.
- The Original Chapel
- The Pilgrim's Service Centre
- The Grand Organ

The tour guide narrated the history of all the places she showed us. After the guided tour, we toured the church on our own.

In the main part of the basilica where Holy Mass was celebrated, I prayed, paused, and reflected. I was spellbound. I included in my prayers family members, relatives, classmates, students, friends, town mates, and everyone I knew who had touched my life, former co-workers, supervisors, directors, et al.

Jardin Botanique (Botanical Garden) in Montreal - We boarded a Choo-Choo train and toured the Botanical Garden by train. The driver of the train started the tour in the Rose Garden, and then drove us all around the park. It was an orientation tour.

After the Choo-Choo train tour, we toured the Botanical Garden by ourselves. Brother Marie-Victorin founded this Montreal Botanical Garden in 1931. Now, it is considered as one of the largest and most beautiful gardens in the world. There are 22,000 plant species and cultivars. The site is on a 75-hectare place.

The Rose Garden was breathtaking. There were many varieties of roses in this garden. I had my picture taken in the midst of the blooming, sweet smelling, and fragrant roses. It was magical to behold. The Chinese Garden was undergoing renovation, but we were able to see and enjoy the many gorgeous plants in the garden. They are a spectacular sight to behold! Next to the Chinese Garden was the Japanese Garden. The bamboo trees standing tall reminded me of my former country, the Philippines. Many flowers typical in Japan were spellbinding to look at.

There are many more gardens, such as the Leslie Hancock Garden, Montreal Botanical Garden, Youth Gardens, First Nation Gardens, Alpine Garden, Fruit Garden, Aquatic Garden, Peace Garden, Monastery Garden, Medicinal Plants, etc. It was absolutely delightful seeing all of these fabulous flowers and plants. Thank God for blessing us with the beauty of nature. It was magical and enigmatic.

The Insectarium at the Botanical Garden was created by Georges Brossard, an entomologist. It was very scientific and interesting. Exhibits on display were various kinds of preserved bugs, beetles, spiders, dragonflies, butterflies, wasps, locusts, crickets, ants, centipedes, bees, you name it. Visitors could see just about every kind of insects. It was really fascinating to read their life, habitant, how they hunt for food, how they survive, protect, and defend their life from danger, etc.

At the Saint Joseph's Oratory of Mount Royal in Montreal in Canada

Ofelia attended Holy Mass at the Notre Dame Cathedral in Montreal in Canada.

Vancouver, British Columbia, Canada

After our stay in Montreal, we flew to Vancouver in British Columbia, Canada. It was a long more than five-hour flight.

In Vancouver, we stayed at the Empire Landmark Hotel in Vancouver. It was a high-rise building, and our room was on the 28th floor. After we checked in, we went to the sleek Cloud 9 Revolving Restaurant & Lounge, atop the hotel on the 42nd floor. What a 360-degree of fabulous and breathtaking sight! You can see the enchanting ocean, the awesome harbor, a gigantic ship and small boats coming and going, the towering skyscrapers, the majestic mountains, the clear blue sky.

I said, "Oh my God, how beautiful!"

This restaurant revolved while having dinner, and the fantastic scene followed the diners. On our first day of stay, I ordered a grilled marinated half chicken seared and topped with a honey and roasted garlic glaze.

I prayed before meal, "Bless us, O Lord, and these Your gifts, which we are about to receive from Your bounty through Christ, our Lord. Amen." Thank God for giving us our daily bread.

The entrée was served with green salad, creamy dressing, asparagus, cherry tomatoes, fresh bread, and green peppers. What a delectable meal. I ordered the same food the next day.

The next day, we customized our sight-seeing tour of lively Vancouver and purchased a forty-eight-two-day pass for a hop-on hop-off tour aboard an open top bus. The bus driver drove us all around town. Listening to the recorded audio guided tour, we learned the places of attractions to see in Vancouver. We toured on a bus all around town twice the second and third days, and saw the places we needed to explore.

On our own, we visited the following attractions frequented by tourists:

The Vancouver Harbour- We went to the port of Vancouver and enjoyed the beauty all around. The scene was beckoning – you can see the vast ocean, colossal ships, an enormous ship from China, private boats, yachts, seaplanes taking off and landing, impressive buildings near the port, stores, souvenir boutiques, fine restaurants, etc. We shopped for souvenirs and bought a shirt, pins, the flag of Canada, refrigerator magnets, key chain with a bottle opener, knife, wine bottle opener, and maple syrup. The Canadians make the best maple syrup in the world.

Stanley Park - We boarded the bus and toured the park twice. The bus only goes in one direction. The audio tour guide said Stanley Park has 400 hectares (about 1,000 acres). It is the top urban park in the world. Lush trees, (some trees are centuries old), evergreen forests, beaches, and astonishing flower gardens are a visitor's delight. Planted in the Rose Garden are numerous varieties of roses. The audio tour guide said many men took their fiancées to the Rose Garden, picked pretty roses and proposed to their would-be bride for marriage. It is a favorite place for fiancés. The audio tour guide also said that picking a rose is prohibited, and you would be fined. I wonder how many would-be bridegrooms have been fined for picking a rose.

There are various kinds of activities guests can do in Stanley Park. You can take a swim in the English Bay, play tennis at one of the twenty-one courts, have lunch or dinner in the fine restaurants, relax, take a long walk, run, take your kids on a picnic, view the splendid harbor, ride the Stanley Park Horse-Drawn Tour, etc.

The First Nations art and totem poles at Stanley Park are one of Vancouver's most fascinating attractions. I personally enjoyed the totem poles. It is interesting to read what they symbolize.

Vancouver Aquarium in Stanley Park - This Aquarium is one of the topmost aquariums in the whole world. There are more than 50,000 incredible aquatic creatures that visitors can revel.

We watched the dolphin show. The dolphins performed their acrobatic diving and jumping to the delight of the onlookers. The penguins were lovable. And oh, the beluga whales were very white. Beluga means "white one" in Russian. I watched them swim nonstop. Beluga caviar anyone?

The Great Escapes: Life in 4-D Show at the Aquarium in Stanley Park - Life is lovely and full of surprises. What a tremendous surprise in attending The *Great Escapes* show. Each visitor was given a pair of 3-D glasses. This show about the innovative ways animals have acquired to survive their life in a potentially harmful environment is not only entertaining, but exciting as well.

The 3-D glasses and the special effects brought us into action. Those big and strong animals on the screen ran right in front of your eyes, as if you were there, and you ran with them.

How could I outrun the African wild dogs? I was breathless running with them. It was jaw-dropping. Then, I felt a mammoth animal, whose paws were on my neck. I knew it was only a 3-D special effect, but it startled me that I got scared, and I got ready to jump and run. It is human nature to protect oneself from danger. Then, I felt an animal hissing and scratching my legs. You could feel there was someone scratching your legs. Suddenly, I smelled an animal smell and water was sprayed on me. Oh, how magical!

Those gigantic, larger than life images of animals vaulting on screen are truly amazing. That is moviemaking at its best! I don't know how the producers of this movie were able to do such a thing, but it is incredible and mind-boggling. I think everybody immersed themselves deeply in the show and were totally absorbed by the fascination of it all. What an exciting, fun adventure. The experience was so unforgettable; it will linger on for a while. I recommend this show. Experience the movie magic for yourselves, eh. Cool!

Science World at Telus World of Science, Vancouver - It was nice there were always taxis in front of the hotel. We didn't have to ask the hotel's desk clerk to call a taxi for us.

We took a taxi and went to the Science World at Telus World of Science. I was so happy the queue was not long. After purchasing our entrance tickets, we toured this scientific tourist attraction. We explored the marvels of science, the exhibits on display, the blasting science movies, the demonstrations, and the additional traveling presentations.

The first place we explored was the exhibits on the human body. There was a figure of the anatomy of the human body, and we could examine it. There was a narrative of the different functions of the body – the brain and nervous system, heart and circulatory system, the digestive system, the respiratory system, the muscular system, the immune system, and the skeletal system. Also on exhibit was a board that explained what the heart does. I put my hand on the exhibit and I could hear the beating of my heart. My heart was beating in a regular rhythm – it means I am fine, no heart disease.

The balloon demonstration was neat. The *Titans of the Ice Age* movie in the big theatre on a large screen with surround sound was incredible. An employee cautioned the people they might get dizzy. The movie had carried visitors to the frozen landscapes of North America, Europe, and Asia several thousand years ago. Close encounter with gigantic creatures such as giant sloths, cave bears, mammoths, toothed cats, etc. are what you would experience in the *Titans of the Ice Age* movie. It is a compelling movie.

The Museum of Vancouver - The Museum of Vancouver houses more than 65,000 items in their collection. It highlights artifacts about the story of the Metro Vancouver area. A planetarium was added to the museum. Science shows are shown in the theatre. I like the collection on the First Nations people.

Vancouver Art Gallery - After paying for the entrance fee, we proceeded to the first level of the Gallery and started enjoying the exhibitions. Many works of art by distinguished artists were resplendent. It was delightful to see the artwork of Pablo Picasso - Picasso: The Artist and His Muses. His paintings were astounding.

The Metropolitan Holy Rosary Cathedral of our Lady of the Holy Rosary in Vancouver - The Holy Rosary Cathedral serves as the Cathedral of the Roman Catholic Archdiocese of Vancouver in British Columbia. The architectural style is Gothic. The interior design resembles the Sainte-Chapelle in Paris. It is majestic.

Ad majorem Dei gloriam – For the greater glory of God, we attended Holy Mass at the Holy Rosary Cathedral. The liturgy was ethereal. I always feel spellbound attending Mass and receiving the Holy Eucharist. It revives me, and it is invigorating. I prayed, paused, and reflected. I always remember in prayer the members of my family, relatives, classmates, students, friends, town mates, former co-workers, supervisors, and directors who have touched my life.

Tom said to me, "Even on our vacation, we always attend Holy Mass on Sunday, and we never miss Sunday Mass."

I said, "Yes, we always attend Holy Mass even on vacation. It was instilled to me in Catholic school that carried to my adult life."

The nuns said, "You only miss Mass if you are sick."

At the Butchart Gardens in Brentwood Bay, British Columbia, Canada

*At the Metropolitan Holy Rosary Cathedral of Our Lady of the Holy Rosary
in Vancouver, British Columbia, Canada*

The Cruise to Victoria, British Columbia, Canada

We signed up for an excursion to Victoria. The driver of the Landsea Tours & Adventures Bus picked us up from our hotel. She was a pretty young lady, and a college student who was our tour guide and driver. She narrated about the tour and the tourist spots we would be seeing. When we got to the port, she drove the bus in the parking lot of an enormous ship I thought resembled the Titanic. She told us to go upstairs, choose a seat, and the ship would sail in a few minutes, and take more than an hour to get to Victoria. Tom and I chose seats close to the window. The cruise was smooth. The wide ocean was calm, and the Sun was shining bright. We enjoyed the enchanting scenery along the way. We cruised through the fabulous Gulf Islands to the Island of Vancouver. After more than an hour, the ship docked in the harbor in Victoria. We got back on the bus, and the tour guide began the tour of Victoria. She drove us to the places of interest in Victoria, and then dropped us off where we would like to stay. Tom and I chose to be dropped off by the port.

Here are the must-see and tourists' attractions we have visited in Victoria:

The Legislative Assembly of British Columbia - We were lucky we were able to be on time for the guided tour. The tour guide was great, and very knowledgeable. She described the architectural and historical importance of these beautiful and working buildings, house to the Legislative Assembly of British Columbia.

As we toured the interior of the building, she described the Legislative Chamber, the British Columbia Coat of Arms, Reception Hall, the Portrait of Her Majesty Queen Elizabeth II, Queen of Canada, Queen Elizabeth II's Golden Jubilee Window, Queen Victoria's Diamond Jubilee Window, Stair Windows, the Memorial Rotunda, the Ceremonial Entrance, etc.

Suddenly, while everyone was looking at the Legislative Chamber Room, a young man (an actor) dressed to the nines interrupted the tour and narrated the life story of Francis Rattenbury, the British architect who won the competition to design and construct the Parliament Buildings in Victoria, British Columbia, Canada. After, the narration, the tour continued.

In front of the stairs of the building, live theatrical plays are presented in vignettes. The actors/actresses are dressed in magnificent historical costumes. We sat on the stairs and watched a play. I enjoyed the nice play. Seeing live theatre play is my special interest. I call it "my cup of tea."

Queen Victoria Memorial - Strolling in the gorgeous gardens in front of the Parliament Buildings is serene and revitalizing. In the gardens on the front lawn is the Memorial Statue of Queen Victoria. It makes one feel like being in London, one of my favorite cities.

The Butchart Gardens in Brentwood Bay, British Columbia near Victoria - WOW! There are fifty-five acres of land in the Butchart Gardens for visitors to explore. The gardens were begun by Jennie Butchart. The Butcharts named their estates "Benvenuto." It means "welcome" in Italian. The gardens have become popular, and annually many visitors come to see them. Touring the gardens is self-guided.

The following are the various kinds of gardens you will see in touring the Butchart Gardens:

- Sunken Garden
- Rose Garden
- Japanese Garden
- Italian Garden
- Mediterranean Garden

Planted in all the expansive and colorful gardens are ample of fabulous and blooming flowers visitors can relish and appreciate. I will mention some of the captivating flowers that captured the deepest core of my heart:

Various kinds of beautiful, sweet-smelling roses in different colors from around the world, Agapanthus (Lily of the Nile or African lily), Aster, Begonia, Camellia, Cleome (Spider flower), Chrysanthemum, Dahlias, Hydrangea, purple Iris, Peony, Painted Daisy, Magnolia, Zinnia, etc.

The gardens are breathtaking. I was awe-struck and ecstatic how spectacular the gardens were. One can't help but feel sheer delight, indeed.

Globetrotting and exploring places have been a valuable tool for learning and acquiring more knowledge. It has been educational, fantastic, fun, exciting, and marvelous. In traveling, you will get to understand, acquaint, and learn more about other people's cultures, foods, languages, traditions, customs, etc. It is wonderful and fascinating meeting people in foreign countries whose lives are entirely different from your own existence. It is very overwhelming, challenging, and actually going out of your anxiety free and comfortable life especially when you go from one airport to the other to catch your scheduled flights to the next country in your itinerary.

In traveling, you will meet numerous people at churches, hotels, motor coaches, historical museums, art museums, theatres, restaurants, cafés, bars, public squares, palaces, botanical gardens, flower gardens, harbours, ports, parks, along the promenades, ships, boutiques, guided tours, trains, or Eurostar trains, etc. Many of them are a joy, courteous, exuberant, and awesome. For us, the best was meeting an Italian Admiral, his wife, and granddaughter who taught Tom Chinese checkers. We correspond with them. They live in Livorno. It is near Pisa.

There has never been a dull moment on travel adventures. Just make the most of it, and you will be enchanted beyond belief.

Finally, traveling helps enhance your life richly and give you more self-assurance and profound courage that you may not have before.

Sources on The Great Travel Adventures: Guided tours by men and women tour guides, audio CD tour guides, pamphlets handed out on tours and writings on the walls inside the museums.

Ms. Jan B., our travel planner is a wonderful travel agent. In appreciation for her assistance in planning our yearly travel, I sent a letter to her supervisors. Here is the letter. I love appreciating and praising nice and marvelous people who touch my life.

15 July 2015

Auto Club Travel Contact Center
Supervisor of Ms. Jan B.
American Automobile Association Travel

Dear Madame Jennifer, or Sir Ron,

I would like to thank Ms. Jan B. for taking care of my travel needs in an outstanding manner. Ms. Jan B. gave me the best customer service in the whole wide world. Every time I called her, the service was always exceptional. She always made my day whenever I talked to her.

Ms. Jan B. is a marvelous travel agent. She is smart and very knowledgeable in the travel business – airline reservations, hotel accommodations, places of interest, etc. She is extremely friendly and courteous. She does an excellent job in taking care of the customers. She gives the best of herself. She provides the most stellar assistance a traveler can dream of. Madame Jennifer, or Sir Ron, you have a great team in the AAA Travel Department! Ms. Jan B. performs her job superbly, and demonstrates amazing support and determination in meeting the customers' needs. Her willingness to go the extra mile to serve the travelers makes her a valued team member of your workplace. She is awesome, super, terrific, and remarkable! She did an outstanding and A+ job for us.

With her dynamic expertise, my husband and I are now ready to go to European countries on August 1, 2015.

Bravo! Kudos to Ms. Jan B. for the amazing travel arrangements she did for us. I wish her a long life, good health, happiness, peace, and continued success in her chosen profession.

Madame Supervisor Jennifer, or Supervisor Sir Ron, I would like to let you know how much I truly appreciate Ms. Jan B.

Please present this email to Ms. Jan B. Please let me know when you get this email and when it was presented to Ms. Jan B. Thanking you in advance for this request.

Wishing you a splendid day and more success in your travel business!

Sincerely,

OFELIA DAYRIT-WOODRING
Retired Technical Editor

"We make a living by what we get, but we make a life by what we give." – By Sir Winston Churchill

"Carpe diem" ("Seize the day"). – By Horace, Roman poet

When you are traveling, it is good to learn to say "thank you" in various languages:

Merci beaucoup - Thank you very much in French
Vielen Dank - Thank you very much in German
Molte grazie - Thank you very much in Italian
Muchas gracias - Thank you very much in Spanish
Dank je wel - Thank you in Dutch
Efcharisto – Thank you in Greek
Spasibo - Thank you in Russian
Gratias tibi - Thank you in Latin
Mahalo – Thanks in Hawaiian
Maraming salamat – Thank you very much in Tagalog (Filipino language)
Dacal a salamat – Thank you very much in Kapampangan (a dialect in the Pampanga province in the Philippines. It is my mother tongue. I speak it fluently.
Arigatogozaimashita – Thank you in Japanese
When you are traveling, it is good to learn to say goodbye in various languages:
Au Revoir – Goodbye in French
Arrivederci – Goodbye in Italian
Auf Wiedersehen – Goodbye in German
Adios – Goodbye in Spanish
Tot ziens – Goodbye in Dutch
Vale – Goodbye in Latin
Paalam – Goodbye in Tagalog
Mamun naco – Goodbye in Kapampangan
Sayonara – Goodbye in Japanese

ANYTHING UNDER THE SUN

A beautiful poem my daughter Susana has written for me when she was fifteen going on sixteen - a teenager. It is a heartwarming and awe-inspiring piece of poetry. I love it.

May 10, 1992
Dedicated to: My Mother
Dedicated by: Sue

You're the One

You're the one who stands beside me in everything I do.

You're the one who lets me know I can make my dreams come true.

You're the one I need when times get really tough.

And for all the things you've done for me, I just can't thank you enough.

You may not understand how much you mean to me.

You're a very special person and I hope that you can see.

You mean a lot more to me than a hug could ever show.

I love you so much and I really want to let you know.

Because you are my mother I'm thankful in every way.

And any time that we're apart, in my heart is where you'll stay.

So have a happy Mother's Day!

Written by: Sue

Mom

For all the times that I forgot to "Thank You,"

For all the special, little things you do,

For all the words that sometimes go unspoken,

I need to say, I love you, Mom...I do.

I love you for the way you stop and listen,

And for your kind support throughout the years,

For teaching me the meaning of compassion,

And sharing my triumphs and my tears.

And if at times I may have seemed ungrateful,

I want to say, I truly hope you see,

That nothing you have done has been forgotten,

And day by day, you just mean more to me.

By Susana

Susana was a thirteen-year-old teen when she penned this poem.

My Daughter – Susana
By Ofelia, Susana's Mom

A daughter is a precious gift from God
who brings joy and sunshine to your life.
A daughter brightens your days and makes you
happy through her loving and thoughtful ways.
A daughter knows how to lift up your heart and mind.
She knows the right words to say – graceful words of
wisdom that give you courage, comfort, and fortitude
to vanish your fear.
A daughter is a marvelous blessing from the heavenly
Father God above, a special, beautiful, awesome,
and precious treasure to love.
And I love Susana, my one and only pretty and
charming daughter I lovingly call my baby "Nene."

The Grandsons – Logan and Kaleb

Grandsons are very special angels sent from God above to fill our hearts and minds with endless love, astounding happiness, splendid comfort, and marvelous peace. Logan and Kaleb melt my heart. They take my breath away.

It is glorious to be grandparents. It is fascinating! It is indescribable! It is jubilant! We are blessed! Thanks be to God!

And we love Logan and Kaleb, our incredibly handsome, nifty, and cherished grandchildren.

Mother – A Daughter's Tribute

This loving tribute was read during the funeral of Librada. Ofelia, Librada's only daughter wrote this tribute to honor her mommy.

Librada Aguinaldo-Dayrit was a very hardworking lady who managed a successful small business – a dress and a tailor shop, for a living, supporting her two children, Nestor and Ofelia, whose father was killed by communist guerillas when Ofelia was four months old. She was the most popular and best dressmaker and tailor in town. She made dresses and men's shirts for doctors, lawyers, teachers, government employees, etc. She also made altar cloths and vestments for the priest. Her artistic and talented abilities in sewing was well-known and enjoyed by all her customers. She made dresses for all occasions from informal to formal, from casual dresses to evening gowns, bridal gowns, party dresses, pantsuits, etc. Throughout the years, she created the most beautiful and exquisite wedding gowns. Many young brides walked down the aisle wearing her elegant wedding gown creations. On special occasions like a formal party, she created the most gorgeous and sophisticated evening gowns. She had received outstanding compliments for her fabulous and evening gown ensembles. Her skills and expertise in sewing made her customers very happy. She won the hearts of the people she serviced and was deeply loved. Her contribution to the fashion world was remarkable.

With this business, Librada raised and educated her two children that she had considered her greatest accomplishment and the fulfillment of her mission in life. She was able to send both of her kids to college.

She came to the United States with her daughter Ofelia and the Woodring Family on 20 May 1977. She had lived in Sacramento for over twenty years and became an American citizen in 1982. She was so happy and proud when she received her naturalization certificate.

In the U.S.A., she made dresses, pantsuits, evening and bridal gowns, etc. for Boutique La Condesa, a fashion store owned by her close friend, Sheri. She also did sewing for family, relatives, and friends. On some occasions, she made the dance costumes for the Filipino members of the Lion's Club. She also made altar cloths for the Blessed Sacrament Chapel and had done alterations for her priest friend, who was a friend of the family. She was praised for her creativity, and her artistry was always complimented.

Librada was a doting grandmother, the best grandmother a grandchild could ever dream of. She took care of her grandchildren while her daughter, Ofelia, was at work. She patiently brought them to the bus stop everyday till they were in junior high school. She adored her grandchildren and beamed with pride when she watched William at piano recitals and Susana on tap, jazz, ballet, and piano recitals, or when she performed, sang, and danced during talent shows. She was equally proud of Emmanuel, her eldest grandson.

She had tremendous courage and strength in facing adversities. When told about her terminal illness (cancer), she was calm and peaceful. She had submitted her fate to the will of God like a meek lamb. She was grateful for the seventy-seven years of precious life the Lord God had bestowed on her. She looked back at her life and reminisced the good times. She said it was wonderful she was able to go on European tours, visited several countries and saw historical places. She particularly loved the magnificence of Rome, the Eternal City, Florence, the Renaissance City, Venice, the Floating City, Paris, the City of Lights, and the splendor of London, Monaco, Germany, Holland, and Switzerland.

She also talked about how much she enjoyed the performing arts. Victor Hugo's *Les Miserables* was her favorite musical because the characters of the story are Catholics. When the French police arrested Jean Valjean for stealing silver at the home of the Bishop of Digne, the bishop told the police Jean Valjean did not steal the silver, that he gave them to him. The kindness of the Bishop of Digne touched her deeply. The Bishop of Digne was her model for compassion. She attended the performance of *Les Miserables* in London in England with her daughter, Ofelia. *La Traviata*, *La Boheme*, and *Carmen* were her favorite operas. She was captivated by the rousing overture of *Carmen*. It was special as it reminded her of her musician father who played the lively overture.

Librada was compassionate and generous. Giving was an important part of her life. She was gregarious. She loved people. One of her happiest moments was being surrounded by people. She enjoyed cooking and baking for friends and relatives. She was an excellent cook and prepared the most delicious dishes, superb pastries, and exotic desserts. She loved giving away samples of her cooking. She met people in the neighborhood, and she was everybody's grandma.

Librada loved and enjoyed being an usher at the Saint Francis of Assisi Catholic Community in California. She felt wonderful greeting the parishioners on a Sunday morning, and handing out the church bulletins. She was thrilled when Cecilia, the Music Director of the Saint Francis of Assisi Catholic Community, asked her a few times to sing solo numbers. She sang Salve Regina and a Spanish song with great joy.

She was a pious woman who spent a lot of time praying. Every day at 5:00 A.M., she was awake and played the CD recording of Pope John Paul II leading the Rosary in Latin. Daily, she played this CD, and prayed the Rosary in Latin with Pope John Paul II leading the Rosary.

Librada has so many wonderful qualities and talents, so much warmth and kindness she shared with everyone in her life. She was a special person blessed by God with a loving spirit she always shared. Her exuberance, goodness, and caring brought the very heart of God to those whose lives she touched, especially to my family. She never stopped caring; she never stopped giving. She was someone to count on. She was always there. She was a passionately devoted mother, mother-in-law, grandmother, and friend indeed. There's love and pride in every thought of her.

It's a blessing to have a wonderful mother like you, Mom, and you're loved and appreciated more than words can say. Thank you, Mom, for all your love, and for the way you made my life special throughout the years.

Librada Aguinaldo-Dayrit graduated from high school from the Grant Joint Union High School District in Sacramento, California on June 4, 1981. It was the fulfillment of a lifelong dream to have more formal education.

The Paragon of Kindness

Be kind to others more than necessary. Nicolasa Mutuc-Aguinaldo, my grandmother, the mother of my mom, was a shining example of kindness. She was a lady who was kind to others more than necessary. She was a jewel, the epitome of what a truly caring person is. I remember vividly in my grandma's home there were always people – relatives from out of town who stayed at her home for several weeks and longer. She provided for them. She cooked for them, and took care of them. Every year in September during the town fiesta, the feast day of the town's Patron Saint - Saint Nicolas de Tolentino, many relatives from out of town came to attend the celebration. After attending Holy Mass, they proceeded to grandma's home for lunch or dinner. Her home was filled with many visitors. She loved and enjoyed the company of relatives and friends. She was an amazing woman.

Grandma's motto was "God will provide. God will return to you abundantly what you give away. God will bestow his prolific blessings upon you, if you are kind, and share what you have with others." It is very true based on my own experience. It is wonderful to emulate her shining example. Grandma Nicolasa was a big-hearted lady. She embodied compassion. She was my paragon of kindness.

Librada Aguinaldo-Dayrit, my Mom was kind to others as well more than necessary. She was very much loved by many people in Sacramento, California. She was generous, and shared what she had with others. She liked to cook, and she loved giving away the food she fixed. Her friends, doctors, nurses, pharmacists, friends at church, et al told me that she gave them her delicious and superb cooking - hopia (Filipino dessert made of mung beans, flour, eggs, etc.), lumpia, (spring rolls), bibingkang kanin (rice cake), puto lason (white bread - dessert), pancit (noodles), etc.

When she was in the hospital, there were so many people who visited her. When the priest who was assigned at Mercy San Juan Hospital in Sacramento came to see her, he told her, "I am looking for the most popular lady who always has lots of visitors. I was told that you are very popular, and many people are coming here to see you." The priest made her day! Mom was very happy upon hearing the kind words of the priest.

Mom also loved giving gifts even if there are no occasions. She bought things and reserved them for anyone who touched her heart. Like her mother, Librada was an amazing woman as well.

Below is a comment from one of her priest friends:

"She was a real lady, proper in every way, kind, and always caring about you and your family and other people. I think it is from her that you have such a generous heart! I will remember her in my prayers today."

Mother Teresa of Calcutta, Librada Aguinaldo-Dayrit, and Nicolasa Mutuc-Aguinaldo are compassionate people, and their kindness and generosity are exemplary. They are my heroes whom I emulate.

Sharing some kind words from employees and supervisor at work, only to touch, move, and inspire...

Peer Award

Ofelia Woodring:

Fely is a rare gem in the world whose actions and writing abilities towards her fellow team members creates the feeling of being as high and spectacular as Mount Everest. Her kindness, generosity, positive attitude, willingness to pass her extensive knowledge, and her delicious feasts are second to none. We appreciate Fely's contributions to our great team.

Note: The Peer Award was displayed on the bulletin board at work for one month with the picture of Fely (Ofelia).

During the Christmas season, our Branch Chief, Ms. R. T., my second-level supervisor wrote a letter to Santa for each of her employees. Below is the letter of the Branch Chief to Santa, letting him know her wish for me.

She is smart and generous and recognizes her co-workers in a kind and eloquent way. This precious, little lady shares the true meaning of Christmas each and every day. Because Ofelia Woodring has this amazing ability to lift and inspire, dear Santa, please give her anything her loving heart should desire.

R. T.

Chief, ENLT

One day, before Christmas, Ms. R. T., the Branch Chief, called us for our monthly safety meeting. After the meeting, she gave us three sheets of paper entitled "MATCH FAMOUS PERSON WITH CO-WORKER." After we were done matching each co-worker with the famous person, she started reading the description she wrote for each of her employee, and the famous person he/she was compared with. Then, we gave her our answers - best guesses.

I will only mention what she wrote about me, not the other employees.

2. _____ is spiritual and caring. Famous person to compare her with is "Mother Teresa," who was a living Saint. Known for being kind, having a strong conviction for providing selfless service, and devoted to the caring and well-being of others.

ANSWER:
2. Ofelia Woodring

R. T.
Chief, ENLT

The Phone Call

Logan, my grandson, was five years old when he left this message (below) on my cell phone. I kept it. I listen to it every now and then, so it does not get deleted. I save it in the archive every month. Logan also left a message on his grandpa's cell phone thanking and telling him he is the best grandpa ever, etc.

Here is the message: "Merry Christmas, Grandma. You are the best! I have received the Christmas present. Thank you so much. I love you so very much. You are the best grandma ever."

His mom told me she did not tell him what to say. Everything he said was all his own. Isn't that wonderful? A five-year old kid knew how to thank his grandparents in such an eloquent, uplifting, and loving manner. He is very articulate, even at five. Logan is an awesome kid.

When he was three years old going on four, Logan and his mom were shopping at the Best Buy Store. The manager heard him speak.

He told his mom, "Your son speaks so articulately. I can give him a job now. I will hire him; he speaks very well. Just tell me when can I hire him."

What a nice compliment from the Best Buy Store manager.

Thanks be to God for blessing Logan with talents.

An Essay By Logan
Logan
Trinity Christian School
4th grade
Short Story

If Animals Could Talk

If animals could talk, we would be able to communicate more easily. Sometimes I think they would like to talk because when I come home, there is my dog, waiting for me as if he was ready to say, "Hello." I would love my animal to talk because then I could ask if he liked where he lived and he'd tell me, or if he wanted to go out, or come inside, or if he were too cold or hungry.

Wouldn't you like to talk to your pet and your pet to answer back? They could ask you for food rather than barking or meowing. If only animals could talk, but they don't. Instead, they can be annoying because they bark and cannot respond with words for us to understand.

There are other animals besides pets that would be fun to listen to. If I were able to speak to a lion I would ask him if he liked living in a zoo, and why he is called a "king." If I saw an elephant, I would love to ask if I could hop on and ride him.

Since animals cannot speak, God has given them something called "instinct." Animals use their instincts and are very smart. My own dog is so smart that when I get the leash, he jumps up and down, going crazy, knowing that we are going for a walk. He is so smart, that when I walk over to get his food, he knows he's going to eat. When my dog smells the barbeque, he knows he will be eating very well, and jumps all over the place. He is so smart that even when I hide his toy, he is able to find it. My dog is fun and smart and is able to win when we have a race.

I love my animal no matter what and he is fun to have around, but I wish animals could talk, don't you?

(Word count-343)

The Budding Writer

Below is the creative writing of Logan that earned him an excellent award for Creative Writing during the Creative Writing Festival sponsored by the Association of Christian Schools International California/Hawaii Region. We are very proud of Logan. God is good. Thank God for blessing Logan with creative writing abilities.

Who knows? Maybe he will be a novelist like J.K. Rowling, the English novelist best known for the Harry Potter fantasy series.

Trinity Christian School
Logan
7th grade
Short Story

A Fishing Trip

It was a clear Friday evening off the coast of Maine approximately at 7:00 P.M. when Jonathan and his best friend of twenty-two years left their dock for a three-day fishing trip. Jonathan had told his wife they would be back before sunset on Monday.

When Monday came around and she hadn't heard from Jonathan or Lucas, she began to panic. Hours turned into days, days turned into weeks. The reality she might never see her husband again was starting to become a constant thought. But that morning at 7:03 A.M. she got the call, a call from Jonathan.

"I thought you said I wouldn't out-fish you, but it sure looks like I am running circles around you here," said Lucas. The two had managed to fill up the belly of the boat with an amazing amount of fish. Never in all their years of fishing had they been so successful, and had so much fun. They had planned on three days, but actually had started heading home after just two and a half days because they could not store anymore fish. They just finished pouring the last bit of ice on the fish when they heard a warning over the radio about a fast-moving hurricane heading right towards them. It was on them before they even had a chance.

Lucas slowly opened his eyes to see Jonathan hovering over him.

"Are you alright, Lucas?" Jonathan asked.

Lucas slowly stood to his feet, brushed away the sand from his face to see an island lush with trees and a huge towering mountain.

Jonathan explained how he had pulled Lucas from the planks of wood they had floated on for a day and a half to shore. Realizing the sense of emergency, the two men made a small shelter then headed out to explore a bit before dark. They managed to find some fruit for dinner and a nearby water fall for a source of water. Very scared and exhausted, Lucas and Jonathan faded into the night. For the next few days, Jonathan foraged for food and built a small hut while Lucas was using his engineering experience to build the two men a boat to get off the island.

Eight days later around 9:00 P.M., Lucas was putting the final touches on the small water craft when he heard a sound he had never heard before. "It sounded like a small tyrannosaurus!" exclaimed Lucas.

Jonathan said he heard something, but had been sleeping, so he was hesitant to believe Lucas.

The next morning, they awoke to see three toed foot prints leading up to a destroyed boat Lucas had built. Jonathan blamed Lucas because Lucas had stored the fish they had caught on the boat and now all was lost. Lucas, feeling totally disheartened, left camp in a rage while Jonathan tried to salvage what he could.

Lost, Lucas tried to find his way back home, but it was already dark and he knew his best chance was to try and find a small shelter to settle down for the night and wait it out until morning. Sometime in the middle of the night, Lucas heard the same sound. Heart pounding, he climbed out of his small cave he had found to follow the sound. He was determined to prove to Jonathan what he was hearing was, in fact, real. The creature he was hearing was too fast, and he lost it. But he saw the same tracks he had seen back at camp. Lucas went back to his small cave and waited out the night. The next morning, instead of heading back to Jonathan, he followed the tracks; he surely wanted to prove to Jonathan what he had heard was real.

The next morning, he began following the tracks he had seen the night before, and after a few hours the tracks led into a small lake that was completely surrounded by thick trees and cliffs. Realizing there was only one way, Lucas began to panic since it became very obvious that the creature was very close. Quickly, he turned around and began running to try and make it back to Jonathan before nightfall. Sometime at dusk, he heard the footsteps and the sound of the creature he had been tracking earlier, and his heart started pounding.

Lucas screamed, "Jonathan!" over and over as he kept running. He came flying around a corner running into Jonathan. He spent the next two hours explaining to him what he had heard and seen.

That next morning, Lucas and Jonathan set out to find the creature Lucas had been hearing. They spent two days trying to get back to the small lake. They ended up finding the lake after dark and decided that there was no place to sleep, so they hiked up a small cliff and made camp.

At sunrise, Jonathan had woken up to the sound that could only be described as a small tyrannosaurus rex. Frightened, he woke up Lucas and explained what he had heard. They gathered their belongings and explored the perimeter of the lake. After finding many carcasses and remains, they decided to leave this area and never come back. While they were heading back to camp, they heard the creature off in the distance. Feeling they could stay far enough away, Lucas suggested to follow it. They followed the sounds and tracks for five hours until they came upon a huge dark path leading to the top of the mountain they had seen from the shore.

Jonathan had tried to convince Lucas not to go, but it was completely unsuccessful. Knowing Lucas would keep going, Jonathan gave up and followed. It was near nightfall; they reached the top and could not believe what they were seeing. Sleeping in a valley of what seemed to be an extinct volcano was a massive creature.

"It has to be fifteen feet tall," whispered Jonathan.

The two maneuvered around the what seemed like quarter mile around ledge at the top of this crater to try and find a safe place to make camp. The hole they found was just big enough for the two men to lie down in with no room to move. Jonathan was awoken from sleep by screams from Lucas yelling:

"Get away from him!"

Jonathan stood up and detected Lucas brandishing a spear as the creature pounced on Lucas. A loud shriek echoed in the hills, and Jonathan ran to Lucas. "Lucas, are you okay?" shouted Jonathan. Both men saw the creature scurry off into the distance, injured from Lucas' spear.

Once they had somewhat relaxed after the creature had gone, they realized what it seemed to have been guarding. Mixed with the stone and ash seemed to be massive amounts of diamonds. Even though they were stranded on an island, all Lucas and Jonathan could think of was getting back to their families and what these diamonds could do for their futures. Both men filled up a medium-sized backpack they had made out of palm branches and leaves. A couple days later, they located the camp they had first built. Both men collapsed. Emotions ran high with the simple comfort of their small home they had built. The next few days were spent fortifying the camp for the possibility the creature would return. Both men never saw it again, and on that last morning they spent there, a small light from a fishing vessel could be seen off in the distance of the night. Jonathan scurried to light the bonfire they had built believing one day they would be saved.

After seeing a blazing fire off in the distance, Captain

James Wetherby of the commercial fishing boat The Avenger sent out a mayday for help. The United States Coast Guard showed up four hours later rescuing the two men and ending the nightmare they both had lived through during the last few weeks. Both men boarded the ship barely saying a word, and left all they had gathered in their time on the island, except a small box they had made of sticks and mud. Nobody ever did ask what was in the box the two men carried on board. After they were settled in Jonathan asked Captain James if he had a phone he could use to call his wife.

Roughly a week had gone by since Jonathan and Lucas were reunited with their families, and on that Sunday evening, Jonathan and his wife had Lucas over for a small welcome home party.

"Sara, can you come in here?" Jonathan hollered from the dining room.

Sara walked into the room to see Jonathan and Lucas on both sides of the table with a crafted wooden chest. Sara was asked to open the chest. She cautiously opened the lid, and to her amazement, a chest full of brilliant diamonds lie before her. She dropped to her knees crying, confused, and amazed.

The Path to Success

An Open Letter to Catholic High School Students

Dear Catholic High School Students,

Your life is ahead of you. Take the path to success! Reach for the stars! Reach for the Moon! They are attainable through hard work and perseverance.

You, the young people, are our greatest assets and the hope for the future. From you will rise our future leaders - Catholic priests, chaplains, ministers, president of the country, senators, congressmen, governors, mayors, ambassadors, diplomats, educators, school teachers, college professors, editors, medical doctors, medical surgeons, nurses, pharmacists, psychologists, engineers, architects, scientists, bank managers, military officers, corporation managers, executives, etc.

My advice to you is study very hard. Stay focus on your studies. Accomplish your school work and homework with zeal and enthusiasm. Develop a strong ethic in your education. Do your best in getting excellent or outstanding grades. Get involved in all aspects of academic endeavors. Join academic clubs such as the Science Club, English, Literary, and Speech Club, Mathematics Club, etc. Participate in extracurricular activities. Accept challenging school tasks. Improve yourself at all times. Accumulate lots of wisdom and knowledge. Learn, explore, and discover continuously.

Take care of yourself – mind, body, and spirit. Be kind to yourself and others. Establish warm and happy relationships with your priest, parents, siblings, teachers, and friends, and have a nice personal support system.

Get involved in your local church and offer to perform volunteer activities. Share your God-given talents in service to God. Be a lector, lead the Rosary prayer, be an altar server, join the church choir, if you can, etc. When your local parish carries out the feeding of the poor program, render your service in the community and assist in cooking the food. Extend your helping hand in serving the food for the poor.

Spend time with God. Include prayers in your daily life. Love, praise, glorify, and give thanks to God always. Do things that are pleasing to the Lord God.

Be good to your priest, parents, and teachers. Give them the respect they deserve. Appreciate and thank them truly for their genuine love and caring. They are there to guide and assist you to succeed! Your priest, parents, and teachers are doing their utmost best to help you become into the self-assured, responsible, courteous, and compassionate men and women you are supposed to be. They unselfishly provide you with the important means and avenues to achieve your nifty goals, and your shining dreams to reach for the brilliant stars, and make your very distinguished place in our society and in the world. They assist you in building your lives, and your bright future.

Plan ahead in making your future as bright as the dazzling stars in the firmament. Go to college. Achieve academic excellence. Persevere!

Someday in the future, when you have completed your Bachelor's Degree and succeeded, and when you have found a good job, share some of your earnings with your family and relatives who may need it. Give stipend to the church. Support your church. Help the poor. There are many references in the Holy Bible about the poor people and poverty. The poor are very close to the heart of God.

It is a Christian duty to serve God and humanity with all your strength. Wishing you all the best young students. May you all succeed!

Sincerely,
Ofelia A.D. Woodring

"Amor vincit omnia, et nos cedamus amori." ("Love conquers all things, so we too shall yield to love." - By Virgil

It is Spring!

Arise, spring is here, a time of renewal.
For see, the winter is over.
The snow is gone.
No more rain, sleet, and hail.
The time of the birds' singing has finally arrived.
Hear the calm and soothing songs of the birds.

It is refreshing! It is breathtaking!
Glory fills the land!
Feel the glorious sunshine.
Enjoy the marvelous fruits of the earth.
See the fabulous flowers of the field.
Smell the resplendent flowers blooming stately in splendor.
Look at the gentler meadows.

Amazing beauty can be seen everywhere –
    amid the gorgeous and fragrant flowers,
    the plants abounding in vitality, the pristine brooks,
    the fantastic streams, and the graceful trees
with their splendid branches.
Rejoice, pause momentarily.
Praise and thank the awesome God,
    and truly enjoy spring,
    the Season of Rebirth.

Madame Butterfly and *Sunflower*

After seeing the opera Madame Butterfly and the movie Sunflower, I felt a profound empathy for Cio-Cio San and Giovanna. My empathy for these two women inspired me to write the poem below.

Note: Cio-Cio San is the leading lady in the opera Madame Butterfly. She fell in love with Lieutenant Pinkerton, but the naval officer was unfaithful. She married Lieutenant Pinkerton in the summer when the cherry blossoms were in full bloom, but he left her.

Giovanna is the leading lady in the movie Sunflower starring Sophia Loren. Marcelo Mastroianni played the leading male character. It is a poignant melodrama.

Summer and Reminiscence

It was a splendid night.
In the garden of sweet, lovely flowers,
while the enchanting moon and twinkling
stars shine brightly in the firmament;
we held each other tightly,
and promised our undying love
for each other forever and ever.

Amidst the flourishing cherry
blossom flowers, below the fascinating windy
magic of a bright summer moonlight;
while flying birds' songs in the blue sky
reflect in the starlit luster, and the zephyr
brushing our cheeks;
our eyes lovingly met, and said
the enigmatic words of faithful love.

You vowed dearly to love me,
   till the end of time – the deepest core of our
joyful hearts traveled the farthest bay of the
paradise seeking for magnificent dreams,
   and a bright future, but you had to leave suddenly. . .
To go to the far-flung, overflowing, rich land with
a sincere and sacrosanct vow to come back to me. . .

Autumn radiance shimmered in
   tranquility – chilly dark winter months
   inevitably came rushing in.
Sweet roses bloomed with the praises
   of enchanting spring.
Another dazzling and rapturous morning
   adorned around the summer nights,
but the faithful vow to return to me
   has blended with the brittle and
   withered of fall leaves,
   carried away by a whistle of
   the strong violent tempest.

You never came back… you're gone…forever!
Painful tears fell into droplets of loneliness.
What is left of the sweet, lovely summer
   dreams we beautifully made together;
the joining of our jubilant hearts… are
now marked with poignant memories.

I can't find my way.

Alone, I am completely lost,

as if I am adrift at sea; feeling like a rover

wandering aimlessly in a shadowy, cloudy

world seemingly, never see the light of day.

But, there is hope that looms in the horizon.

In due time, by the grace of God,

I shall heal; I shall heal. . .

I bought the DVD movie Les Miserables from Amazon.com. Amazon.com requested me to write a preview of the movie. I have complied with the request. I wrote the preview below. I recommend the movie.

Les Miserables

I love the world-renowned and marvelous stage play *Les Miserables*. I have seen it London, England at the Palace Theatre with my mom. In the United States, I have seen it five times. It was great that the stage play was made into a movie. I also love the movie version. When the Bishop of Digne told the French police Jean Valjean did not steal the silver he gave them to him, and told Jean Valjean he forgot the candlestick and left the best behind, Jean Valjean turned his life around. The depth of the kindness of the Bishop of Digne inspired him to be a better person. He began a new life. His conversion was powerful and moving.

The actors and actresses in the movie *Les Miserables* played their roles in an outstanding manner. They portrayed the characters of the story convincingly. Hugh Jackman was nominated for an Academy Award for his portrayal of Jean Valjean. His voice was powerful and his acting was superb and phenomenal! Anne Hathaway won the Oscar for Best Supporting Actress playing the role of Fantine. She was remarkable in her role as Fantine. Russell Crowe was super in his role as Inspector Javert. And I loved Amanda Seyfried's portrayal of Cosette. Her voice was ethereal and absolutely delightful. The score of the movie was splendid and grand. The songs have gorgeous melodies. The scenes in the movie were fantastic and breathtaking. Amazing story! I loved the final words at the end of the movie:

"TO LOVE ANOTHER PERSON IS TO SEE THE FACE OF GOD."

There are plenty of words of wisdom in this movie you can learn and use in your daily life, whoever you are.

Don't miss this sublime and awesome movie! Everybody should see *Les Miserables*. Go buy the Blu-ray or DVD. The production is lavish, and it is spectacular. Above all, this movie is grace-filled, spellbinding, and inspiring. You will be so happy you did!

Be Not Afraid – Conquer the State

"The sea is dangerous and its storms terrible, but these obstacles have never been sufficient to remain ashore... Unlike the mediocre, intrepid spirits seek victory over these things that seem impossible... It is with an iron will that they embark on the most daring of all endeavors... to meet the shadowy future without fear and conquer the unknown."
        - By Ferdinand Magellan, Explorer (circa 1530)

We lived in California for twenty-two years. When the place where Tom and I worked was slated for closure, and our future was unknown and uncertain, I have memorized these words of wisdom by Ferdinand Magellan. I often recited them. These words convinced me everything would be fine, that I should not be afraid, and somehow we would end up with a job somewhere. Lo and behold, my husband's organization was transferred to another state. My organization was also transferred to another state. He was able to retain his job, and I was able to retain my job. We just had to move!

When we were moving, I told myself, "Fely, Be not afraid. It is okay to move. You are only moving to another state. You are not moving to the boondocks! Conquer the state. Make new friends, and have a challenging and fun adventure, etc."

Indeed, the move worked out so well. And yes, the good Lord God was with us through it all! At the new workplace, after we moved, and I started working, I met some of the best, amazing, and indefatigable co-workers, supervisors and directors in the world. They are the best employees I have ever known and worked with. They are amazing and terrific.

I am so happy God has put these awesome supervisors, directors, and co-workers in my path who have touched my life. God has truly blessed me abundantly in moving to another state. I have met such marvelous men and women at the new workplace.

I have prayed for my co-workers, supervisors, and directors at several major basilicas in Rome and the basilicas in Paris that we have visited. I prayed that God may bless them all with good health, long life, happiness, peace, and more wisdom. They have blessed me countless times in many ways.

My Farewell Letter When I Retired

Dear Supervisors and Co-workers,

"Parting is such sweet sorrow." Juliet said this line in Romeo and Juliet, a play by William Shakespeare, my favorite author.

I have mixed feelings about retirement. Indeed, it is such sweet sorrow. I am happy, and I am also sort of sad.

You are one of those treasures. For your many acts of caring and kindness, many, many thanks. Your caring and kindness to me are beyond words. You are the epitome of goodness - everything that is good - high degree of intellect, exuberant, super, remarkable, awesome, fantastic, magnificent, incredible, marvelous, exceptional, outstanding, phenomenal, dynamic, exemplary employees, etc. I will not run out of adjectives to describe you. You are a world class!

You are real troopers! It was a real joy to have worked for you, my dear supervisors. You are an employee's dream! It was a real joy to have worked with you, my dear co-workers. You are a co-worker's dream!

My thoughts are with you always and hope for good things for all of you. You are all truly the best! The best supervisors and the best co-workers I have ever known!

After thirty-three years and nine months of working for the federal government, it is now time to give it all up in favor of retirement. I love my job so much. There has never been a dull moment. I have worked for a total of thirty-eight years and nine months (thirty-three years and nine months in the federal government, four years as a school teacher teaching fourth grade children in the Philippine Public School, and one year and three months in private company).

I need to take life at a slower pace now and watch the world go by. I would like to spend more time with Logan and Kaleb, my grandkids. They are awesome, and they are handsome hunks. Praise and thanks be to God for blessing me with these grandkids. Logan played "The First Noel" during the Christmas Program at Trinity Christian School, a private Christian School. He played in an outstanding manner. Although I was not there to see him, I saw him on YouTube. WOW! Isn't that incredible? Computer magic!

Con Te Partiro – (It's time to say goodbye).

I will quote an anonymous author, "People come into our lives and quietly go. Others stay a while and leave footprints in our hearts, and we are never the same."

Your footprints are in my heart, and I am never the same. I'll remember you all fondly!

A million thanks for the monetary gift. I will send it to the following charitable organizations that are dear to my heart in honor of you all:

Association of the Miraculous Medal - $20.00

Christian Foundation - $5.00 (I have sponsored a boy in Mexico and an elderly lady in Guatemala)

Catholic Relief Services - $5.00

Oblates of Mary Immaculate - $5.00

Boys/Girls Town - $5.00

Holy Infant Jesus of Prague - $5.00

Cancer Research - $5.00. My mom and brother both died of cancer.

My goodbye in several languages. I love languages. (I lived in Europe, and it was fascinating to hear people speak in various languages).

Farewell - English (obviously)

Vale - Latin

Arrivederci - Italian

Adios - Spanish

Au Revoir - French

Auf Wiedersehen - German

Antio sas - Greek

Do widzenia - Polish

Sayonara - Japanese

Paalam - Tagalog, Filipino language

Mamun naco - Kapampangan, Filipino dialect - my mother tongue

Aloha - Hawaiian

Con Amor (With love),

Sincerely,

Fely

OFELIA DAYRIT-WOODRING

Technical Editor

ENLTB

"Carpe diem" - "Seize the day!" - By Horace, Roman poet

Dawn Will Come

A Short Story

He vividly took a glimpse at the massive façade of the National Penitentiary in Muntinglupa, Rizal. At long last he was blessed with a Christmas gift – the gift of freedom which he had much yearned.

Alexander quickened his footsteps, walked as fast as he could to get away from that building; to bury into complete oblivion the multifarious hours, days, and years he had spent there. He trekked the path of nowhere wandering aimlessly while the obstinate nocturne fog caressingly brushed his dry, frosty cheeks. He looked frozen stiff as the chilly December breeze raged over his frail body. He tucked his worn gray coat closely to his quivering body, but the nippy weather still made him shiver. He bent slightly, and placed his two very cold hands in his pockets feeling a little relieved. Then, he stared nonchalantly at the glowing tinsels supplemented with long strings of blending multicolored lights, lamenting, weeping, and feeling sorry for himself.

Gleeful laughter of children and teenagers filled the air sweetly. They were enjoying the yielding bliss of the Yuletide season. From a well-decorated department store, music like the soothing wind of dawn was played. It seemed to be spreading intense happiness to the whole world…the dreamy Christmas songs - "Silent Night," "Hark! The Herald Angels Sing," "O Come All Ye Faithful," the gorgeous melodies echoed loudly in his ears.

It was still six and a half hours before Christmas, yet every nook he passed by with the joyful warmth of the merry season was meaningless to him. He seemed to be carried away and lost as he couldn't mingle through the jovial faces of people strolling jubilantly on the streets because he felt them sneering at him, or mocking him… he who was confined in jail for several years. The beautiful and glorious atmosphere that surrounded him, the inevitable falling of the cool mist from the vast sky, and the scintillating, bright, and colorful lanterns brought him no more cheers. As the reflections of the mirthful voices coming forth from all angles grew louder and louder, and had hurt his inner bones and poignantly pained deeply the firmness of his whole being that he had to walk away, to hasten fast. He walked continuously as fast as he can till he lounged himself in a bus stop bench. Sighing deeply and enjoying the smoke of his one last cigarette, he was unable to contain his mournful eyes from crying. Far away, his thoughts travelled fast. Blithe and lachrymose reminiscences of the past rushed back in his reverie.

More than a decade ago, Alexander Rivera was a man of honor. He was a college student, an incredibly handsome hunk, robust, and young. On a sparkling night across the "Lovers Lane" in town, he met Christina Jalandoni, the pretty heiress of Don Alberto Jalandoni, a distinguished lawyer, politician, and a wealthy landowner in Cebu in the Visayan Island. She was standing happily by the lane viewing the luminosity of the full and lovely moon spreading lavishly on the fragrant and enchanting flowers. She was stunning and dashingly irresistible that before Alexander realized it, a slug of Cupid's delicate and magical arrow penetrated the deepest core of his heart.

"Oh, hello," she greeted him back in a melodious tone that was musical, mystifying, and pleasant to his ears.

"It's nice meeting you," he said to her. "Are you enchanted by the magnificent scene?"

She was beautiful, petite, and marvelous that she fascinated Alexander's silence. One of those wonderful and extraordinary love-at-first-sight episodes blossomed into a lyrical, lackadaisical romance between the young couple.

As the days inevitably fell from the boughs of the weeks, their love grew stronger. Standing in a captivating world that seemed never to end, they were just meant for each other. They spent good time watching the setting sun, wishing for their very own bright stars gleaming through the silvery moonlight. Christina was speechless when Alexander slipped a sparkling diamond engagement ring set in gold on her finger. The two shared together the nectar of love...drive-in movies, picnics, glittering social gatherings, jovial dance parties, church prayers and activities, and attending Holy Masses.

Their love for each other was enduring. It was meant to last forever, but a violent tempest came. It was a sunny day. Alexander was seated on a chair in an empty room at his home grateful for a few moments of solitude to contemplate. He began to ponder of his nightmare he would lose Christina. Wanting to dispel the dreaded illusion, he tried to block it out of his mind. The illusion proved to be true.

Don Alberto did not like Alexander. Alexander's family was not rich. Christina was born with a silver spoon in her mouth, but not Alexander. Don Alberto felt Alexander was not the right choice for his gorgeous and wealthy daughter, an opulent heiress. Alexander was in this meditative plight when he heard a loud thumping on the door. He opened it.

Don Alberto entered. He asked Alexander to listen carefully to what he had to say. He told Alexander, "Ambitious young man, who would like to soar quickly and easily by marrying into wealth, and who would wish to mingle with a prominent and affluent clan, I am here to pay you to leave my daughter Christina. Name a price. I will gladly give it to you." He dislodged his revolver and directed it at him. Don Alberto said, "Forget her, or else..."

Alexander nearly lost his temper, but he calmed himself down. He told Don Alberto, "My love for your daughter Christina is genuine. Death a million times, I would gladly challenge, but my true love for your daughter would not change. With sincerity from the bottom of my heart, I truly love her; I love her dearly."

Their agitated argument compelled Don Alberto to leave the house.

The next moments were filled with unpredictable suspense. Alexander wrote Christina a letter telling her about the poignant encounter. There was no reply. He had exerted tremendous efforts to get hold of Christina, his loved one, but to no avail. Everything metamorphosed into a debacle. He found out from Christina's cousin that Don Alberto sent Christina to the United States to stay with relatives to forget Alexander.

He was stunned by the horrid news. He thought he could not manage to live. The deep wound was extremely painful that it vibrated with unknown harshness in his whole body.

Time flies fast. It brings a silhouette of multifarious changes. It changes the course of a person's life; it alters an individual's unknown destiny.

Alexander vowed to aim higher. "I must rise. I must be ambitious; I need to be wealthy. I must be somebody, and become someone who is larger-than-life. I must show Don Alberto that I could make my life in parallel with his luxurious standard of living. To search for greener pastures, I must seek my fortune and my luck in other land, in Manila," he promised himself. It was the first time his eyes caught Manila. It was awesome, spectacular, and fabulous. The city was raucous and very busy. There were various pedestrians walking on the busy and crowded streets, deafening noises, honking vehicles rushing off everywhere. Only the Almighty God knew where everyone was going. He saw the city of towering skyscrapers, many amazing, and variety of department stores, awesome colleges and universities, captivating parks with stunning flower gardens, magnificent, sublime, and awe-inspiring Roman Catholic Churches, the charming city with a unique barrier on the fantastic bay and a vigorous rocky shoreline. On the surface, it is always very bright, the neon lights continuously burning intensely and blinking the whole night through. Darkness he perceived later is in the realm of the overpopulated, but lovely metropolis.

Alexander came to the city to forget Christina, to hunt for a good job, to become rich, to make his life in parallel with that of Don Alberto. He wanted to reach the blazing stars and the bright moon in the vast firmament. He told himself it can be done by hard work and self-sacrifice. And he found the big fortune he was looking for.

The problem of unemployment which likewise abounds in Manila herded him to join illegal occupation – smuggling. The cooperation of crooked cops and law enforcement officers facilitated the smuggling activities of his associates. Hence, he was able to amass lots of money.

He became rich within a brief span of time. He started spending nights at bars, shimmering nightclubs, spending long, endless bouts with beautiful women with their mischievous, enticing laughter and intoxicating perfume. In addition, there was the ever flowing champagne, with strong wine bottles and fine, crystal goblets. He was lost completely! He visited gambling dens practicing the luring vices…billiard, black jack, etc. He savored worldly pleasures. He gloated the transient world up to the brim, forgetting all about Christina, his lofty, honorable dreams, and his noble ambitions. He got sidetracked; he slipped and fell into grave sins.

In contrast with the infinity of God, all earthly things are ephemeral. Alexander's zestful essence ended when one somnolent night while listening delightfully to a fairyland of wondrous and resplendent music, around the hot, burning touch of an alluring hostess at the Roxas Boulevard Cocktail Lounge, he suddenly came across a rugged, drunken man who grabbed the woman who was entertaining him, dragged and forcefully danced with her. With bursting anger, Alexander went ballistic. He choked the drunken man by putting his big and strong hands to his throat till the man shook all over, his knees buckled, and his body collapsed from the force or pressure. The drunken man fell writhing, his blood spurting from all over his body.

Alexander killed the drunken man. He gasped; for a moment he could not stir. He held on to the scattered chairs, breathless from terrible exhaustion and intense madness.

The influential family of the victim sought justice. Authorities left no stones unturned in prosecuting the culprit. Justice was not delayed. With swift court procedures he was tried. The findings divulged that he was guilty of homicide. That infamous and notorious day when the judge of the Manila Court of First Instance read his verdict, he could not contain his tears from rolling down his pale cheeks. He cried out incessantly in a loud voice like a baby.

Thus, he served in prison for many years. He waited to be free, waited and waited until doomsday. He had tenaciously clung to the hope that his gloomy days in prison will soon be over, so he manifested patience, humility, and good behavior that he was recommended for parole.

After his mind had plunged into the morsel of undefined contemplation, he stood up. He murmured to himself, "Oh, my Lord God, what shall I do? Guide me, forgive me, and have mercy on me."

He lifted his heavy feet, stood up, and walked a few steps again and again till he found himself inside a magnificent well-lit Roman Catholic Church. It was full of worshippers when he entered. There was a large comet that dangled above the altar, strings of glittering multi-colored lights and ornaments. A Christmas tree on the right side of the altar was filled with pretty decorations such as ribbons, Christmas cards, various shapes of bells, garlands, a mini Santa Claus, paper angels, lanterns, little twinkling stars, dolls, toys, chocolate candies, etc. In the sanctuary was a conventional manger. The figure of the sweet baby Jesus lying on the manger was surrounded by the figures of Mary, Joseph, the three kings, and the shepherds. He knelt down on his knees, and he prayed earnestly.

The church bells rang out across the starlit brightness indicating the birth of Jesus Christ – the Savior. And on such a jolly, marvelous, and triumphant Christmas, he rejoiced with the faithful parishioners. Then, he paused momentarily, and for his long-awaited freedom, he had found a new hope, a hope that looms in the new horizon. A new dawn has finally come to his shattered life. Life for him began anew!